PHYSICAL EDUCATION for CHILDREN

Daily Lesson Plans for Middle School

Second Edition

Amelia M. Lee, PhD
Louisiana State University

Katherine T. Thomas, PhD
Iowa State University

Jerry R. Thomas, EdD
Iowa State University

Human Kinetics

Library of Congress Cataloging-in-Publication Data

Lee, Amelia M., 1938-
    Physical education for children : daily lesson plans for middle school / Amelia M. Lee,
Katherine T. Thomas, Jerry R. Thomas.--2nd ed.
      p. cm.
    Jerry R. Thomas' name appears first on earlier ed.
    ISBN 0-87322-683-6
      1. Physical education and training--Study and teaching (Middle school)--United States.
2. Lesson planning--United States. I. Title. II. Thomas, Katherine T., 1948- III. Thomas,
Jerry R.

GV223 .L42 2000
796'.071'273 21--dc21

                                        99-044613
                                        CIP

ISBN: 0-87322-683-6

Table F4.2 is reprinted with permission from the *Journal of Physical Education, Recreation & Dance*, volume 56, number 1, p. NCYFS-24. *JOPERD* is a publication of the American Alliance for Health, Physical Education, Recreation and Dance, 1900 Association Drive, Reston, VA 20191.

Table F4.3 is reprinted with permission from the *Journal of Physical Education, Recreation & Dance*, volume 56, number 1, p. NCYFS-23. *JOPERD* is a publication of the American Alliance for Health, Physical Education, Recreation and Dance, 1900 Association Drive, Reston, VA 20191.

Table F4.4 is reprinted with permission from the *Journal of Physical Education, Recreation & Dance*, volume 56, number 1, p. NCYFS-22. *JOPERD* is a publication of the American Alliance for Health, Physical Education, Recreation and Dance, 1900 Association Drive, Reston, VA 20191.

Acquisitions Editor: Scott Wikgren; **Developmental Editor:** Kristine Enderle; **Managing Editor:** Amy Flaig; **Copyeditor:** Arlene Miller; **Proofreader:** Julie Marx; **Permissions Manager:** Heather Munson; **Graphic Designer:** Stuart Cartwright; **Graphic Artist:** Denise Lowry; **Cover Designer:** Keith Blomberg; **Photographer (cover):** Tom Roberts; **Art Manager:** Craig Newsom; **Illustrator:** Argosy; **Printer:** Versa Press

Printed in the United States of America   10 9 8 7 6 5 4 3 2 1

Human Kinetics
Web site: http://www.humankinetics.com/

United States: Human Kinetics, P.O. Box 5076, Champaign, IL 61825-5076
1-800-747-4457
e-mail: humank@hkusa.com

Canada: Human Kinetics, 475 Devonshire Road, Unit 100, Windsor, ON N8Y 2L5
1-800-465-7301 (in Canada only)
e-mail: humank@hkcanada.com

Europe: Human Kinetics, P.O. Box IW14, Leeds LS16 6TR, United Kingdom
+44 (0)113-278 1708
e-mail: humank@hkeurope.com

Australia: Human Kinetics, 57A Price Avenue, Lower Mitcham, South Australia 5062
(08) 82771555
email: liahka@senet.com.au

New Zealand: Human Kinetics, P.O. Box 105-231, Auckland Central
09-523-3462
e-mail: humank@hknewz.com

CONTENTS

This book contains a physical education program for six, seventh, and eighth grades with lesson plans for each day of the school year. The basis of the program is our developmental view of physical education, which considers the needs and behaviors of children as they mature, grow, and change. The developmental perspective of our program can be seen in two ways: first, the same skills become more challenging as the children become older and experienced; and second, new activities are incorporated for the older children. The activities in the lessons are based on our knowledge of what is developmentally appropriate.

Many different activities are presented in the four levels of this program (Grades K-5 can be found in *Physical Education for Children: Daily Lesson Plans for Elementary School,* Second Edition). The program provides breadth by the number of different activities and skills included and depth by presenting these skills in increasingly complex tasks throughout the elementary and middle school years. The program can serve as a curriculum guide or model for physical education programs from kindergarten through eighth grade. Individual teachers or schools can expand or extend the program as appropriate.

The program was developed for classroom teachers and physical education specialists, either pre-service or practicing. Teachers using this program should select units of instruction that they are confident teaching and then repeat these lessons to allow students to master the skills. Our hope is that this program will accomplish three objectives:

- Allow teachers to focus on the teaching/learning process.
- Encourage quality physical education by serving as a guide for developmentally appropriate physical education programs.
- Help teachers understand the process of children's development and use that knowledge to be effective teachers.

To help teachers obtain positive results from the lesson plans, some basic concepts about motor development and teaching practices are presented in the introductory section. With this knowledge, a teacher can perceive how program planning, lesson-plan development, and effective teaching can be linked for a quality program.

The lessons are based on two assumptions: first, that the teacher has become familiar with the material in this introduction; and second, that the children have had previous physical education experience. All the teacher needs to do is review the overall content of the lessons at the beginning of the year, gather the necessary equipment (most is readily available), review the lesson plan prior to teaching each day, and then enjoy teaching physical education. The children will become more skilled and physically fit, everyone will have fun, and the children and parents will love the program.

Teachers who use the lesson plans can make a long-term contribution to the health, physical fitness, and motor skills of their students. Children who gain motor skills and fitness tend to develop lifelong habits of regular physical activity, an important element of physical health, mental health, and a healthy lifestyle.

This book is a collection of daily lesson plans for sixth, seventh, and eighth grade physical education. The units present a complete set of lessons, enabling you to organize and teach a daily program for middle school students. These lessons have proven successful for many teachers. As you become more comfortable with their content and approach, you will be able to incorporate your own ideas into new lessons or expand upon the ideas presented here.

THE VALUE OF PHYSICAL ACTIVITY

The Surgeon General's Report on Physical Activity and Health released in the summer of 1996 indicates that physical inactivity, a major cardiovascular disease risk factor in adults, is at epidemic proportions in the United States; the report challenges educators to play a key role in designing programs to increase physical activity levels among citizens of all ages.

Evidence suggests that school age children's activity patterns continue into adulthood and that increases in children's physical activity might lead to changes in their activity patterns as adults, reducing their risk of cardiovascular disease. Because there is evidence that physical activity during childhood can promote overall health and well-being, physical activity is included as a national health promotion objective in *Healthy Children 2000* (U.S. Department of Health and Human Services 1992). This report was the result of a national effort to enhance the quality of life for all American children. The report challenges parents and teachers to involve children in physical activity programs beginning at an early age.

Childhood is a critical time for fostering the development of a healthy lifestyle. Teachers play a vital role in helping children develop attitudes and behaviors related to physical activity, diet, and health; and these attributes and behaviors often extend into adulthood. Teachers can also help students feel positive about their own movement skills and confident about reaching their movement goals.

Regular physical activity is beneficial for overall health and well-being. Physically-educated children are more likely to become and remain active. A physical education program should consist of basic information regarding exercise and the effects of exercise, plus a set of basic movement skills. People are less likely to participate in activities they do not know about, do not know how to do, or do poorly. Thus, positive experiences during childhood and adolescence are important determinants of an active lifestyle during adulthood. We must provide children with the knowledge and skills they need to make healthy decisions regarding exercise. A child's competence (i.e., skill) and enjoyment regarding physical activity have been identified as prime determinants of physical activity during adulthood.

GOALS AND OBJECTIVES OF PHYSICAL EDUCATION

The activities and decision-making experiences presented in this book are designed to move children along the path toward physical education skills and knowledge. With participation in the curriculum outlined for sixth through eighth grades, we can expect the students to demonstrate competence in combining the locomotor and manipulative skills into specific sport, rhythmic, and gymnastics skills. The lessons provide opportunities for refining the specific skills, stunts, and dance steps by introducing game-like drills and structured dance activities.

The first goal at this level is to make the movement and sport patterns efficient enough to use in specialized sport activities and a variety of folk and square dances. Students should become proficient in traditional tumbling and balance stunts and should participate in advanced partner stunts. Creative expression is also emphasized so that students can invent new forms of games, rhythmic sequences, and tumbling routines. The second goal for this level is to develop and maintain physical fitness. A variety of vigorous physical activities are incorporated into the daily lesson plans. There are several options for implementing the fitness program, including fitness units, fitness contracts, and homework.

In addition to developing motor skills and physical fitness, which are the primary goals of physical education, growth in the cognitive and affective domains is also important. Children should understand the principles involved in physical fitness development and begin to plan their own exercise programs. Students need to understand the health benefits of regular exercise and to participate in moderate to vigorous activities both in and out of class. Another goal is to teach students to think critically about their own learning. The lessons in this curriculum offer learners many opportunities to identify errors in their own performance and in the performance of others.

Finally, we know that students must feel good about themselves and must be confident about their success before they can move forward toward a healthy lifestyle. Our program uses specific strategies to build confidence and avoid anxiety. Social interaction is emphasized, and students are encouraged to appreciate the successes and achievements of others.

ORGANIZATION OF THE LESSON PLANS

The lesson plans can be organized in many different ways as long as the lessons (e.g., tennis or rope jumping) within a unit are presented in numerical order. The lower numbers represent basic skills, while higher numbers represent skills that build on the previous lessons in the unit. There are four broad categories of activities: nine weeks of games and sports lessons; six weeks

each of gymnastics and rhythmical activities; and six weeks of fitness and health. Many lessons should be repeated so students can master the skills and enjoy doing the activities again.

Some teachers may prefer to do lessons in units, so that the year begins with organization and fitness testing (weeks 1-4); gymnastics (weeks 5-10); fitness, including moderate to vigorous games, Fitness Hustles, circuit training, and fitness challenges (weeks 11-14); games and sports (weeks 15-23); health (weeks 24-25); rhythmic activities (weeks 26-31); fitness testing (weeks 32-33); and then perhaps repeating favorite lessons (weeks 34-36). This plan may work well in situations where you must rotate equipment, share facilities, or plan indoor units around the weather. We suggest another plan that alternates activities in table I.1.

Beginning the School Year

We recommend that you teach the organizational and management techniques presented in the organization unit of the lessons during the first week of each school year. Organizational and management techniques should be reinforced as needed throughout the year. You should establish five aspects of management and organization: the signals you will use, getting into and changing formations, handling equipment, the social skills you expect, and other rules (and consequences) for good behavior. Five lesson plans are provided for the first week of school to accomplish these tasks. You will also want to consider how you will manage routines such as getting water, entering and leaving the gym or playground, using the bathroom, and taking attendance (if necessary). The purpose of organization and management is to provide greater time for instruction and to prevent problems. Additional information about making teaching better and easier is presented in the section titled "Practical Knowledge About Teaching."

Three other activities are suggested for the beginning of each semester: teaching and reviewing the Fitness Hustles, administering the fitness test, and developing the semester fitness contract. Weeks two, three, and four can be used for assessing growth and physical fitness, teaching the Fitness Hustles, and developing the physical fitness contract for each child.

The purpose of the growth and fitness assessment is to monitor growth and fitness by measuring height, weight, degree of fatness, aerobic endurance, muscular strength, muscular endurance, and joint mobility (flexibility).

Table I.1: A Sample Weekly Format for Grades 6-8

Month one	Month two	Month three
Week 1–Organization: review and teach routines Week 2–Fitness: introduce Hustles Week 3–Fitness: testing Week 4–Fitness: testing	Week 5–Games and sports: tennis Week 6–Games and sports: soccer Week 7–Rhythmic activities: dance steps Week 8–Games and sports: football	Week 9–Gymnastics: tumbling and stunts Week 10–Gymnastics: tumbling and stunts Week 11–Rhythmic activities: folk dances Week 12–Games and sports: basketball

Month four	Month five	Month six
Week 13–Games and sports: basketball Week 14–Fitness: Hustles Week 15–Free days: repeat or choice Week 16–Fitness: circuit training	Week 17–Fitness: fitness challenges Week 18–Rhythmic activities: tinikling Week 19–Rhythmic activities: tinikling Week 20–Gymnastics: partner stunts	Week 21–Gymnastics: partner stunts Week 22–Games and sports: volleyball Week 23–Games and sports: softball Week 24–Rhythmic activities: advanced tinikling

Month seven	Month eight	Month nine
Week 25–Fitness: moderate to vigorous games Week 26–Free days: repeat or choice Week 27–Gymnastics: small equipment Week 28–Gymnastics: large equipment	Week 29–Health: health concepts Week 30–Health: health concepts Week 31–Fitness: testing Week 32–Fitness: testing and Hustles	Week 33–Fitness: testing and Hustles Week 34–Rhythmic activities: rope jumping Week 35–Games and sports: track and field Week 36–Games and sports: track and field

During this time, the Fitness Hustles can be introduced and the fitness test can be taught and practiced. The test includes the mile run, sit-ups, backsaver sit-and-reach, and push-ups. Children need to practice these items several times before the actual test is administered. The objective of practicing the mile run is to learn about pace.

During the third week, the fitness test can be administered and a fitness contract developed with each child. The contracts can focus on maintaining or increasing each fitness component, depending upon individual needs and test results. The Fitness Hustles, which are exercises to music, are also used to supplement lessons during this week. By this point the Fitness Hustles should be well learned; they can be used throughout the semester.

Health and Fitness Lessons

The health and fitness lessons presented are as follows: 10 health concept lessons, 10 lessons for practicing fitness tests, 5 lessons for introducing the Hustles, 5 lessons for circuit training, 5 lessons of moderate to vigorous games, and 5 lessons of fitness challenges. Each of these lessons, or units, can be repeated or expanded. The health and fitness lessons were designed to be used in the classroom, but they can be adapted for use on the playground or in the gym. The 10 health concept lessons can be put together in a unit, or the concepts can be integrated with the fitness or skills lessons. These lessons are not meant to represent a comprehensive health education program, and many teachers will want to supplement the plans with the introduction of other materials. However, the ideas presented will help you get started and offer meaningful content for those students who get no other formal health instruction.

We believe that physical fitness is an important goal. The fitness lessons include warm-ups and moderate to vigorous activities that encourage being physically active. Physical fitness is like any other motor skill; it must be practiced to be learned well enough so that we can enjoy participating in the activities. We believe that children and adults are more likely to continue participating in activities in which they feel competent. The goal is to first teach the skills necessary to be physically fit, and second, to make physical activity fun and challenging. For some programs a third goal is to actually achieve physical fitness. This can be a goal when you have enough time devoted to physical education to meet the criterion of three days per week of aerobic activity, as well as additional days to teach other skills (Plan D is an example). Since very few schools designate this much time for physical education, we offer three alternative plans (A, B, and C).

Plan A

The year begins with two weeks of fitness training and testing as previously described. The process of practicing and taking the fitness test can be repeated at the end of the school year (weeks 31-33). Three fitness units are presented in the fitness section: circuit training, moderate to vigorous games, and fitness challenges. Two of these units can be used in the fall, and one can be used in the spring. With the Fitness Hustles, this will provide fitness activities for use throughout the year. The Hustles can also be used during the free choice weeks to include more fitness lessons.

Plan B

Fitness testing would occur at the beginning and end of each year. Fitness would be done one or two days each week, rotating through the Hustles, challenges, circuits, and moderate to vigorous games. Each of those lessons would be used approximately two times in 36 weeks. Other activities would be taught the other three or four days per week: gymnastics, rhythmic activities, and games and sports. The children would have fitness homework or fitness contracts to complete the fitness training if a program goal is to achieve physical fitness.

Plan C

Fitness testing would be conducted at the beginning and end of the year. Fitness would be done as a unit scheduled during four weeks, with one week each for the Hustles, circuits, challenges, and moderate to vigorous games.

Plan D

Fitness testing would occur at the beginning and end of the year. Fitness would be scheduled three days per week; rhythmic activities, games and sports, and gymnastics would be scheduled on the other two days each week for the entire school year. Many options for scheduling could be used to rotate the fitness lessons throughout the year. An example is provided in table I.2, using the 15 fitness lessons six to seven times throughout the year. The Fitness Hustles could also be included in a rotation. This plan was designed for schools with five days of physical education scheduled and physical fitness as a major goal of the program. To maximize training benefits, the three days of fitness training should be scheduled alternate days (Mondays, Wednesdays, and Fridays).

Table I.2: A Sample Fitness Training Program for the Year

Weeks	Monday	Wednesday	Friduay
4, 9, 14, 19, 24, 29, 34	Moderate to vigorous games 1	Moderate to vigorous games 2	Moderate to vigorous games 3
5, 10, 15, 20, 25, 30	Moderate to vigorous games 4	Moderate to vigorous games 5	Challenges 1
6, 11, 16, 21, 26, 31	Challenges 2	Challenges 3	Challenges 4
7, 12, 17, 22, 27, 32	Challenges 5	Circuit 1	Circuit 2
8, 13, 18, 23, 28, 33	Circuit 3	Circuit 4	Circuit 5

Fitness Testing

It is important to consider how the fitness testing information will be used. If you do fitness two days per week with fitness homework or fitness contracts; or if you do fitness three days per week; or if you do fitness units (eight or more weeks), you can expect fitness to be maintained or improved by the program. However, if you are not including at least the minimum amount of fitness in the program (i.e., three days per week for eight or more weeks), you should not expect improved fitness test scores at the end of the year. If fitness scores do improve, it is likely due to growth. When fitness is done less than three days each week, fitness test information would be used more for informational or monitoring purposes than for evaluation of the program or grading.

It is important for you to understand your goal for fitness activities and testing and to explain this goal to your students. If you are monitoring fitness, explain that to the students. If you are doing fitness activities two days per week, explain to the children that they must do at least one more workout in order to be physically fit. We do not advocate grading on physical fitness (grading is especially problematic if the program is not meeting the criteria to train for physical fitness). We suggest reporting physical fitness scores to children and parents and using the scores to monitor behavior and health and to develop fitness contracts.

Fitness Contracts, Homework, and Journals

Fitness contracts can be used to encourage students to adopt an active lifestyle. Students, with your help, plan individualized fitness programs to be completed on weekends and after school. This places responsibility on the students and empowers them. Lifetime fitness is the result of self-discipline and the decision to be physically active; fitness contracts can be the beginning of this process for your students. Programs should be individualized; some children will have very challenging goals, while others will have more moderate goals. The children should be encouraged to keep journals that describe their personal feelings about the activities. Careful assessment of the contract program is needed so that revisions can be made as needed.

Fitness homework can be presented on a calendar or assigned daily. Fitness homework is helpful for long breaks. Examples of fitness homework might be

- taking a 30-minute walk with a family member,
- doing 10 push-ups and 30 curl-ups, or
- playing a game for 20 minutes.

Children write down what they did (e.g., where did they walk, when, and with whom?), and turn in the written report. Remind children that the fitness test will indicate whether they have been keeping their contract and doing their homework.

Instructional Program

This program includes nine weeks of games and sports lessons and six weeks each of rhythmic activities and gymnastics. Units have five lessons each week. As we planned this curriculum, we used a five-day week for physical education; however, you may want to continue a unit by repeating lessons for mastery. The lessons were designed to be repeated, and for many activities repetition is necessary for mastery.

Some teachers like to set aside Friday for either (a) using the Fitness Hustles, or (b) a fun choice. The Fitness Hustles are fun and vigorous, and the students enjoy doing them regularly. Some teachers have helped to motivate students by offering Friday as a "fun choice" day if they worked hard Monday through Thursday. Teachers can offer a choice of activities for "fun choice" days, or they can allow the students to choose.

Organizing the Lessons

You can decide how to organize the lessons based on several factors. The schedule for physical education is one factor; for example, some schools do not have physical education every day. Also, consider that children enter physical education with varying backgrounds. Children who had developmental physical education in earlier grades should be ready for the activities presented here. However, children vary, and some children may need to master basic skills before doing the activities in these lessons. Facilities and equipment also influence what you can teach. The lessons demand basic equipment; however, some schools may not have all the equipment for all of the lessons.

Schools and school systems may have curricular goals that will also influence your choices. For example, one school may emphasize cooperative learning while another gives priority to physical fitness. Finally, you must consider your own skills, strengths, and values when selecting what to teach. The lessons in this book represent a wide variety of physical activities, all of which are developmentally appropriate for children from grades six to eight.

The lesson plans are arranged sequentially within each activity category, or unit. Thus the later lesson plans assume that the previous lesson plans have been taught. In addition, it is assumed that the children have mastered fundamental motor skills and have had broad experiences in a variety of games and rhythmic and gymnastics activities. If your students have not had previous formal work on the fundamental skills, remedial practice will be necessary. In this situation you may need to use lessons from the elementary physical education lessons (grades kindergarten through fifth) found in *Physical Education for Children: Daily Lessons Plans for Elementary School*, Second Edition, to teach your students what they missed in previous years.

This book contains lessons for grades six, seven, and eight for two reasons. First, acquiring motor skills requires practice and repetition; thus, it is worthwhile to introduce a large variety of skills over a year's time and then have the children repeat most of the lessons during a subsequent year or two. Second, at the end of most activities, suggestions for expansion are provided for children ready to try more advanced skills. These suggestions may be used during a second or third year.

Schools with physical education scheduled less than five days per week will not be able to complete all of the lessons in a year. In those schools teachers should plan to use all of the lessons over the three grades, perhaps allowing children to spend more time on an activity one year and not doing that activity at all the next year.

Classroom Lesson Plans

Ten classroom lesson plans are included for times when you need to teach physical education in the classroom, or some other confined space, due to weather or other activities in the gymnasium. One theme classroom lessons reinforce is the value of physical activity. When teachers are dedicated to presenting opportunities for physical activity on a regular schedule, children can sense the value teachers are assigning to such activity.

USING THE LESSON PLANS

Now we will discuss "what" to teach. Lesson plans are divided into these sections: student objectives, equipment, warm-up activities, skill- or concept-development activities, and conclud-

ing activities. You should read the entire lesson before you teach the lesson. Some teachers make notes about the lesson to take to class; others take the entire lesson plan. The lesson objectives are stated in behavioral terms so that you can see the exact purpose of the lesson; informing the students about the objectives of the lesson (i.e., what they should expect to learn) facilitates learning.

All equipment needed in the lesson is listed together to help you gather the equipment quickly before class. Cones are usually used to mark the instructional area; we recommend using cones to mark boundaries even when lines are available. The warm-up activity is explained the first time it is presented in the lessons; if the warm-up is used again, a reference to the lesson explaining the warm-up is presented. Most of the warm-up activities focus on physical fitness by requiring moderate to vigorous movement or stretching.

The body of the lesson is called the skill-development activity. This is where you demonstrate, present instructions, and provide practice opportunities and opportunities for feedback. The lessons describe the correct movement (the process or qualitative aspect of the movement). You should stress doing the movements correctly (this applies to the warm-up, too). In this section the following symbols are used:

italicized words or phrases = statements by the teacher to students and

(words in parentheses) = answers to questions

Finally, most lessons have a concluding activity, which is often a game where students use the skills practiced during the lesson.

MOTOR DEVELOPMENT INFORMATION FOR TEACHERS

Children are not miniature adults. While it is easy to assume that children are just smaller versions of adults, this assumption can lead to inappropriate expectations. Motor development concerns how children grow, mature, become more efficient, learn, respond to exercise, and feel about physical activity. Many books provide useful information about motor development. In this section we will provide some key developmental information to help you understand the lessons and maximize the physical education experience for your students.

GAMES AND SPORTS

Student objectives

Equipment

LESSON 9
SOCCER

Student Objectives

- Show increased skill in Goal Kicking.

Equipment

- 1 soccer ball for every 6 children
- 10 cones to mark goals
- Chalk, flour, tape, or cones to mark lines
- Jump ropes and cones for warm-up activities

Warm-up activities

Warm-Up Activities (5 minutes)

Circuit Training

Increase the time at each station. See Grades 6-8: Games and Sports, Warm-Ups, page 80.

Reviewing an activity

Skill-development activities

Skill-Development Activities (15 minutes)

Goal Kicking

Arrange the children in groups of six at a playing area, each group with a soccer ball.

1. The students practice Goal Kicking from a stationary position with a goalie defending; have them start with a 20-foot wide goal and a kicking line 30 feet away.
2. Gradually decrease the size of the goal and increase the distance to the kicking line.
3. Rotate students from kicker to goalie to ball chaser. Repeat.

Concluding activities

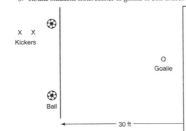

106　Physical Education for Children: Daily Lesson Plans for Middle School

Concluding Activities (10 minutes)

Introducing an activity

Line Soccer

Arrange the children into teams of six, each team with a soccer ball, with two teams assigned to each playing area. The children on each team are numbered from 1 to 6. Each playing area is marked by two parallel lines 30 feet apart. The teams line up opposite each other behind the lines.

1. Call a number from 1 to 6 to identify active players. The players with that number attempt to dribble and kick the ball below shoulder level over the opposing team's line.
2. The line players act as goalies and can use their hands to pick up the ball and throw it to an active player.
3. Only active players can score. A player stays active, and thus can score, until a new number is called or a score is made.
4. Variations:

   Increase the size of the playing area.

   Call more than one number at a time.

   Use a square formation and have four teams.

Games and Sports　107

Growth and Maturation

Each child grows and matures on an individual schedule. The environment, specifically exercise, has little effect on height or maturation; however, exercise can help children develop more skeletal mass, more muscle, and less fat. During the elementary school years growth and maturation is steady. Rapid changes in growth and maturation occur around puberty. Girls enter puberty between 9 and 11 years of age, and most girls are finished growing by age 13. Boys enter puberty between 11 and 13 years of age and are still growing at age 15. Some children mature earlier, others later. For boys, early maturation may present a short-term advantage in sports and physical education. Sometimes these boys are shorter and more muscular as adults than boys who mature later. For girls, early maturation may be a disadvantage; earlier maturing girls tend to be more pear shaped and may have larger amounts of body fat. Later maturing children (male and female) may have an advantage in sports and physical activity as adults because they are often taller (they grow over a longer time period) and more linear (leaner for their height).

Rapid growth is usually a sign of maturation, which means a number of other changes will be forthcoming. In grades six through eight, most of the girls will go through puberty, as will some of the boys. Most of the boys will start puberty by eighth grade. Teachers may want to talk to the class or individual children about normal differences in the timing of maturation and growth. Girls may feel uncomfortable because they are fully mature and tall, while boys may feel uncomfortable because they are not yet maturing and are short. Knowing that this is normal often increases their comfort level. A simple comment to the tallest girls like, "It is nice to be tall," can help them adjust to the changes associated with puberty.

Body Proportions

Children have different body proportions than adults. Teachers need to understand that certain skills may be more difficult for young children than for adults because of differences in body proportions that influence balance and leverage. Young children have relatively larger heads, relatively shorter legs, and shoulders that match their hips so they look "straight up and down." As children grow and mature their legs become longer, which means their heads appear smaller on their bodies. In young children the head is heavy and sometimes difficult to control when doing balance activities. At puberty, male shoulders grow broader, which is an advantage in many physical activities. Early maturing males will have longer legs and broader shoulders to help them perform better than later maturing children. Longer legs and arms help them run faster and throw farther.

Bones, Muscles, and Fat

Bones, muscles, and organs grow during childhood; we can observe the bones getting longer as children increase in height. The bones should also increase in breadth and density during growth. Exercise has a positive influence on bone growth.

During childhood many girls and some boys may have too much fat. Too much fat may be a sign of a health problem or, more likely, the result of environmental factors related to diet and exercise. All of us need some fat, however, there is no reason to expect anyone to gain large amounts of fat during childhood or adolescence. At puberty, males experience rapid gains in muscle, and females tend to gain fat. The observed differences in fat between males and females at puberty are due in part to environmental factors, for example, too little physical activity. Teachers should encourage young females to remain physically active.

It is important for the teacher to realize that there are few biological reasons to explain motor performance differences between boys and girls before puberty. Most observable differences in motor performance between boys and girls, even in the primary grades, are the result of different treatment and encouragement by parents, teachers, and others. Girls, just like boys, need to develop motor skills and receive the benefits of regular exercise.

If there are large variations in physical size and maturation in your class, you may want to consider these as you group children for activities. Pairing more mature children may provide better matched partners, which may be safer. Alternatively, if you are grouping children and want the groups to be similar to each other, you may have to place one more mature child in each group. Finally, smaller and less mature children should be encouraged and given the same opportunities as more mature children. A simple comment like, "When you reach your growth spurt this will be easier, so don't give up," can motivate children and keep the issues related to growth and maturation in perspective. Teachers should

- expect normal variations in physical growth and maturation,

- recognize the influence of body proportions on leverage and balance,

- consider physical size and maturation when grouping students for practice,

- encourage females to be physically active,

- talk to children about the effects of growth and maturation on performance, and

- have similar expectations for males and females prior to puberty.

Cognitive and Psychological Factors

If we look closely, we can see the differences in body proportions between children and adults. However, it is impossible to see the differences in the way children think and feel. Sometimes, we can infer these from observing the child's behavior. As children approach puberty, it is easy to forget that 11- to 13-year-old children are not adults. Before we can do a skill, we must understand what to do and remember what to do. By 11 years of age, children are using a variety of methods to help themselves solve their movement problems. For children still having trouble solving problems, teachers can provide additional information to help with understanding.

Most adults understand the relationship between practice and learning. Children may not see the relationship. When children are not able to perform a task they may assume they "just can't" do it. Teachers can help by identifying places in lessons where difficulty is expected ("I think the most difficult part of this to learn is the . . .") and by making statements about the benefits of practice ("It took me a long time and a lot of practice to learn this."). This helps children to see the relationship between practice and learning. Furthermore, it helps children to feel "normal" when they need to practice to learn a task. Observe your students; when you give them time to practice, what are they doing? Older children may avoid practice because they are afraid they will fail. From their viewpoint, it may be better to have a behavior problem (not cooperating) than to fail at the task.

Using Feedback

Teachers provide feedback during practice. Often teachers focus on encouragement, which is good. However, specific feedback about the skills is also helpful. Children want to improve; getting better at skills is important to them. Children appreciate information that will help them improve, although young children may not always be able to use the information. It takes younger children longer than older children and adults to use feedback to make corrections. Thus, allowing more time and focusing on the quality of practice, not just the quantity, is often helpful.

Children under 12 years of age need more time than you do to answer questions and respond to feedback. As a rule, provide at least 10 seconds for young children to formulate solutions. Facial expressions and body language tend to "override" other sources of feedback. So if a teacher is saying "good job" but has negative body language, the child may interpret the expression to mean "the teacher is unhappy with me."

Motivation

In addition to differences in learning, children have different feelings about and motivations for physical activity than adults. Young children focus on the task; they are motivated to learn new skills to help them determine if they are normal and if they are improving. Some children shift from being motivated by learning the task to being motivated by the status performance brings. Children who are task motivated tend to persist in physical endeavors longer than children who are ego or status motivated. Teachers should encourage children to focus on task mastery and the positive feelings associated with improvement. Teachers can help children identify improvement; children should relate improvement to practice and hard work.

Children under age 12 have difficulty seeing another person's perspective and therefore can have trouble with teamwork. Learning to cooperate is important, but learning to understand another person's feelings is difficult. Competition is not important to young children, but improvement and fun are. Children will be excited during game play in the absence of competition. Children learn about competition from adults. Competition can be stressful for children, in part, because motor skills are very public; everyone sees how you are doing. We are not suggesting that all competition is bad, but we believe that competition should be minimized during physical education. The lesson plans include very little competition, focusing instead on cooperation and skill development.

Children's perceptions about their ability influence their motivation in physical education. Children who perceive themselves as poorly skilled may spend instructional time thinking, "I am the worst student, everyone is looking at me, I am different because I am so bad." Children who perceive themselves as skilled may spend instructional time listening to the teacher. This leads to a negative spiral; first, the low-skilled child is not paying as much attention to the instruction as the high-skilled child, so the high-skilled child probably improves, making the low-skilled child feel even worse. Teachers need to help children focus attention on the task. Children can be taught to redirect their attention from negative self-thoughts to the task at hand.

Children enter school with a persistent optimism about their chances for success; this leads to a keen level of eagerness in most learning situations. Children believe that increased effort can improve their ability, and their beliefs about their performance actually exceed their performance. By fourth or fifth grade their beliefs and performance levels begin to match. Girls tend to have slightly lower self-confidence about motor skills than boys. Girls tend to have higher self-confidence about more "female" activities (e.g., dance) as compared to more "male" activities. In addition, girls' self-confidence tends to lessen with age.

Children make choices about activities; they decide whether or not to participate, whether or not to try, and how to approach learning. These decisions are influenced by their beliefs about their performance. Thus, if girls are expected to do poorly in a sport, they will have less self-confidence; this could lead to the decision not to try very hard, which results in low skill learning. Low skill leads to lower self-confidence and so forth. Teachers must actively seek to change the perceptions of children who view certain tasks as being inappropriate for them. Teachers should

- allow children time to formulate decisions about movement problems,

- provide children with the strategies (solutions) they need to learn and remember,

- relate practice to improvement and learning,

- provide general encouragement and specific feedback about skill,

- provide opportunities to cooperate with others,

- have similar expectations for boys and girls and low- and high-skilled children,

- provide equal feedback and encouragement to all children regardless of skill level, and

- make it clear to students that you value them and believe they can succeed.

The Effects of Exercise

Physical fitness is one result of a physically active lifestyle. Sedentary people are at greater risk for cardiovascular disease and other health problems. Health risk is reduced as individuals become physically active. There are many ways to be physically active: walking, gardening, housework, sport, etc. Moderate to vigorous physical activity has immediate benefits—a better conditioned and more trim body, a healthier lifestyle, better mental health—as well as long-term benefits—reduced blood pressure, a more efficient heart, weight control, and a possible longer life span.

A major goal of many middle school physical education programs is to promote physical fitness in students. Physical fitness has five components: cardiovascular fitness, muscular strength, muscular endurance, flexibility, and body leanness.

Cardiovascular Fitness

The body makes two major adjustments to prolonged rhythmic exercise, such as running, cycling, or swimming. First, muscles do their work during exercise by using fuel and oxygen. The more intense the work, the more oxygen and fuel used. The oxygen is used very rapidly, so the blood must deliver more oxygen (and fuel, too, at high exercise intensity levels) as work continues or increases. This means the lungs and heart must work harder. Generally, heart and respiration rates increase as the intensity of exercise increases. Fatigue sets in when the circulatory system can no longer keep up; work must then be stopped or reduced.

Second, exercise produces heat. The body dissipates some heat through breathing, but most heat is lost through sweating. The circulatory system increases the blood flow to the skin, and heat is lost by radiation and evaporation of sweat. Children have less ability to handle heat than adults. During exercise, especially during hot, dry weather, dehydration can occur. Fluid loss should be replaced by regular intake of water during exercise. Children should always be permitted as much water as they want during and after exercise. Water is as good for fluid replacement as sports drinks.

Children (8-15 years of age) may not respond to training as adults do for several reasons. First, children tend to be very active, so they may be more fit than adults. Second, children have higher resting and maximal heart rates. Boys' average heart rate at age 6 is 86 beats per minute; this drops to 66 beats per minute by age 13. Girls follow a similar pattern beginning at 88 beats per minute and dropping to about 70. It is thought that children have to train at a higher rate than adults to get the same benefits. Another issue is that a large part of cardiovascular capacity (aerobic capacity) is inherited; therefore, much of the difference between individuals is genetic. Therefore, since individual adults respond differently to training, it is likely that children do, too. In summary, becoming fit may be more difficult for some children than for others, and children may have to train harder than adults to get the same benefits.

Three criteria describe the minimum amount of work necessary to train the cardiovascular system: an individual must train for at least 20 minutes (duration), three times per week (frequency), at a training heart rate. Training heart rate is calculated using the following formula: (220 minus age in years) multiplied by intensity. Intensity can be any percent between 75 and 90. So for a 13-year-old, the training heart rate should be 166 beats per minute at an intensity of 80 percent (207 multiplied by 80 percent). By middle school, students should be able to take their pulse at the carotid artery (the large artery in the neck) to get their heart rate and calculate the training heart rate. Cardiovascular fitness occurs after 8 to 12 weeks of training at the appropriate intensity, frequency, and duration.

Muscular Strength and Endurance

Muscular strength and endurance develop as a result of training. Muscular strength refers to doing a movement against resistance at least one time; muscular endurance refers to doing the movement more than once. Muscular endurance influences our ability to train the cardiovascular system; for example, the heart rate may be low, but the legs are too tired to keep running. In this example, muscular endurance is low. In addition to the heart muscles associated with cardiovascular training, fitness focuses on two other muscle groups. These include the abdominal muscles, because weak abdominals are associated with lower back pain in adults; and the arm muscles, significant in such activities as chin-ups and push-ups.

For some people the first fitness issue is muscular strength, because they are unable to do one repetition of the task (e.g., one sit-up). After gain-ing the muscular strength necessary to do one repetition, the focus shifts to muscular endurance. Muscular endurance is achieved by low intensity (weight) and more repetitions, for example 10 repetitions, rest, 10 more repetitions, rest, and a final set of 10 repetitions. Strength training uses fewer repetitions and more intensity (weight or resistance). Children and females do not gain as much strength from training as males do after puberty. Therefore, the males in your class who have reached puberty will benefit more from strength training than the males who have not reached puberty and the females.

Flexibility

Flexibility is the range of motion in a joint. Good flexibility is associated with injury prevention and, in some sports, with superior performance. Flexibility varies greatly from joint to joint within individuals and is relatively easy to improve. The most common test of flexibility is touching the toes. Flexibility of the legs and lower back is important in preventing and reducing lower back pain.

Summary

During fitness instruction and training teachers should

- allow children to drink water during and after moderate to vigorous exercise,
- be aware of individual differences in response to training,
- teach children to count their heart rates by counting the carotid pulse, and
- teach children the short- and long-term values of regular exercise.

Changing Movement Patterns

We are all too familiar with the term "throw like a girl," which means the thrower did not take a step, or stepped on the same foot as the throwing hand, or exhibited very little body turn, or may have moved the object more like a shot put or dart than a baseball. Ironically, it is normal for all children to throw using this pattern when they are young; with practice the pattern becomes more efficient and vigorous. Most motor patterns follow a similar trend.

Think about how a baby walks; the steps are short and the feet are spaced far apart. Babies often move with their arms held rigid at shoulder height. Most motor skills have been described in two ways in the research literature. First is the ideal pattern: to produce the most efficient and effective outcome. This is the way experts try to do the skill. Second are the common stages observed as individuals learn the skill. Unfortunately, many of us never reach the ideal technique in a motor pattern. However, the ideal is helpful for teachers and students as a goal. Understanding the typical stages, however, is also helpful to teachers so they can identify normal performance progression and know what to expect and encourage next as the child practices.

We have included in the lessons information about the various movement patterns and what is appropriate for this age and developmental level. Experienced teachers may have studied or learned through experience the normal progression of motor patterns. They can use this information to help children by altering lessons or providing feedback. As you observe children, you will notice the orderly progression of skill development, and soon you will be able to make predictions about what the child will do next. You will notice we have not mentioned movement outcome, but only the process and qualities of the movement patterns. This is because changes are more rapid in the qualitative area; children can obtain outcome (product) information for themselves.

To teach and provide feedback about movement patterns, teachers should

- use information about individual student technique to identify the qualitative goal of the movement pattern being learned,
- understand the progression of movements so they know what to expect, and
- focus on the qualitative aspects of movements for feedback and instruction.

PRACTICAL KNOWLEDGE ABOUT TEACHING

To be an effective teacher, you need to be aware of "who," "how," and "what" you teach. The previous section covered "who": the students and the developmental changes you could expect to see. This section will cover "how" (and the lessons themselves will present "what" to teach). Ideas for arranging the environment to facilitate learning will be presented: developing a management system, getting started, and making sure that students stay on track. The guidelines presented in the following sections can be applied directly in most teaching settings but may have

to be modified slightly for other teaching situations.

Developing a Management System

Teachers should use management techniques to assure each child the opportunity to learn. As you might anticipate, every child will not behave perfectly during instructional time. Wise teachers develop a management plan before the first day of teaching. They then teach the behaviors associated with the plan during the first classes of the year and follow the plan consistently throughout the school year. Because children feel comfortable with routine and rules, good management helps children to feel comfortable and to know what to expect. A good management plan includes the following topics:

- A plan for entering and leaving the gym or play area
- A signal for starting and stopping
- A plan for distributing and gathering equipment
- A set of rules for behavior
- A standard set of consequences for violating the rules

Rules for behavior facilitate a positive learning environment, and it is important to enforce the rules and procedures at all times. Rules can be stated in a positive way and should describe the expected behaviors, for example, following directions, stopping on a designated signal, and using equipment as intended. You must clearly state that you expect students to show respect to others, listen, cooperate with a partner or in a group, encourage others to succeed, and generally behave in a socially responsible way. The list of rules should be posted in a prominent place, and time should be spent teaching each desirable skill at the beginning of the school year. Here is an example of a set of physical education rules:

1. Follow directions the first time they are given.
2. Stop and listen on the signal.
3. Use equipment only as it is intended.
4. Listen and respect others.
5. Avoid using hostile gestures, fighting, or disruptive activity.

A chart of the rules is helpful; it can be used both to teach the rules the first day of class and to remind children about the rules throughout the year. Explain that the rules ensure that everyone has an opportunity to learn, help students to know what to do, and keep class safe. Children appreciate having rules and knowing the rules because this establishes boundaries and allows them to fit in (to avoid embarrassing themselves by having negative attention directed at them). Have the students practice the rules and think of examples that would violate the rules.

Children must understand the consequences for rule violations. The following consequences might be appropriate in schools where consequences are not already established schoolwide:

- First time a child breaks a rule: a warning
- Second time a child breaks a rule: 5 minute timeout
- Third time a child breaks a rule: 10 minute timeout
- Fourth time a child breaks a rule: talk to the parent

Giving a warning should be a private event; moving into the child's space and explaining the warning is recommended. Some teachers prefer to warn children so the entire class can hear. This may embarrass a child and result in further misbehavior. General statements like, "Someone is breaking the rule," are ineffective, because children do not know who is breaking the rule. Teachers who make a regular habit of speaking to individual children can provide a warning that is indistinguishable from feedback, reinforcement, or conversation. Timeout areas can be set up in the activity area, but away from the other children and the activity. Timeout means that the child is removed from the activity. During timeout a child should not receive any positive reinforcement. Asking the child to sit on the edge of the play area with her back turned to the group is appropriate.

A key to managing children's behavior is communicating clearly and specifically what you want the children to do. Be firm and assertive when you present the discipline guidelines, and make sure the children understand the system. The following guidelines can help you maintain control of the learning environment:

- Have a designated place to gather for all instructions (e.g., under the tree, against the wall, standing on the circle).
- Provide instruction or directions only when all eyes are on you and there is absolute silence.

- Make sure that your directions are clear and complete (e.g., who goes where, how many in a group, what to do when you finish, how long you exercise).
- Have the practice area ready (e.g., clearly marked).
- Establish a plan for the distribution and collection of materials (e.g., equipment).
- Practice various formations so children can quickly get into a line, a circle, a square, and so forth.
- Use a signal to tell the children when you are finished with instructions and ready for them to move.

Classes should be organized so that children get the maximum amount of practice. Maximum practice considers both quality and quantity. Quantity is the number of turns or time doing the task; while quality is related to the process of improving, which is usually a result of student understanding, feedback, and error correction. The following guidelines are helpful in maximizing practice:

- Select some simple activities and some that are more difficult and challenging.
- Encourage children to master all tasks, but allow each child to progress at his or her own rate.
- Select activities that have wide appeal so that children will see others excited, and thus be motivated to participate themselves.
- Have enough equipment and practice area(s) so that children do not wait in line.
- Keep groups small so there is more opportunity for participation.

Getting Started

Effective teachers begin by getting the students' attention. This can be done by using a signal to stop, look, and listen. Call individual students by name if necessary, but do not start instructions until all of the students appear ready to receive information. After they appear ready to learn, use simple and precise terminology to explain the task they will be learning and what the goal or objective is. Relate the task to something they already know and can do. The following hints set the stage for a successful learning environment:

- Be certain the children understand the goal of the activity; in other words, the child must know what he or she is supposed to do. A question such as, "Can anyone tell me the important points you need to remember to perform the skill correctly?" will help.

- Be explicit about what you want the students to think about during instruction and practice. Select important cues, repeating them several times, and have the children repeat the cues aloud. Remind the children that they should remember the points because each point contributes to success.

- Give clear and concise verbal instructions in language the child can understand. However, do not talk too much. For example, when explaining the basic jump in jump rope, simply say, "Twirl the rope overhead and jump over it when it hits the ground."

- Provide a demonstration of the task. You can demonstrate or use a skilled child to demonstrate. Limit demonstrations to three repetitions.

- Provide time for the children to think about what you have said. Ask a question to determine if the children understand the activity. Try counting to 10 before calling on a student or assuming there are no questions; this amount of time allows children to formulate questions.

- Use "part practice," which means that a task that is long or has several parts should be practiced in parts. You might explain the first step, pause, and then ask the children to practice that step. Give adequate time for children to practice and think about the first step before introducing the second step using the same process. Usually the second part is added to the first part for practice.

- Explain the "why" as well as the "how" of tasks. Children need to understand how a skill will be used. Knowing the use of a skill often motivates children during practice drills. For example, explain that crunches (or sit-ups) improve the endurance of the abdominal muscles and push-ups improve endurance of the arm muscles.

- Help students attach meaning to a verbal description and demonstration of a skill by using good metaphors. The arm position for the forearm pass in volleyball could be likened to a platform that is level and firm. This helps students to perceive the movement needed for a successful pattern.

- Help children identify the parts of the activity that are critical to good performance. Using verbal labels often helps. When teaching them the forehand stroke in tennis, you might say, "Ready; turn; step; swing," to help children establish good rhythm. Counting can be used to help students establish the desirable rhythm and to focus attention.

- Help children relate new skills to skills they have already mastered. For example, say "Remember how we tossed the frisbee in our last class? Today we are going to learn the backhand drive in tennis and the movement is similar."

Staying on Track

During the course of instruction, it is the teacher's responsibility to guide learning. Managing behavior, asking critical questions so children think about what they are doing, encouraging children to make self-corrections, and providing specific feedback about performance are ways in which teachers guide learning. Providing verbal and nonverbal feedback will let the children know about acceptable behavior. Examples are: "Good job, you are all following the rules today" or "I like the way Katie put away her equipment." Deal with unacceptable behavior quickly the first time it becomes evident. Be consistent with rewards and punishments. Set limits for children, but always maintain a warm and supportive environment. For example, "I want to hear what you have to say, but don't shout. You must raise your hand." Avoid sarcasm and hostility. Use eye contact and physical touch to send a message that you are serious about your rules for behavior. Never argue with a child; instead make a statement like, "I understand, but you . . . ," which will allow you to repeat what you want the child to do. Do not use threats; for example, rather than saying, "If you don't follow the rules, I will . . . ," say, "If you line up quickly so we can begin on time, we will have time to play your favorite game at the end of class."

Help children make self-corrections, as this will allow them to become independent learners. Encourage children to monitor their own progress and to handle distractions. Spend time teaching the children self-management skills so they do not depend upon the teacher. Students can be encouraged to ask themselves a series of questions about the task, such as, "What is the goal of this task? What am I supposed to do?

What are the key elements to remember?" Some students will think about what others think of them, rather than thinking about the instructions or the task. This is true for students who may consider themselves different from the rest of the class (e.g., girls, low skilled children, or minority students). The plan may also include some self-rules to follow:

- Always pay attention to the task I'm working on.
- Avoid students who encourage me to be inattentive.
- Set a goal I want to achieve.
- Get help from the teacher if I get confused and make errors.
- Stop and think about the task when I start to think about other people.

Teachers should provide positive reinforcement for children who can manage their own behavior and regulate their own learning. Specific praise for those children who are focusing and trying hard can be a strong motivator. Feedback about the performance also helps learning. When a child makes a mistake, give the information necessary to do the skill correctly (or at least better) on the next trial. Giving corrective feedback sends a message to the child that you care about his or her learning and that you believe he or she can learn the skill. Corrective feedback is best given using the sandwich technique where you provide encouragement, corrective information, and encouragement. An example is, "Robert, I can see improvement; next time step farther forward; I know you can do it!" Allow time for children to think about feedback and make corrections before they take another turn. Watch for early signs of frustration from lack of success, and help children set realistic goals. At times the task might need to be broken down into smaller steps, or the equipment or environment might need to be changed. For example, the child could use a larger faced racket for practicing the forehand drive.

Developing Positive Feelings

An environment that encourages discussion is comfortable and nonintimidating. Children can relate interpersonally without fear of reprimand or judgment. We want children to feel good about themselves and others and have positive experiences in physical education. The following guidelines create a learning environment that stimulates discussion and critical thinking:

- Demonstrate the behavior so the children can copy you (e.g., say "please" and "thank you;" make mistakes and admit that it is okay and normal to make mistakes).
- Recognize that the contributions of each child are important. Send a message that you value each child and are interested in what each child has to say.
- Personalize the lesson whenever possible. Help the children to relate new learning to their own experiences. Encourage children to talk about themselves.
- Give each child an opportunity to share. Never allow one or two children to dominate a discussion.
- Be tactful and patient in handling incorrect responses. Try to dignify the answer and get the student back on track.
- Encourage children to talk about their favorite things or people (e.g., pets, trips, parents, movies). Ask open-ended questions that cause children to think ("What do you think about . . ."; "Think about a time when . . ."; "What do you do when . . .").
- Provide adequate "wait time" for children to respond. Ask a question, but encourage the children to think before responding.
- Encourage children to laugh with each other, but never at each other. Children should not be allowed to make fun of others because of poor or inaccurate responses.
- Watch and listen for signs that children want to include you or have special needs. For example, when a child says, "There is room to sit over here," the child is probably saying, "I want you to sit with me, but I am afraid or embarrassed to ask."
- Stand where you can see all of the children as much of the time as possible. While this is an important safety and instructional concern, your position also reflects how important all of the children are to you. Children positioned behind you or out of your view may feel left out. Some children prefer a position out of the teacher's view, while others move closer so they can demand more attention. Moving around the outside of the area allows you to see the entire group and to share your attention evenly among students.

Try to use these teaching tips as you use the lessons.

In a positive learning environment, the teacher is in control and plans in advance how to motivate students and get them actively involved in the lesson. Students of any age learn more and are more satisfied with school if they fully understand what is expected of them. As teachers, we need to be clear about the types of behavior we expect from students. Procedures for entering the gym, selecting partners and groups, working with task cards, and rotating among activity stations are examples of routines that should be taught for a more efficient, productive learning environment. A list of clear rules with consequences for breaking these rules should be posted in the gym and discussed with the students. It is important to emphasize working cooperatively in a learning group, and time should be spent teaching students the importance of listening to and showing respect for others.

UNIT ORGANIZATION

This organizational unit includes five lessons designed to show teachers how they can plan and use certain strategies to maximize students' opportunities to learn. These lessons can be used at the beginning of the school year and should be revisited any time students drift from the expected procedures.

LESSON DESCRIPTIONS

Lessons 1 and 2 introduce formations; teach a signal for start, listen, and stop; and emphasize the importance of each student taking responsibility for his or her own behavior. Students practice moving from squad to circle formation and practice changing directions on visual and verbal sig-

nals. Lesson 3 presents task cards and spacing concepts, such as close and spread. Lesson 4 continues work on task cards, teaches a station formation, and introduces journal writing as a way to get students to share their thoughts and feelings about physical education. Lesson 5 reviews cooperative group work and provides opportunities for students to work in learning groups.

ORGANIZATIONAL CONCEPTS

After deciding what to teach, teachers must decide how students will be organized for instruction and how the information will be communicated to them. At times it is appropriate to teach students in a large group. However, this whole-class concept limits the students' own choices if all students perform the same task the same way at the same time. If the task is presented to the class as a problem statement, students have more individual choice concerning response. Arranging students in small groups or in individual learning environments puts more responsibility on the learners, since the teacher cannot always correct the actions of all groups or all students at once. Whether the students will be taught as a whole class or arranged in small groups, teachers must teach a management system at the beginning of the year so students will know the exact behaviors expected of them.

Many movement tasks and sports skills can be practiced effectively in small groups. The teacher must make decisions concerning group size and opportunity for activity. Squad formation and stations are both effective ways to practice in small groups. In station work, students are divided into groups, and each group is assigned to a practice area marked in the gymnasium or on the playground. Usually each station is planned with progressive tasks; tasks can be communicated to the learners with task sheets or posters. This arrangement allows students to progress at their own rates. A different task or physical activity is practiced at each station, and usually the teacher signals when the groups are to rotate.

During physical education class, students make choices concerning which activities to participate in, how hard to try, and how to go about learning the material. Teachers need to be sensitive to the feelings and attitudes students have and help them build confidence in their abilities. Cooperative discussion groups and journal writing are examples of ways in which students can express what they feel and believe.

LESSON MODIFICATIONS

These lessons might need to be modified for students who can manage their own behavior from the beginning. Some students do not require strict rules and consequences in order to behave appropriately. On the other hand, even with rules and routines in place, there might be times when some students seem to be unable or unwilling to be productive participants in class. In this case teachers must have a specific discipline plan, perhaps involving the school principal and the parents.

ORGANIZATION

LESSON 1

SIGNALS, BOUNDARIES, GROUPINGS, AND RULES

Student Objectives

- Move among squad, line, circle, scatter, pairs, and station formations.
- Start, listen, and stop on a visual signal.
- Move in, across, around, and outside boundaries.
- Explain why a physical education class needs rules.

Equipment

- Physical Education Rules poster
- 5 balls
- 4 cones
- 10 hoops

Warm-Up Activities (5 minutes)

Movement Tasks

Use four cones to outline a large square. Divide the students into four groups, and line up one group on each side of the square.

1. The groups execute the following tasks.
2. For each task, a point is awarded to the first team to successfully complete the task.
3. Give a start signal for each task that follows:

   Run around the outside of the area.

   Run across the area and stop on the other side.

   Run around a cone that is on the side opposite you, and then return.

   Run and stop on a signal, jump three times, and skip back to your place.

   Hop across the area and stop.

   Jump across the area.

4. Give a stop signal.

Skill-Development Activities (20 minutes)

Physical Education Rules

Arrange the students in an information formation.

1. Read the rules to the students.
   - Rule 1: *Follow directions the first time they are given.*
   - Rule 2: *Keep hands, feet, and objects to yourself.*
   - Rule 3: *Stop, look, and listen on the signal.*
   - Rule 4: *Avoid hostile gestures, fighting, or game disruption.*

2. Have a discussion to help students understand why rules are important and stress that it is each student's responsibility to manage his or her own behavior.

3. Ask the following questions:

   What might happen in a class that does not have rules?

   What are some examples of behaviors that students who do not take responsibility for their own behavior might exhibit? (not paying attention when the teacher is explaining an activity, disturbing others when they are practicing, using equipment in ways that it is not intended, arguing about the rules of a game, or pushing and shoving when lining up to go back to the classroom.)

   What are some examples of behaviors that students who are responsible for their own behavior might exhibit? (listening to the teacher, always stopping on a signal, trying all activities without complaining, including all students in a game, helping students who need help, or using the equipment in the correct way.)

Formations

Use the balls for squad markers. Students should line up behind the balls. Ask the students to make the following formations:

Form five short lines (squads), with no more than six people per line, behind the five balls.

Form one long line in front of me, facing me.

Return to squads.

Each squad form a circle.

Form one large circle.

Return to squads.

Move to scatter formation.

Stand facing a partner in scatter formation.

Make a double circle with partners.

Return to squads.

Moving and Freezing by Groups

Using four groups, line up one group on each side of the square marked with four cones. Assign each group a number.

1. Call the number of a group (e.g., "Squad 1"). That group moves around within the boundaries (in the area marked by cones) until you provide a visual signal (for example, holding your hand in the air).

2. On the visual signal, the squad freezes and returns to starting position. Repeat these two steps until all groups have had at least one turn.

3. Repeat this procedure, giving directions to run around the outside of the boundaries, to move across the area, and so on.

Concluding Activities (5 minutes)

Cooperative Hoop Moves

Arrange the students in groups of four or five at one end of the play area. Give each group two hoops.

1. Each team starts by standing in a hoop behind a starting line, with a person toward the front of the team holding a second hoop.
2. Mark a finish line 30 feet away.
3. The second hoop is placed on the ground toward the finish line, but where team members can step or jump into the hoop.
4. When the whole team is in the second hoop, a team member reaches back and picks up the first hoop.
5. This hoop is placed on the ground toward the finish line, and the team moves into it. This continues until all the teams have traversed the distance from the starting line to the finish line.
6. If a team member falls or touches the ground outside the hoop with any body part, that team must return to the starting line and begin again.
7. The first team to cross the finish line wins.

LESSON 2
SIGNALS, BOUNDARIES, GROUPINGS, AND RULES

Student Objectives

- Change direction on a visual signal.
- Move diagonally, lengthwise, and cross-wise across an area.
- Move in an area within an area.
- Give situational examples of rules.
- Cooperate in a discussion group.

Equipment

- Physical Education Rules poster
- Four cones

Warm-Up Activities (5 minutes)

Moving to Visual Signs

Arrange four cones to form a rectangle. In response to the following visual signals, the students move in the indicated directions and stop. Movement should be continuous unless the stop signal is given.

Thumb pointed over your shoulder. (Students move forward.)

Finger pointed right. (Students move left.)

Finger pointed left. (Students move right.)

Finger pointed straight ahead. (Students move backward.)

Hand held up with palm facing front. (Students stop.)

Finger pointed to either back corner. (Students move diagonally.)

Hand held up with palm facing front. (Students stop.)

Skill-Development Activities (20 minutes)

Form Two Teams

Students form a line on a boundary line and count off by twos.

1. The number ones move across the area to the other boundary line.
2. The ones are Team 1 and the twos are Team 2.

Touch Down

Team 1 lines up on a boundary line with each player holding both hands out in front, hands placed together to form a pocket. Team 2 lines up on the opposite boundary line. You hold a small object that is used as the bait.

1. Holding the small object, walk to each student pretending to drop the object in the student's hands.
2. Give the object to a student, but don't let the opposing team know who that person is.
3. On a signal the teams run to the opposite boundary lines, with each player on Team 2 attempting to tag a player on Team 1.
4. If the player with the object gets to the opposite boundary line without being tagged, Team 1 scores a point.
5. Repeat with Team 2 as the carrying team.

Moving Within a Rectangle

Arrange the students in four groups. Divide the rectangle into quarters (point out imaginary lines), and place one group in each of the quarters.

1. Ask the students to move within their own areas.
2. The students stop on a signal, and on the next signal they move together to another area.
3. Repeat, with the rule that they cannot go to the same area twice.

Concluding Activities (5 minutes)

Rules

Ask the students to recall and verbally list the rules. Watch for situations in the remainder of the organization lessons that are examples of good rules behavior; stop the class and point them out.

Cooperative Discussion Groups

Arrange the students in groups of four to six to form heterogeneous discussion groups. Have equal representation of students of different races, ethnic origins, social classes, and gender.

1. Establish guidelines for cooperative discussion groups. Tell the children that

    everyone must participate in the discussion;

    only one student can talk at a time, and the others must listen; and

    everyone must show respect for others.

2. Present a topic for the groups to discuss. Here are some examples:

    Describe a student who takes responsibility for his or her own behavior.

    What should we do with students in our class who fail to take responsibility for their own behavior?

    How should we deal with students who do not follow the class rules?

    How should we deal with students who do not try?

    How should we deal with students who do not take care of the equipment?

LESSON 3
SPACING, EQUIPMENT, STATIONS, AND RULES

Student Objectives

- Use task cards.
- Demonstrate three spacings.
- Relate rule-infraction consequences to rules.
- Cooperate in a discussion group.

Equipment

- Physical Education Rules poster
- Four cones
- Task cards

Warm-Up Activities (5 minutes)

Distances

Use four cones to outline a rectangle. Arrange the students with partners in scatter formation inside the rectangle.

1. Ask the students to respond to the following commands:

   Stand 1 or 2 steps from your partner. This is close.

   Stand 5 or 6 steps from your partner. This is spread.

   Walk 10 steps away from your partner. This is distant.

   Remember how far away you are from your partner when you are close, spread, and distant.

2. Have the students respond quickly to the following commands: *Close, distant, close, spread, distant, close, spread, close.*

Skill-Development Activities (20 minutes)

Partner Relay

Arrange the students with partners and assign each pair to either Team 1 or Team 2. The teams line up in pairs on a boundary line designated as the starting line. One person in each pair is identified as Player A; the other is identified as Player B.

1. Hold up a task card that describes the movement to be used in the relay and identifies the direction of movement for the two players.
2. Each pair must look to see what the task is and what the direction for each player is.
3. Use the following symbols to represent direction of movement:

   X = Forward

   O = Backward

   < = Sideways
4. Here are some examples of tasks and directions:

   Player A Run X

   Player B Jump O
5. The players must move to the return line and back to the starting line using the correct movement and direction. Players moving incorrectly must start over.
6. The second pair cannot start until both Player A and Player B return to the starting line.
7. Change the card after two or three pairs have finished a turn. The first team to have all players return to the starting line wins.

Concluding Activities (5 minutes)

Rules

1. Ask the students to recall and recite the rules. See Grades 6-8: Organization, Lesson 1, page 4.
2. Describe the consequences for infractions:

   First offense: 5-minute timeout

   Second offense: 10-minute timeout

   Third offense: call to parents

   Fourth offense: removal from class, 15 minutes in isolation

   Fifth offense: visit to principal
3. Ask if there are any questions.

Cooperative Discussion Groups

Arrange the students in groups of four to six to form heterogeneous discussion groups. See Grades 6-8: Organization, Lesson 2, page 7. Present a topic for the groups to discuss. Here are some examples:

Describe a student who doesn't try in physical education.

What should we do if some students don't try?

What would our class be like if nobody tried?

How should we deal with students who always want to argue with other students and the teacher?

How should we deal with students who shove and hit other students?

LESSON 4
FORMING GROUPS AND JOURNAL WRITING

Student Objectives

- Use tasks cards in a station formation.
- Share their feelings about physical education in writing.

Equipment

- Task cards
- A notebook and pencil for each child

Warm-Up Activities (5 minutes)

Forming Groups

Review forming groups with adaptations. Cards are made before class and distributed to the children as they enter the gym. Each card should be either red, blue, yellow, or green; cards should have different team names printed on them (e.g., Cubs, Cardinals, Rangers, or Orioles). Cards should be numbered from 1 to 28 or the number of children who are in the class. With 28 students in the class, there should be 7 red, 7 blue, 7 yellow, and 7 green cards. Each team name should be printed at least once on each color.

1. Present the following tasks:

    Find a partner who has the same color card. Students should ignore the team name and the number.

    Now find a partner who has the same number on the card. Students should ignore the team name and the color.

2. Form two groups. Cardinals and Cubs make up one group, and Rangers and Orioles make up the second group. Students should ignore the color and the number.

3. Continue with other combinations.

4. Form two groups. Group 1 = numbers 1 through 14 and Group 2 = numbers 15 through 28.

5. Form four groups. Group 1 = Cardinals, Group 2 = Cubs, Group 3 = Rangers, and Group 4 = Orioles.

Skill-Development Activities (20 minutes)

Task Cards

Fitness tasks are printed on cards large enough for the students to read (8 1/2 inches by 11 inches or larger).

1. Place one of the cards at each of the four stations.
2. Students are assigned to a station and on a signal move to the next station. Allow two or three minutes at each station.

    Task Card #1: Run in place 50 steps or more without stopping.

    Task Card #2: Moving in circles or figure-eights, gallop or skip for 50 steps without stopping.

    Task Card #3: Hop 25 times on the right foot and 25 times on the left foot.

    Task Card #4: Jump in place at least 50 times.

Partner Relay

Arrange the students in pairs and assign each pair to one of five relay teams. Mark a starting line and a return line.

1. At the return line, place a stack of cards for each relay team.
2. The cards (one for each pair) should specify how the pair will return to the starting line. Here are some examples:

    Run with one person going forward and one going backward.

    Hold hands, face each other, and slide.

    Gallop with opposite feet forward.

Concluding Activities (5 minutes)

Feelings About Physical Education

Arrange the children in scatter formation. Each child needs a notebook and a pencil.

1. Ask the children to think about their own feelings when they were in physical education last year.
2. Stimulate the students' thinking by asking some of the following open-ended questions:

    I feel good in physical education when I . . .

    My favorite activity is . . .

    If I were the teacher, I would change . . .

    Some things I do not like about physical education are . . .

3. This should be a serious activity and students' responses should be private and not discussed in class.
4. You should read the journals to get ideas about how the students think and feel about their experiences in physical education.

LESSON 5
COOPERATIVE TEAMS AND DISCUSSION GROUPS

Student Objectives

- Work successfully in a student learning group.
- Cooperate in a discussion group.

Equipment

- Six playground balls

Warm-Up Activities (5 minutes)

Forming Groups

Review forming groups with adaptations. See Grades 6-8: Organization, Lesson 4, page 10.

Skill-Development Activities (20 minutes)

Cooperative Learning Groups

Arrange the students in groups of four to six to form heterogeneous learning teams.

1. Review the guidelines for cooperative group work (see Grades 6-8: Organization, Lesson 2, page 7).

2. Discuss that in group work cooperative effort is important.

   Each student is responsible for his or her own work and the work of the team. The group is not successful unless all students accomplish the goal.

   Students must help each other.

   Each student must try hard.

3. Present a problem for the groups to solve. Here are some examples:

   Create a ball game that uses throwing and catching.

   Create a ball game that uses kicking.

   Discover ways to explain the meaning of balance.

   Discover ways to explain the meaning of strength.

Concluding Activities (5 minutes)

Cooperative Discussion Groups

1. Continue work with cooperative grouping by asking students to discuss a variety of topics.

2. Present open-ended questions for the groups to discuss and arrive at a solution. All groups discuss the same question. Here are some examples:

   What should we do about students in our class who do not like physical education?

   Why is physical education important?

   What are the most important things we can learn in physical education this year?

   What does playing fair mean?

   Why is it important to follow the rules when playing a game?

3. A representative from each group shares the solution with the entire class.

Improving student fitness has long been a priority for school physical education. Healthy lifestyles begin with positive exercise values developed early in life. A glance at the media in the United States and other countries indicates a major emphasis on moderate to vigorous physical activity and its immediate benefits, which include a better conditioned and trimmer body, a healthier lifestyle, and better mental health; as well as its long-term effects of reduced blood pressure, a more efficient heart, weight control, and a possible longer life span. Physical fitness promotes good health and provides the resources for individuals to successfully perform their daily activities without undue fatigue. Most authorities agree that physical fitness involves cardiorespiratory function, muscular strength, muscular endurance, flexibility, and leanness.

UNIT ORGANIZATION

This section includes lessons and activities for use in the fitness phase of the program. There are descriptions of a Fitness Hustle Warm-Up, three Fitness Hustles, and several lessons designed to help students learn the Hustles. Fitness Hustles are simply aerobic exercises to music. You can use the steps described here to put together different sequences, you can adapt the steps described to make them more challenging to the students, or you can create new steps of your own. In addition, after some practice the students can create their own steps.

The program provides two weeks for assessing growth and health-related fitness; a day-by-day plan for accomplishing the assessment is described in this section. During these two weeks, you have time to practice the Fitness Hustles so that the students can perform the sequence rhythmically. It is also suggested that you take time to practice the health-related fitness test, especially the mile run. Other assessment items described in this section are those for height, weight, degree of fatness, strength, muscular endurance, and flexibility.

There are 15 other fitness lessons; they include a variety of activities such as circuit training, rope jumping, jogging, and moderate to vigorous games. Each lesson has a warm-up routine and approximately 12 to 15 minutes of spirited activity designed to provide a good workout. The concluding activity for each fitness lesson introduces a fitness concept and provides ways for the students to learn the information needed for planning their own fitness programs. Students are given numerous opportunities to work in cooperative groups to solve fitness problems. These 15 lessons can be grouped together into a fitness unit, or they can be distributed throughout the year, depending on your needs and personal choice.

LESSON DESCRIPTIONS

Lessons 1 through 5 present the Fitness Hustles and provide opportunities to practice them. Lessons 6 through 10 introduce assessment items, including height, skinfolds, flexibility, the one-mile run, and sit-ups; these are used in combination with the Fitness Hustles. Lessons 11 through 15 outline procedures for administering the tests and developing individual fitness contracts.

Lessons 16 through 20 introduce an Individual Stretching Routine and a beginning level circuit. The circuit includes exercises for cardiovascular endurance, agility, muscular strength, and muscular endurance. A progression plan is presented so that the circuit can be used throughout the year as a warm-up or fitness activity. A variety of partner fitness activities are also offered for variety. Each lesson introduces a fitness concept as a concluding activity.

Lessons 21 through 25 continue with the same format, offering an advanced circuit and additional fitness concepts. Lessons 26 and 27 use rope jumping and jogging for cardiovascular endurance. Lesson 28 introduces Chinese rope jumping and uses cooperative jogging as a cardiovascular activity. Lesson 29 continues with Chinese rope jumping, progressing to intermediate level skills. Fitness stunts are used in this lesson for the development of muscular strength and endurance. Fitness games and additional stunts are presented in Lesson 30. Each of the last 15 Fitness lessons includes 5 or 10 minutes of concluding activities designed to develop conceptual information about health and fitness.

FITNESS CONCEPTS

Physical fitness is part of total well-being and implies the ability to carry out the usual day's activities without undue fatigue. Other aspects of well-being include mental, social, and emotional health. A healthy diet, regular exercise, saying "no" to drugs and alcohol, and making responsible decisions can contribute to a better quality of life.

Physical fitness includes five components: cardiorespiratory endurance, flexibility, muscular endurance, muscular strength, and leanness. Cardiorespiratory, or aerobic, fitness is the ability of the circulatory system to pump oxygen-rich blood to the muscles. Flexibility is the ability to move a joint through a full range of motion. Muscular endurance is the ability of a muscle to repeat a movement many times. Muscular strength is the greatest amount of weight a muscle can lift. Leanness refers to a lack of excess body fat.

Anaerobic endurance is the ability to exercise at high intensity levels for a short period of time. Jogging, cycling, and swimming are examples of anaerobic exercise. Running the 100-yard dash is an example of an anaerobic exercise.

To increase aerobic fitness, the overload prin-

ciple should be considered. To *overload* is to place greater than usual demands on the cardiorespiratory system, or to work harder than usual. The overload principle should also be considered when exercising for gains in strength, muscular endurance, and flexibility.

The frequency of exercise refers to how often exercise is done. The recommended frequency to achieve aerobic fitness is three to four times a week. Intensity of exercise refers to how much work is done during an exercise session. To achieve aerobic fitness, an overload must be placed on the cardiorespiratory system.

Skill-related components of fitness include agility, speed, and balance. Agility refers to the ability to change directions quickly. Speed is the ability to move from one place to another in a short period of time. Balance is the ability to maintain a position for a certain period of time.

The development of muscular strength and muscular endurance requires a different type of exercise. To increase strength, heavy weights should be used. To develop endurance of the muscle, many repetitions should be done with lighter weights. In strength training the size of the muscle increases; in endurance training muscle size does not change much, but the muscle can work longer.

To increase flexibility, the overload principle must be applied. Stretching exercises lengthen the muscles and thereby increase the range of motion in a joint. A slow stretch should be used, rather than a ballistic, or bouncing, stretch.

A healthy level of body fat is required for high-level wellness and good health. Exercise plays a role in weight management.

TEACHING TIPS

Students should be encouraged to discover and find answers to their own fitness problems, realizing that every individual has special needs. It is important to make students feel comfortable with their own abilities and competence, while guiding them toward healthy decisions about their lives. You might want to spend a little extra time trying to change the students' negative ability perceptions. Students must believe that increased effort can improve their fitness and health.

Table F4.1: Unit Plan for Level Four: Fitness

Week 2: Hustles	Week 3: testing	Week 4: testing
Monday: introduce warm-up Tuesday: introduce Hustles I, II Wednesday: practice Hustles I, II Thursday: introduce Hustle III Friday: practice Hustles	Monday: Hustle I, skinfolds, height Tuesday: Hustle II, weight, skinfolds Wednesday: flexibility and sit-and-reach test, Hustle I or II Thursday: introduce one-mile run and sit-ups Friday: practice one-mile run and sit-ups	Monday: one-mile run Tuesday: sit-up test Wednesday: fitness contracts Thursday: introduce jogging Friday: fitness circuit

Week 14: Hustles	Week 16: circuit training	Week 17: fitness challenges
Monday: warm-up Tuesday: review Hustles I, II Wednesday: practice Hustles I, II Thursday: review Hustle III Friday: practice Hustle III	Monday: stretching, Circuit I, partner fitness Tuesday: stretching, Circuit I, partner fitness Wednesday: stretching, Circuit I, obstacle Thursday: stretching, Circuit I, follow leader, five-minute jump Friday: stretching, Circuit I, follow leader, 10-minute jump	Monday: stretching, advanced circuit training Tuesday: stretching, advanced circuit training Wednesday: stretching, advanced circuit training Thursday: stretching, advanced circuit training Friday: stretching, advanced circuit training

Week 25: moderate to vigorous games
Monday: stretching, rope jump, jogging Tuesday: stretching, rope jump, five-minute jump, jogging Wednesday: stretching, Chinese jump, jogging Thursday: stretching, Chinese jump, fitness stunts Friday: stretching, fitness stunts, fitness games

Note: This is one way to organize these lessons. More likely you will want to use lessons throughout the year rather than planning all fitness instruction in one unit. In any curriculum plan, the fitness assessment is repeated at the end of the year.

LESSON 1
FITNESS WARM-UP

Student Objectives

- Demonstrate the steps to the Hustle Warm-Up.
- Demonstrate the Hustle Warm-Up routine.

Equipment

- Music: "Thriller" from *A Thriller for Kids* (side B), Georgiana Stewart, Kimbo Records (KIM 7065)

Skill-Development Activities (25 minutes)

Steps for Grades 6-8 Hustle Warm-Up

Arrange children in a scatter formation.

1. Teach the steps to the warm-up routine individually.
2. Combine the steps and have the children perform them to music as indicated.

Alternate Heel Lift

Standing with feet comfortably apart, the student lifts the right and left heels alternately, similar to walking in place.

Heel Lifts

Standing with feet together and hands on hips, the student lifts both heels up so that weight is on toes and then returns to starting position.

Knee Touch

Standing with feet comfortably apart, the student lifts the left knee and touches it with the right elbow and then returns to starting position. The movement is repeated, using the right knee and the left elbow.

Count 1: Lift knee and touch.

Count 2: Return to starting position.

Twisting Knee Bend

Standing in a straddle position with heels flat, the student holds arms parallel to the floor with elbows bent, bends the knees, and at the same time twists the body to the left, and then returns to starting position. The movement is repeated with a bend and twist to the right.

Count 1: Bend and twist to the left.

Count 2: Return to starting position.

Count 3: Bend and twist to the right.

Count 4: Return to starting position.

Grades 6-8 Hustle Warm-Up Routine

1. Play "Thriller."

2. Have the children perform the following sequence of steps:

   Heel Lifts (16 counts)

   Alternate Heel Lift (16 counts)

   Heel Lifts (16 counts)

   Alternate Heel Lift (16 counts)

   Knee Touch (16 counts)

   Twisting Knee Bend (16 counts)

   Knee Touch (16 counts)

   Twisting Knee Bend (16 counts)

   Heel Lifts (16 counts)

   Alternate Heel Lift (16 counts)

   Heel Lifts (16 counts)

   Alternate Heel Lift (16 counts)

   Knee Touch (16 counts)

   Twisting Knee Bend (16 counts)

   Knee Touch (16 counts)

   Twisting Knee Bend (16 counts)

3. Demonstrate and have the children practice the Warm-Up Routine.

LESSONS 2 AND 3
FITNESS HUSTLES I AND II

Student Objectives

- Demonstrate Fitness Hustles I and II.

Equipment

- Music: "Flashdance" from *A Thriller for Kids* (side B), Georgiana Stewart, Kimbo Records (KIM 7065)
- Music: "Breakin . . . There's No Stopping Us" from *A Thriller for Kids*, Georgiana Stewart, Kimbo Records (KIM 7065)

Skill-Development Activities (25 minutes)

Steps for Fitness Hustle I

Arrange children in a scatter formation. Teach the steps to be used in Hustles I and II.

Break
The student does a double bounce with feet together, clapping on the first bounce.

Step-Kick and Reach
The student steps slightly to the left on the left foot, kicks the right leg forward, and reaches toward the kicking foot with the opposite hand. The movement is repeated on the other side.

Jog-Karate Kick

The student jogs in place three steps then kicks to the side, alternating the kicking leg (i.e., jog right, left, right, kick left; jog left, right, left, kick right).

Double Scissors

Scissors: The student jumps to a stride position with one arm swinging forward and up and the other arm swinging down and back, then jumps again, changing forward and back legs and arms, continuing to alternate right and left legs.

Double Scissors: The student executes the Scissors step with a double bounce before changing legs and arms. That is, the student jumps to a stride position with one arm swinging forward and up and the other arm swinging down and back, and then jumps or bounces in that position.

Twist and Bounce

With feet together, the student bounces in place while twisting feet and hips to the left and arms and shoulders to the right. The movements are repeated to the other side, alternating on each bounce.

Grasshopper

The student hops on the left foot while lifting the right knee up to the side; repeats, hopping on right foot and lifting left knee up to side; and continues, alternating right and left.

Heel and Arm Swing

The student jumps in place, extending the right foot forward and touching heel to floor while the left arm swings forward and up and the right arm swings down; jumps again, changing legs and arm swings; and continues, alternating right and left.

Knee Dip With Elbow Pull

Standing with feet comfortably apart and heels flat, the student bends the knees halfway, keeping the back straight, and then returns to standing position, keeping elbows bent with arms parallel to the floor. With each knee bend, elbows are pulled backward.

Knee Touch

The student step-hops on the right foot, lifting the left knee forward while touching the right elbow to the left knee. The step-hop is repeated on the left foot, with the left elbow touching the right knee. The movement continues, alternating right and left.

Diagonal Jog Right, Left

The student jogs diagonally forward eight steps to the right-hand corner of the room and then jogs diagonally back to the starting point. The Diagonal Jog is repeated to the left-hand corner and back. This jogging motion is the same as straight-ahead jogging.

Rocker Step

The student bounces on the right foot with the left leg extended to the side, then bounces on the left foot with the right leg extended to the side, then repeats on the right foot, hopping on the last rock (i.e., rock right, left, right, hop on right). The movement is repeated with the hop on the left foot.

Fitness Hustle I

1. Play "Flashdance."
2. Perform the following steps:

   Break (16 counts)

   Repeat (16 counts)

   Jog-Karate Kick (16 counts)

   Grasshopper (16 counts)

   Jog-Karate Kick (16 counts)

   Grasshopper (16 counts)

   Heel and Arm Swing (16 counts)

   Rocker Step (16 counts)

   Heel and Arm Swing (16 counts)

   Rocker Step (16 counts)

   Break (16 counts)

   Repeat (16 counts)

   Jog-Karate Kick (16 counts)

Grasshopper (16 counts)

Jog-Karate Kick (16 counts)

Grasshopper (16 counts)

Heel and Arm Swing (16 counts)

Rocker Step (16 counts)

3. Demonstrate and have the children practice Fitness Hustle I.

Fitness Hustle II

1. Play "Breakin . . . There's No Stopping Us."

2. Perform the following steps:

Twist and Bounce (16 counts)

Repeat (16 counts)

Grasshopper (16 counts)

Heel and Arm Swing (16 counts)

Grasshopper (16 counts)

Heel and Arm Swing (16 counts)

Diagonal Jog Right (16 counts)

Diagonal Jog Left (16 counts)

Diagonal Jog Right (16 counts)

Diagonal Jog Left (16 counts)

Knee Dip With Elbow Pull (16 counts)

Knee Touch (16 counts)

Knee Dip With Elbow Pull (16 counts)

Knee Touch (16 counts)

Diagonal Jog Right (16 counts)

Diagonal Jog Left (16 counts)

Diagonal Jog Right (16 counts)

Diagonal Jog Left (16 counts)

3. Demonstrate and have the children practice Fitness Hustle II.

LESSON 4
FITNESS HUSTLE III

Student Objectives

- Demonstrate the Hustle Warm-Up.
- Practice Hustle I.
- Demonstrate the steps for Hustle III.

Equipment

- Music: "Thriller" and "Flashdance" from *A Thriller for Kids* (side B), Georgiana Stewart, Kimbo Records (KIM 7065)
- Music: "Beat Street Strut" from *A Thriller for Kids* (side B), Georgiana Stewart, Kimbo Records (KIM 7065)

Warm-Up Activities (5 minutes)

Fitness Hustle Warm-Up

Arrange children in a scatter formation. See Grades 6-8: Fitness, Lesson 1, page 20. Perform the Fitness Hustle Warm-Up to "Thriller."

Skill-Development Activities (20 minutes)

Fitness Hustle I

Arrange the children in a scatter formation. See Grades 6-8: Fitness, Lessons 2 and 3, page 21.

1. Review the steps to Hustle I: Break, Jog-Karate Kick, Grasshopper, Heel and Arm Swing, Rocker Step.
2. Perform Hustle I to "Flashdance."

Fitness Hustle III

1. Play "Beat Street Strut."
2. Review the steps in Hustle III: Twist and Bounce, Double Scissors, Knee Dip With Elbow Pull, Knee Touch, Grasshopper.
3. Describe and demonstrate the step sequence for Hustle III.
4. Perform the following steps:

   Twist and Bounce (16 counts)

   Repeat (16 counts)

   Double Scissors (16 counts)

Knee Dip With Elbow Pull (16 counts)

Double Scissors (16 counts)

Knee Dip With Elbow Pull (16 counts)

Knee Touch (16 counts)

Grasshopper (16 counts)

Knee Touch (16 counts)

Grasshopper (16 counts)

Twist and Bounce (16 counts)

Repeat (16 counts)

Double Scissors (16 counts)

Knee Dip With Elbow Pull (16 counts)

Double Scissors (16 counts)

Knee Dip With Elbow Pull (16 counts)

Knee Touch (16 counts)

Grasshopper (16 counts)

Knee Touch (16 counts)

Grasshopper (16 counts)

5. Demonstrate and have the children practice Fitness Hustle III.

LESSON 5
PRACTICING HUSTLES IN COOPERATIVE GROUPS

Student Objectives

- Cooperate with a learning team to reach a goal.
- Demonstrate the steps for the Fitness Hustles.

Equipment

- Music: Hustle Warm-Up—"Thriller" from *A Thriller for Kids*, Georgiana Stewart, Kimbo Records (KIM 7065)
- Music: Hustle I—"Flashdance," from *A Thriller for Kids*, Georgiana Stewart, Kimbo Records (KIM 7065)
- Music: Hustle II—"Breakin," from *A Thriller for Kids*, Georgiana Stewart, Kimbo Records (KIM 7065)
- Music: Hustle III—"Beat Street Strut," from *A Thriller for Kids*, Georgiana Stewart, Kimbo Records (KIM 7065)

Warm-Up Activities (5 minutes)

Fitness Hustle Warm-Up

Arrange the children in scatter formation. The children perform the Fitness Hustle Warm-Up (see Grades 6-8: Fitness, Lesson 1, page 20).

Skill-Development Activities (20 minutes)

Practice Hustle Steps in Cooperative Learning Groups

Arrange the children in groups of four to six to form heterogeneous learning teams. See Grades 6-8: Organization, Lesson 2, page 7.

1. Review the guidelines for cooperative group work.
2. Explain that the goal today is cooperative effort, and each person is responsible for both his or her learning and the team's learning. Every student in the group must master all steps before the team can be successful.

3. Print the name of each step in each Hustle on a task card. Make enough packets to distribute a packet of cards to each group. Each group should have an 8 1/2-inch by 11-inch card for each step.

4. Children in each group take turns showing the cards to the others in the group.

5. The step on the card is practiced until another step is shown.

6. The children are encouraged to help each other because the group is successful only when each child in the group has mastered the skills.

7. Students report to the teacher when the group is ready to take a mastery test. A group reward is given to the group with the best overall performance.

Concluding Activities (5 minutes)

The group winning the performance award selects one of the Fitness Hustles for the entire class to perform.

LESSONS 6-10
GROWTH AND HEALTH-RELATED PHYSICAL FITNESS TESTING

Monday

Measure height and skinfolds.

Equipment: Measuring tape and skinfold calipers, music for Fitness Hustle I

Organization: Divide the children into four groups of five to seven children each.

Activities: Perform the following activities:

1. Briefly review Fitness Hustle I (see Lessons 2 and 3) for the total group (5 minutes).
2. Have three groups practice the hustle; keep the fourth group with you and measure the height of each child. Rotate groups until all children have been measured (15 minutes).
3. Start rotation again and measure skinfolds at the triceps and subscapular sites (10 minutes).

Tuesday

Measure weight and skinfolds.

Equipment: Scale and skinfold calipers, music for Fitness Hustle II

Organization: Use the same four groupings used Monday.

Activities: Perform the following activities:

1. Briefly review Fitness Hustle II (see Lessons 2 and 3) for the total group (5 minutes).
2. Have three groups practice the hustle; keep the fourth group with you and measure skinfolds, picking up from Monday (15 minutes).
3. Start rotation again. Weigh the students (10 minutes).
4. Continue measurement of skinfolds at the triceps and subscapular sites.

   • Take the sum of the triceps and subscapular sites and, using table F4.2, find the percentile reading to the left for each child.
   • You should be concerned about children who fall below the 25th percentile.

Table F4.2: NCYFS Norms by Age (in Years) for the Sum of Triceps and Subscapular Skinfolds—Boys and Girls (in Millimeters)

Percentile	10	11	12	13	14	15	16	17	18
Boys									
99	9	9	9	9	9	10	10	10	11
90	12	12	12	11	12	12	12	13	13
80	13	13	13	13	13	13	13	14	14
75	14	14	14	13	13	14	14	14	15
70	15	15	15	14	14	14	14	15	15
60	16	16	16	15	15	15	15	16	17
50	17	18	17	17	17	17	17	17	18
40	20	20	20	19	18	18	18	19	19
30	22	23	22	21	21	20	20	21	22
25	24	25	24	23	22	22	22	22	24
20	25	26	28	25	25	24	23	24	25
10	35	36	38	34	33	32	30	30	30
Girls									
99	10	11	11	12	12	13	13	16	14
90	13	14	15	15	17	19	19	20	19
80	15	16	17	18	19	21	21	22	21
75	16	17	18	19	20	23	22	23	22
70	17	18	18	20	21	24	23	24	23
60	18	19	21	22	24	26	24	26	25
50	20	21	22	24	26	28	26	28	27
40	22	24	24	26	28	30	28	31	28
30	25	28	27	29	31	33	32	34	32
25	27	30	29	31	33	34	33	36	34
20	29	33	31	34	35	37	35	37	36
10	36	40	40	43	40	43	42	42	42

Reprinted from Ross, Dotson, and Katz 1985.

Wednesday

Measure flexibility with the backsaver sit-and-reach test.

Equipment: Sit-and-reach box, music for Fitness Hustle I or II

Organization: Use the same four groupings as on Tuesday.

Activities: Perform the following activities:

1. The same as for Tuesday, except measure flexibility.
2. Sit-and-reach test
   - The sit-and-reach test is performed in a sitting position without shoes (see figure on next page). The first figure shows a more detailed view of the box used in the test.
   - The child attempts to reach as far down the box as possible while keeping one leg extended straight out from the body. Bend the other leg at the knee and place that foot by the knee of the extended leg.
   - There is a measurement scale on the top of the box; the child reaches forward as far as possible with the palms down and fingers extended for four tries.

- The child holds the position of maximum reach (for at least one second) on the fourth try; this score is recorded (to the nearest inch). Table F4.3 gives the norms for the sit-and-reach test.

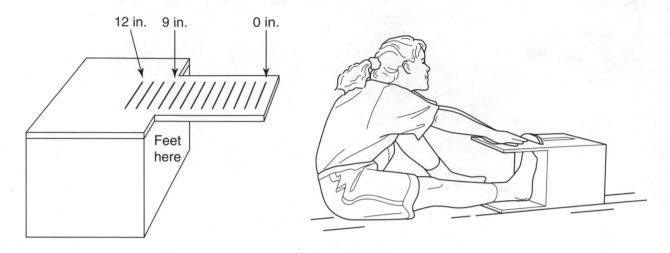

Table F4.3: NCYFS Norms by Age for the Sit-and-Reach—Boys and Girls (in Inches)

Percentile	10	11	12	13	14	15	16	17	18
Boys									
99	18.0	18.5	18.5	19.5	20.0	21.5	22.0	21.5	22.0
90	16.0	16.5	16.0	16.5	17.5	18.0	19.0	19.5	19.5
80	15.0	15.5	15.0	15.0	16.0	17.0	18.0	18.0	18.0
75	14.5	15.0	15.0	15.0	15.5	16.5	17.0	17.5	17.5
70	14.5	14.5	14.5	14.5	15.0	16.0	17.0	17.0	17.0
60	14.0	14.0	13.5	13.5	14.0	15.0	16.0	16.0	16.0
50	13.5	13.0	13.0	13.0	13.5	14.0	15.0	15.5	15.0
40	12.5	12.5	12.0	12.5	13.0	13.5	14.0	14.5	14.5
30	12.0	12.0	11.5	12.0	12.0	12.5	13.5	13.5	13.5
25	11.5	11.5	11.0	11.0	11.0	12.0	13.0	13.0	13.0
20	11.0	11.0	10.5	10.5	11.0	11.5	12.0	12.5	12.5
10	10.0	9.5	8.5	9.0	9.0	9.5	10.0	10.5	10.0
Girls									
99	20.5	20.5	21.0	22.0	22.0	23.0	23.0	23.0	22.5
90	17.5	18.0	19.0	20.0	19.5	20.0	20.5	20.5	20.5
80	16.5	17.0	18.0	19.0	19.0	19.0	19.5	19.5	19.5
75	16.5	16.5	17.0	18.0	18.5	19.0	19.0	19.0	19.0
70	16.0	16.5	17.0	17.5	18.0	18.5	19.0	19.0	18.5
60	15.0	15.5	16.0	17.0	17.5	18.0	18.0	18.0	18.0
50	14.5	15.0	15.5	16.0	17.0	17.0	17.5	18.0	17.5
40	14.0	14.0	15.0	15.5	16.0	17.0	17.0	17.0	17.0
30	13.0	13.5	14.5	14.5	15.0	16.0	16.5	16.0	16.0
25	13.0	13.0	14.0	14.0	15.0	15.5	16.0	15.5	15.5
20	12.0	13.0	13.5	13.5	14.0	15.0	15.5	15.0	15.0
10	10.5	11.5	12.0	12.0	12.5	13.5	14.0	13.5	13.0

Reprinted from Ross, Dotson, and Katz 1985.

Thursday

Practice the one-mile run and sit-ups.

Equipment: Cones for marking a one-mile running course, stopwatch. There are several layouts of fields that can be used to administer the run.

Organization: Divide the children into two groups.

Activities: Perform the following activities:

1. Discuss the need for pacing in the one-mile run.

2. Demonstrate (or have a child demonstrate) the correct technique for sit-ups.

   - The knees must be bent, with the heels 12 to 18 inches from the buttocks.
   - Feet must remain in contact with the testing surface. This is easily accomplished by having a partner hold the feet. The partner can also count the number of sit-ups done.
   - Arms must remain folded and in contact with the chest.
   - The child should perform the sit-up using a curling up motion.
   - One sit-up is completed when the child curls up correctly, touches the elbows to the thighs, and returns to the testing surface until the mid-back makes contact.
   - Norms for the times (seconds) for modified bent-knee sit-ups are presented on the following page in table F4.4.

3. Have one group practice the pacing on the mile run. Encourage each child to find the fastest pace she or he can maintain while running the total distance.

4. Have the other group select partners. In each pair, one partner does sit-ups for 60 seconds while the other partner counts; then they switch roles.

5. After 10 minutes in each activity, have a 2-minute rest and then have the groups switch activities.

6. If the weather is hot, make sure the children have the opportunity to get water when they want it.

Friday

Repeat Thursday's lesson.

Table F4.4: NCYFS Norms by Age for the Timed Bent-Knee Sit-Ups—Boys and Girls (Number in 60 Seconds)

Percentile	10	11	12	13	14	15	16	17	18
Boys									
99	60	60	61	62	64	65	65	68	67
90	47	48	50	52	52	53	55	56	54
80	43	43	46	48	49	50	51	51	50
75	40	41	44	46	47	48	49	50	50
70	38	40	43	45	45	46	48	49	48
60	36	38	40	41	43	44	45	46	44
50	34	36	38	40	41	42	43	43	43
40	32	34	35	37	39	40	41	41	40
30	30	31	33	34	37	37	39	39	38
25	28	30	32	32	35	36	38	37	36
20	26	28	30	31	34	35	36	35	35
10	22	22	25	28	30	31	32	31	31
Girls									
99	50	53	66	58	57	56	59	60	65
90	43	42	46	46	47	45	49	47	47
80	39	39	41	41	42	42	42	41	42
75	37	37	40	40	41	40	40	40	40
70	36	36	39	39	40	39	39	39	40
60	33	34	36	35	37	36	37	37	38
50	31	32	33	33	35	35	35	36	35
40	30	30	31	31	32	32	33	33	33
30	27	28	30	28	30	30	30	31	30
25	25	26	28	27	29	30	30	30	30
20	24	24	27	25	27	28	28	29	28
10	20	20	21	21	23	24	23	24	24

Reprinted from Ross, Dotson, and Katz 1985.

LESSONS 11-15
TESTING HEALTH-RELATED PHYSICAL FITNESS

Monday

Administer the one-mile run.

Equipment: Stopwatch, cones to mark testing area, recording forms, and music for Fitness Hustle I

Organization: Partners, in two groups; one partner from each pair in each group

Activities: Perform the following activities:

1. One child from each pair runs the mile. The other child counts the number of laps. You call out each child's time as he or she crosses the finish line. Each child's partner records the time called. Then switch and let the other group run. (The children will need a short break and the opportunity to get water after the run.)

2. The total group practices the Fitness Hustle.

Tuesday

Administer the sit-up test.

Equipment: Recording forms, music for Fitness Hustle II

Organization: Partners, in two groups; one partner from each pair in each group

Activities: Administer the sit-up test:

1. The partners in one group count the number of sit-ups their partners complete in 60 seconds. Then the partners switch roles.

2. The total group practices the Fitness Hustle.

Wednesday

Develop fitness contracts.

Equipment: Materials for contracts, pencils

Organization: Total group

Activities: Create fitness contracts:

1. Discuss the importance of exercising on a regular basis and work with students so they can develop realistic goals for exercise.

2. Encourage each child to sign a written agreement to try to improve his or her fitness level outside of class.

3. Explain that the fitness tests will be given later during the year so that they can see improvement.

4. Use the contract shown here, or develop one that meets your needs.

Cardiovascular Endurance Program Contract

I, _____ , do hereby contract to exercise for 20 minutes three times a week for 10 weeks. My exercise heart rate will be _____ .

Week	Days	Type of Exercise	Duration
1			
2			
3			
4			
5			
6			
7			
8			
9			
10			

Approved by _____

Date _____

Thursday

Develop appropriate activities for jogging.

Equipment: None, unless some area is to be marked as a jogging route

Organization: Total group

Activities: Teach the children the following ways of organizing a jog to increase interest:

1. Jog for a certain number of minutes (8, 10, 12, 15), the number of minutes to be increased as cardiovascular endurance improves.

2. Jog a certain number of laps around a specified area, the number of laps to be increased with improved endurance.

3. Jog a certain route around the school campus; the route can be marked by you or drawn on a map with key landmarks.

4. Keep a record of the total distance jogged by a group (groups could compete); for example, the total mileage of a group might equal the distance to a certain city.

5. Jog single file. Groups of five to seven children run in a line; on a signal, the child in the rear weaves through the line to the front to become the new leader.

Friday

Practice various circuits to increase strength and muscular endurance.

Equipment: As required, from the list of circuit activities cited below

Organization: Groups, the number of groups depending on the number of stations in the circuit

Activities: Establish a circuit requiring students to do strength and muscular endurance activities. For example:

Station 1: Sit-Ups

Station 2: Push-Ups

Station 3: Jump for Distance

Station 4: Bent-Knee Push-Ups

If playground equipment is available, use Pull-Ups or hand-walking horizontal ladders.

LESSON 16
INDIVIDUAL STRETCHING AND CIRCUIT TRAINING

Student Objectives

- Define the five components of physical fitness.
- Participate in circuit training activities.

Equipment

- Chalk or tape to mark lines
- Six cones

Warm-Up Activities (5-8 minutes)

Individual Stretching Activities I

Arrange children in a scatter formation.

1. Describe and demonstrate the Neck Roll, Shoulder Shrugs, Side Stretch, Front Lunges, and Standing Heel Stretch.
2. Have the children complete the Individual Stretching Activities I.

Neck Roll

Sit tall, with one hand on each side of the head covering the ears. Slowly roll the head around in a circle, supporting the head with the hands, first clockwise and then counterclockwise. Repeat several times.

Shoulder Shrugs

Lift the shoulders to the ears and then return to normal position. Repeat several times.

Side Stretch

Stand with feet apart, toes pointed straight ahead, and knees slightly bent. Place one hand on the hip and extend the other arm up over the head. Slowly bend to the side toward the hand on the hip. Hold for 10 seconds and relax. Repeat on the other side.

Front Lunges

Facing forward, bend to a squat with the right leg under the chest and the left leg extended back. As you bend, place your hands on the floor on each side of your right foot. Look forward, keeping the head up. The back should be parallel to the floor. Hold this position for 5 to 10 seconds. Return to starting position and repeat with the left leg forward.

Standing Heel Stretch

Stand with one foot directly in front of the other with about one foot length between them. With both feet flat on the ground and the body positioned directly above the back foot, bend the knees. Bend as far as you can without allowing the heels to leave the floor. Hold for 5 to 10 seconds. Reverse feet and repeat.

Skill-Development Activities (12-15 minutes)

Circuit 1

Divide children into six groups, and assign each group to one of the six stations.

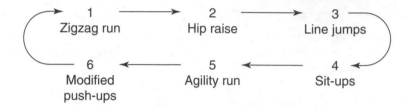

1. Describe and demonstrate each exercise in the circuit.
2. On a signal, children exercise at the assigned station for one minute, counting the number of repetitions.
3. Call "stop" after one minute; children stop and change stations.
4. Allow 15 seconds for them to rotate to new stations.
5. Children complete as many repetitions of the exercise as possible at each station. The time at each station should be increased as the children make gains in fitness.

Zigzag Run

Arrange cones in a zigzag pattern. Each child runs around the cones and then straight back to the starting line.

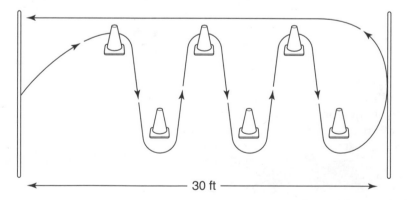

Hip Raise

Sitting with the upper body supported by the arms, lift the trunk until the body is straight and then return to sitting position.

Line Jumps

Two lines are marked on the ground about 12 inches apart. Standing on the outside of one line with feet together, jump sideways over both lines and then jump back to starting position.

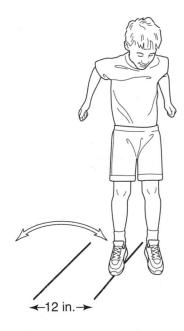

←12 in.→

Sit-Ups

Lie on the back with arms folded across the chest, hands placed on shoulders, and knees bent. Raise the body until the arms touch the thighs and then return to starting position.

Agility Run

Two lines are marked about 10 feet apart. Beginning at the starting line, run, touch the second line with the hand, turn around, run back, touch the starting line, and continue running back and forth, touching each line until 10 lines have been touched. Rest and repeat.

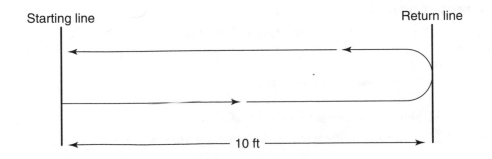

Starting line   Return line

10 ft

Modified Push-Ups

Beginning in a kneeling front-support position (on hands and knees with the knees extended back as far as possible) with the back straight, lower the chin and chest to the ground, keeping the back straight, and then return to starting position.

Partner Fitness Activities

Assign each child a partner of equal size and strength. Have the children move to an area with a cushioned surface, such as a grassy area or a floor covered with mats.

Partner Push

Partners stand facing each other. Each child must grasp his or her own left ankle with the right hand behind the back. The left arm must also be placed behind the back grasping the right elbow. The object is for each child to push the partner off balance, using parts of the body other than the hands or arms.

Partner Hopping

Partners stand facing each other. Each child grasps the opponent's left ankle with his or her right hand and lifts the leg. The lifted leg is held straight. The object is to make the partner lose balance. Repeat, grasping the opponent's right ankle with the left hand.

Partner Dodging

One partner is the "chaser"; the other is the "runner." On a signal, the runner attempts to run away from the chaser. The chaser tries to stay as close as possible. The object is for the chaser to be as close to the runner as possible on the signal to stop. Children then reverse roles.

Progressive Walking Cool-Down

Mark an area (40 feet by 60 feet) in the grass or use a basketball court. Children jog one lap, walk one side, jog the remaining three sides, jog two sides, walk two sides, jog one side, walk three sides, jog one side, walk four sides, and stop.

Concluding Activities (10 minutes)

Physical Fitness Concept

Arrange children in information formation. Review the following concept: *Regular exercise helps to maintain physical fitness. Fitness includes five components and each component needs different kinds of activities to improve it.*

> *Cardiorespiratory endurance is the ability of the circulatory system to provide oxygen-rich blood for energy.*
>
> *Flexibility is the range (or amount) of movement in a joint.*
>
> *Muscular endurance is the ability of a muscle to repeat a movement many times.*

Muscular strength is the greatest amount of weight a muscle can lift.

Leanness means a lack of excess fat.

Exercise Decisions

Arrange children in cooperative groups of four to six children.

1. Review the guidelines for cooperative group work:

   All students must participate in the discussion.

   Students must respect others.

2. Present the following questions for the groups to discuss and arrive at a solution:

   What kinds of activities enhance cardiorespiratory endurance?

   What are some exercises that you can do to improve your flexibility?

   How do you make gains in muscular strength and muscular endurance?

LESSON 17

INDIVIDUAL STRETCHING AND CIRCUIT TRAINING

Student Objectives

- Define anaerobic and aerobic endurance.
- Explain that different exercises are needed for the development of aerobic and anaerobic endurance.
- Participate in circuit training activities.

Equipment

- Chalk or tape to mark lines
- Six cones

Warm-Up Activities (5-8 minutes)

Individual Stretching Activities I

See Grades 6-8: Fitness, Lesson 16, page 38.

Skill-Development Activities (12-15 minutes)

Circuit 1

Divide the children into six groups and assign each group to one of the six stations. See Grades 6-8: Fitness, Lesson 16, page 40. Have children complete the circuit with one minute at each station and 15 seconds to rotate to new stations.

Partner Fitness Activities

Assign each child a partner and have them participate in Partner Push, Partner Hopping, and Partner Dodging. See Grades 6-8: Fitness, Lesson 16, page 42.

Progressive Walking Cool-Down

See Grades 6-8: Fitness Lesson 16, page 42.

Concluding Activities (10 minutes)

Physical Fitness Concept

Arrange children in information formation.

1. Introduce the concept: *Different exercises are needed for the development of aerobic and anaerobic endurance.*

2. Explain that *if the circulatory system is not able to supply the oxygen needed for the exercise, the body can continue to work for a short time without oxygen. Exercising without enough oxygen is called anaerobic activity and can be continued for a short period of time. During anaerobic exercise the body builds an oxygen debt that must be repaid after completion of the exercise.*

3. Explain that *anaerobic endurance is the ability to exercise at a high-intensity level for a short time. Exercise at a high-intensity level is exercise that is very vigorous. An example is running up a flight of stairs quickly.*

4. Explain that *aerobic endurance is the same as cardiorespiratory endurance. It is the ability of the heart and lungs to supply oxygen to the working muscles. Aerobic exercises use the large muscles of the body and are performed for a long period of time. Aerobic means using oxygen. A strong heart can supply more oxygen, so the person with a strong heart has more aerobic endurance. Some aerobic exercises are swimming and jumping rope.*

5. Explain that *some exercises are performed so fast that the circulatory system cannot provide the amount of oxygen the body needs. Some people can exercise for a long time, but aerobic endurance has limits.*

Exercise Decisions

See Grades 6-8: Fitness, Lesson 16, page 43.

1. Present the following questions for the groups to discuss and arrive at a solution:

   What makes an activity aerobic?

   Select five aerobic activities that we could participate in (e.g., jogging, cycling).

   What makes an activity anaerobic?

   Select five activities that could be considered anaerobic (e.g., running bases in softball or running the 100-yard dash).

2. Ask each group to share their responses.

LESSON 18
INDIVIDUAL STRETCHING AND CIRCUIT TRAINING

Student Objectives

- Explain that aerobic exercise should be done for at least 20 minutes.
- Explain that aerobic exercise can help lower blood cholesterol.
- Participate in circuit training activities.

Equipment

- 24 hoops
- 24 cones
- 12 long jump ropes
- 6 jumping boxes
- Chalk or tape to mark boundaries

Warm-Up Activities (5-8 minutes)

Individual Stretching Activities I

See Grades 6-8: Fitness, Lesson 16, page 38.

Skill-Development Activities (12-15 minutes)

Circuit 1

Divide children into six groups and assign each group to one of the six stations. See Grades 6-8: Fitness, Lesson 16, page 40.

1. Have the children complete the circuit with two minutes at each station.
2. Give the children 15 seconds to rotate to new stations.

Obstacle Course

Provide each of the six groups with a variety of equipment (e.g., four hoops, four cones, two long ropes, and a jumping box).

1. Ask each group to create an obstacle course to move through.
2. One child from each group explains the course, and then the children run through each of the courses.

Progressive Walking Cool-Down

See Grades 6-8: Fitness, Lesson 16, page 42.

Concluding Activities (10 minutes)

Physical Fitness Concept

Arrange children in information formation.

1. Review the following concept: *Aerobic exercise should be done for at least 20 minutes.*
2. Review the other guidelines for aerobic exercises.

    Frequency: The exercise must be done at least three times a week.

    Intensity: The exercise must make you sweat and breathe hard.

3. Discuss exercise and blood cholesterol. *Cholesterol is a white, powdery, fatty material found in many foods. The body also makes cholesterol. Our bodies need some cholesterol, but if we take in too much in the foods that we eat, it gets into the bloodstream and can clog the arteries. Aerobic exercises can lower the amount of cholesterol in our blood.*

Aerobic Quiz

Arrange the children in cooperative groups of four to six children each.

1. Present the following statements.
2. Each group should discuss the statement and decide if it is true or false.
3. If the group agrees that the statement is true, they will put thumbs up on a signal.
4. If the group agrees that the statement is false, they will put thumbs down on the signal.

    Aerobic exercise must be done every day. (down)

    Aerobic exercise should be done for five minutes. (down)

    Cholesterol in the blood can clog the arteries. (up)

    Shooting free throws in basketball is an aerobic exercise. (down)

    Aerobic exercise will increase the amount of cholesterol in the blood. (down)

    Jogging is an aerobic exercise. (up)

    Aerobic exercises can be done sitting down. (down)

    Intensity means how hard you exercise. (up)

LESSON 19
INDIVIDUAL STRETCHING AND CIRCUIT TRAINING

Student Objectives

- Define agility, speed, and balance.
- Explain the difference in health-related and skill-related components of fitness.
- Participate in circuit training activities.

Equipment

- Chalk or tape to mark lines
- Six cones
- Short jump rope (8 feet long) for each child

Warm-Up Activities (5-8 minutes)

Individual Stretching Activities I

See Grades 6-8: Fitness, Lesson 16, page 38.

Skill-Development Activities (12-15 minutes)

Circuit 1

Divide children into six groups and assign each group to one of the six stations. See Grades 6-8: Fitness, Lesson 16, page 40.

1. Have children complete the circuit with two minutes at each station.
2. Give the children 15 seconds to rotate to new stations.

Follow the Leader

Arrange children in groups of four to six.

1. One child leads and the others follow, imitating the leader's actions. The leader can run, leap, jump, or hop.
2. Change leaders after one minute.

Partner Dodging

Arrange children with partners in a scatter formation. Designate the partners in each pair as 1 and 2. See Grades 6-8: Fitness, Lesson 16, page 42.

1. On a signal Partner 1 runs and dodges, attempting to get away from Partner 2.
2. Partner 2 attempts to stay as close to Partner 1 as possible. Exchange positions and repeat.

Five-Minute Jump

Arrange children in groups of six to eight. Each child has an individual jump rope.

1. In each group at least half of the children must be jumping rope at all times. The remaining children can be resting.
2. The group goal is to jump for five minutes. Any type of jump can be used.
3. The groups must cooperate to allow rest for those needing it.

Progressive Walking Cool-Down

See Grades 6-8: Fitness, Lesson 16, page 42.

Concluding Activities (10 minutes)

Physical Fitness Concept

Arrange children in information formation.

1. Review the following concept: *Physical fitness has five elements that are important to your health. These components are cardiorespiratory endurance, flexibility, muscular strength, muscular endurance, and leanness.*
2. Discuss how the skill-related components of fitness are different. *The skill-related components are important for performing various motor tasks. They are agility, speed, and balance.*

   Agility is the ability to change directions quickly.

   Speed is the ability to move from one place to another in a short period of time.

   Balance is the ability to maintain a position.

Exercise Decisions

Arrange children in cooperative groups of four to six.

1. Review the guidelines for cooperative group work.

   All students must participate in the discussion.

   Students must respect others.
2. Present the following questions for the groups to discuss.

   What are some activities that require agility? (e.g., soccer, badminton)

   What are some activities that require speed? (e.g., sprinting)

   What are some activities that require balance? (e.g., gymnastics)

LESSON 20

INDIVIDUAL STRETCHING AND CIRCUIT TRAINING

Student Objectives

- Explain that physical health is only one part of wellness.
- Distinguish between physical, social, and mental health.
- Work with a group to describe a person who is working toward a high level of wellness.
- Participate in circuit training activities.

Equipment

- Chalk or tape to mark lines
- Six cones
- Six to eight long jump ropes (12 to 16 feet long)

Warm-Up Activities (5-8 minutes)

Individual Stretching Activities I

See Grades 6-8: Fitness, Lesson 16, page 38.

Skill-Development Activities (12-15 minutes)

Circuit 1

Divide children into six groups and assign each group to one of the six stations. See Grades 6-8: Fitness, Lesson 16, page 40.

1. Have children complete the circuit with two minutes at each station
2. Give the children 15 seconds to rotate to new stations.

Follow the Leader With Jumping and Hopping

Arrange children in groups of six.

1. With jumping stunts, one child leads and the others follow. The stunts can be

jump in place, feet together;

jump forward and back;

jump side to side;

stride jump (one foot forward and one back, exchanging forward foot with each jump);

jump and slap heels before landing;

jump and make a one-quarter turn with each jump;

hop on right foot (in place, forward and back, side to side); or

hop on left foot (in place, forward and back, side to side).

2. Change leaders after one minute.

10-Minute Jump

Arrange children in teams of three.

1. The object of the activity is for one team member to be jumping at all times. One person should start jumping while the other children turn the rope.

2. When he or she begins to tire, the second child should begin jumping.

3. Continue taking turns and resting for 10 minutes.

Concluding Activities (10 minutes)

Physical Fitness Concept

Arrange children in information formation.

1. Introduce the following concept: *Adequate levels of physical fitness are needed for high-level wellness.*

2. Discuss what it means to be healthy. *Being healthy means more than freedom from disease. Being healthy means a state of wellness. It means being the best person you can be. Wellness includes your relationships with other people, what you choose to eat, how you deal with drugs, your exercise habits, and how you deal with stress. Your level of wellness is influenced by the decisions you make about your life. The three important parts of high-level wellness are physical health, social health, and mental health.*

3. Ask the children: *What is involved in good physical health?* (Keeping your body fit, choosing to exercise regularly.) *What is involved in good social health?* (Getting along with others.) *What is involved in good mental health?* (Feeling good about yourself.)

Defining High-Level Wellness

Arrange children in cooperative groups of four to six.

1. Review the guidelines for cooperative group work.

   All students must participate in the discussion.

   Students must respect others.

2. Ask each group to describe a 13-year-old who is working toward a high level of wellness. A representative from each group will share the description the group agreed on.

LESSON 21
ADVANCED CIRCUIT TRAINING

Student Objectives

- Explain the difference between isometric and isotonic exercises.
- Participate in advanced circuit training activities.

Equipment

- Chalk or tape to mark lines
- 6 cones
- 24 hoops
- 6 boxes or 1 bench 16 inches high

Warm-Up Activities (5 minutes)

Individual Stretching Activities II

Arrange children in a scatter formation.

1. Describe and demonstrate the One-Half Knee Bends, Raggedy Ann, Upper Leg Stretch, Upper Body Stretch, and Shoulder Stretch.
2. Have the children complete the stretching exercises, performing several repetitions of each.

One-Half Knee Bend

Stand with the feet shoulder width apart and feet pointed straight ahead. Bend the knees slightly. Hold this position for 20 counts and then relax.

Raggedy Ann

With the knees bent, reach forward and touch the floor. Slowly straighten the knees and hold for 20 counts. Do not straighten the knees all the way; keep a slight bend in the legs.

Upper Leg Stretch

From a standing position, bend the left knee, grasping the ankle. Stretch the upper leg by pulling on the leg; lean forward slightly. Relax and change legs.

Upper Body Stretch

Assume a position on hands and knees. Bend the knees, sitting back. At the same time reach forward with the hands, keeping the arms straight. Hold for 10 counts, relax, and repeat.

Shoulder Stretch

Standing straight, the arms should be behind the body, clasping the hands together. Lift the arms slightly and pull the shoulders back. Hold for 10 seconds., relax, and repeat.

Skill-Development Activities (20 minutes)

Advanced Circuit Training

Divide children into six groups, and assign each group to one of the six stations. The children should exercise at the assigned station for one and a half minutes. The children will jog between each station.

1. Mark off a jogging area.
2. Between each station have children jog for two minutes.

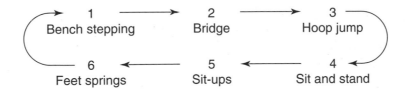

Bench Stepping

Step up on a bench or box that is approximately 16 inches high.

1. *Step with one leg and then the other, extending your legs when on the box.*
2. *Step down with the original leading leg, followed by the other leg.*

3. *The exercise should be done in four counts: up, up, down, down.*

4. *One point is scored each time both feet are on the box.*

Bridge

The children start in a push-up position with the back straight.

1. *Lift your right hand and touch the left hip.*

2. *Return to starting position and repeat with your left hand touching the right hip.*

3. *One point is scored each time a hand touches a hip.*

Hoop Jump

Arrange four hoops in a pattern for each participant at the station.

1. *Jump with your feet together through the hoops.*

2. *When finished, turn around and jump back.*

3. *One point is scored for each hoop you jump into.*

Sit and Stand

The students should sit down with the back straight and the legs extended.

1. *Stand up straight and sit back down, extending your legs.*

2. *One point is scored each time you stand.*

Sit-Ups

One point is scored for each Sit-Up completed with bent knees.

Feet Springs

Mark a line on the floor for each participant.

1. *Begin in a push-up position with your feet on one side of the line.*

2. *Jump your feet across the line, taking weight on your arms.*

3. *Continue jumping back and forth across the line.*

4. *One point is scored for each jump.*

Lap Cool-Down

Do seven laps of an area approximately 40 feet by 60 feet using the following movements:

Slow jogging

Jogging backward

Sliding with right side leading

Skipping

Sliding with left side leading

Walking forward

Walking backward

Concluding Activities (5 minutes)

Physical Fitness Concept

Arrange children in information formation.

1. Introduce the following concept: *Muscles can get stronger and gain endurance from isometric exercise. Isometric exercises are those exercises where you just hold a position. You contract muscles without actually moving. Isometric exercises should be held for 10 seconds.*

2. Discuss the difference between isometric and isotonic exercises: *There are two different kinds of exercises for muscular strength and endurance. Isotonic exercises are moving exercises like push-ups or sit-ups. Isometric exercises are those during which you contract your muscles without moving your body to another place. An example is to push your right fist against the palm of your left hand and not allow your left hand to move.*

Isometric Exercises

1. Describe and demonstrate isometric exercises.
2. Practice isometric exercises.

Stomach Pull

Sit straight with your legs crossed. Pull in your stomach as hard as you can (try to press it against your backbone) and hold for 10 seconds. Relax and repeat.

Finger Pull

Sit straight with your legs crossed. Grasp your fingers together in front of your body. Your elbows should be straight out to the side. Pull against your fingers, trying to move your elbows out. Hold for 10 seconds and repeat.

FITNESS

LESSON 22
ADVANCED CIRCUIT TRAINING

Student Objectives

- Explain the guidelines for performing muscular endurance exercises.
- Explain how exercises for strength development will be different from exercises for muscular endurance development.
- Participate in advanced circuit training activities.

Equipment

- Chalk or tape to mark lines
- 6 cones
- 24 hoops
- 6 boxes or 1 bench 16 inches high
- 1 barbell (commercial or homemade) for every two children

Warm-Up Activities (5 minutes)

Individual Stretching Activities II

See Grades 6-8: Fitness, Lesson 21, page 52.

Skill-Development Activities (20 minutes)

Advanced Circuit Training

Divide children into six groups, and assign each group to one of the six stations. See Grades 6-8: Fitness, Lesson 21, page 53.

1. Have children complete the circuit.
2. Have the children jog for two minutes between each station of the circuit.

Lap Cool-Down

See Grades 6-8: Fitness, Lesson 21, page 54.

Concluding Activities (5 minutes)

Physical Fitness Concept

Arrange children in information formation.

1. Review the difference between muscular endurance and muscular strength, and the types of exercises needed to make gains in each component.

- *Muscular endurance is the ability to repeat a movement many times, so exercises for the development of endurance should be performed many times. A good way to increase muscular endurance is to exercise with weights.*
- *Strength exercises using weights should be performed 6 to 8 times (called repetitions). If the exercise can be performed more than 12 times, the weight should be increased. Remember, these exercises are for strength.*

2. Discuss the guidelines for performing muscular endurance exercises.

- *Endurance exercises should be performed 20 to 25 times when using a weight. If the exercise cannot be performed at least 20 times, then the weight should be reduced.*
- *With both forms of exercise (strength and endurance), the entire group of exercises should be repeated two or three times. One complete group of exercises is called a set.*
- *For endurance exercises with weights, you should perform 20 repetitions in each set and complete two or three sets.*

Arm Curls for Endurance

Arrange children in groups of four to six. Each group should have two or three barbells of different weights.

1. Grip the bar with palms up and lift the weight.
2. Each child selects a weight and performs 20 repetitions of Arm Curls.
3. Each group is asked to demonstrate the difference in the kinds of exercises you would use to develop muscular strength and muscular endurance.

LESSON 23
ADVANCED CIRCUIT TRAINING

Student Objectives

- Explain how muscular strength is developed.
- Explain how muscular strength is measured.
- Participate in advanced circuit training activities.

Equipment

- Chalk or tape to mark lines
- 6 cones
- 24 hoops
- 6 boxes or 1 bench 16 inches high

Warm-Up Activities (5 minutes)

Individual Stretching Activities II

See Grades 6-8: Fitness, Lesson 21, page 52.

Skill-Development Activities (20 minutes)

Advanced Circuit Training

Divide children into six groups, and assign each group to one of the six stations. See Grades 6-8: Fitness, Lesson 21, page 53.

1. Have children complete the circuit.
2. Have the children jog between each station for two minutes.

Lap Cool-Down

See Grades 6-8: Fitness, Lesson 21, page 54.

Concluding Activities (5 minutes)

Physical Fitness Concept

Arrange children in information formation.

1. Review the relationship between muscular strength and muscular endurance. *Muscular strength and muscular endurance are related but different. Muscular strength is the*

greatest amount of weight your muscles can lift at a given time. Muscular endurance is how long a group of muscles can perform.

2. Explain that a larger muscle is a stronger muscle. *You are born with a certain number of muscle cells. We all have different numbers of muscle cells. It is not possible to grow new muscle cells or new muscles. It is possible to enlarge the size of the muscle cells you have. When the muscle cells get larger, the muscle becomes larger. When the muscle becomes larger, it is stronger.*

3. Ask the children these questions: *Who remembers the best way to enlarge the size of muscles and build strength?* (Exercise with weights.) *How can you measure how strong your muscles are?* (Determine the heaviest weight you can lift.)

4. Explain that the ability to support your body weight takes strength. For example, the ability to perform one push-up requires enough strength to lift your entire body weight.

Exercise Decisions

Arrange children in cooperative groups of four to six.

1. Review the guidelines for cooperative group work.

   All students must participate in the discussion.

   Students must respect others.

2. Present the following questions for the groups to discuss:

   What kind of exercise program would you recommend to a friend who could not perform one push-up?

   What are some specific exercises you would recommend?

   How often should your friend exercise?

   Does your friend need to make gains in strength or endurance?

   How can your friend measure the improvement he or she makes?

LESSON 24
ADVANCED CIRCUIT TRAINING

Student Objectives

- Define flexibility as the range of motion in a joint.
- Explain that flexibility is developed by stretching the muscles and ligaments around a joint.
- Participate in advanced circuit training activities.

Equipment

- Chalk or tape to mark lines
- 6 cones
- 24 hoops
- 6 boxes or 1 bench 16 inches high

Warm-Up Activities (5 minutes)

Individual Stretching Activities III

Arrange children in a scatter formation.

1. Describe and demonstrate the Toe Touch, Body Bend, Leg Lift, Double Leg Lift, and Total Body Stretch.
2. Have the children complete the stretching exercises, performing several repetitions of each.

Toe Touch

Sitting with legs straight and feet together, reach toward toes, lower face to knees, and hold for five seconds. Relax. Repeat several times.

Body Bend

Begin standing with feet shoulder width apart and arms by the sides. Bend down to the right as far as possible and hold for five seconds. Return to starting position and bend to the left and hold. Repeat several times to the right and to the left.

Leg Lift

Lie on the back and with the right leg flexed pull it up toward the chest. Hold for 20 counts and relax. Keep the lower back flat. Repeat with the left leg.

Double Leg Lift

Lie on the back and with both legs flexed pull them to the chest. Hold for 20 counts and relax. Repeat.

Total Body Stretch
Lie flat on the floor with the arms extended overhead, the legs straight, and the toes pointed. Stretch, hold for 10 counts, and relax. Repeat.

Skill-Development Activities (20 minutes)

Advanced Circuit Training

Divide children into six groups, and assign each group to one of the six stations. See Grades 6-8: Fitness, Lesson 21, page 53.

1. Have children complete the circuit.
2. Have the children jog for two minutes between each station of the circuit.

Lap Cool-Down

See Grades 6-8: Fitness, Lesson 21, page 54.

Concluding Activities (5 minutes)

Physical Fitness Concept

Arrange children in information formation.

1. Review the definition of flexibility as the range of motion in a joint.
2. Explain that *tendons are connectors and they connect muscles to bones. Ligaments are connectors and they connect bones to bones.*
3. Discuss how flexibility is developed. *The amount of movement in a joint depends first on the type of joint. A hinge joint is the type of joint found at the elbow and allows movement in only two directions. You can bend and extend your elbow (demonstrate this), but notice the ways it will not move. A ball and socket joint is the type of joint found at the shoulders and hips that permits movement in all directions.*
4. Ask the children: *How many ways can you bend your elbow? Now stand up and try bending at the hip. How many ways can you bend at your hip joint?*
5. Explain that *the amount of movement in a joint is also limited by the amount of muscle and ligament around the joint. We cannot change the way the joint is put together, but we can stretch the muscles and ligaments. By stretching the muscles and ligaments around the joint, we will increase the flexibility. If muscles are never stretched beyond a resting position, then the muscle is short and the range of motion is limited, which means the flexibility is poor.*

Cooperative Fitness Discussion

Arrange children in cooperative groups of four to six.

1. Review the guidelines for cooperative group work.

   All students must participate in the discussion.

   Students must respect others.
2. Ask each group to list sport or movement activities that require shoulder flexibility. (Throwing a football or baseball, swimming, performing a handstand or cartwheel, rowing a boat, or climbing a rope.)
3. Ask each group to share their responses.

LESSON 25
ADVANCED CIRCUIT TRAINING

Student Objectives

- Distinguish between static and ballistic stretching.
- Participate in advanced circuit training activities.

Equipment

- Chalk or tape to mark lines
- 6 cones
- 24 hoops
- 6 boxes or 1 bench 16 inches high

Warm-Up Activities (5 minutes)

Individual Stretching Activities III

See Grades 6-8: Fitness, Lesson 24, page 60.

Skill-Development Activities (20 minutes)

Advanced Circuit Training

Divide children into six groups, and assign each group to one of the six stations. See Grades 6-8: Fitness, Lesson 21, page 53.

1. Have children complete the circuit.
2. Have the children jog for two minutes between each station of the circuit.

Lap Cool-Down

See Grades 6-8: Fitness, Lesson 21, page 54.

Concluding Activities (5 minutes)

Physical Fitness Concept

Arrange children in information formation.

1. Explain that *flexibility exercises should use static rather than ballistic stretching. A static stretch is a slow stretch held for a period of time. A ballistic stretch is a bouncing stretch.*
2. Discuss why static stretching is recommended. *With a slow, gradual stretch you are less likely to stretch too far and injure the muscle being stretched. Also, there is less muscle sore-*

ness when you use a slow stretch. When you stretch, you need to move slowly to a position in which the muscle pulls a little because of the stretch. Hold the position for 10 to 20 seconds. Relax and repeat the exercise. Always try to relax the muscles being stretched.

Partner Assistance

Arrange children in pairs. One child in each pair is the teacher and the other is the student.

1. Using the Sitting Stretch, the child who is the teacher describes to the student things to remember when stretching.
2. Then they exchange places, and the second student acts as the teacher. The second teacher describes the principles for doing the Sideways Stretch.

Sitting Stretch

Sit with the legs straight and the toes pointed up. Bend from the hip to get a slow, easy stretch. Hold for 10 seconds. Relax and repeat. Do not bounce. Do not dip the head forward.

Sideways Stretch

Sit with the feet shoulder width apart and the toes pointed straight ahead. The knees should be slightly bent. Place one hand on the hip and extend the other arm up over the head. Slowly bend to the side toward the hand on the hip. Hold for 10 seconds and relax. Repeat in the opposite direction.

FITNESS

LESSON 26
ROPE JUMPING AND JOGGING

Student Objectives

- Define obesity.
- Explain that eating extra calories results in gaining weight.
- Practice rope jumping.
- Jog for 8 to 10 minutes.

Equipment

- Six to eight long jump ropes (12 to 16 feet long)
- Cones to mark a large oval.

Warm-Up Activities (5 minutes)

Individual Stretching Activities IV

Arrange children in a scatter formation.

1. Describe and demonstrate the Sitting Stretch, Side Stretch, Upper Leg Stretch, Grasshopper Stretch, and Squat.
2. Have the children complete the Stretching Activities.

Sitting Stretch

Sit with the legs straight and toes pointed up. Bend from the hips to get a slow, easy stretch. Hold for 10 seconds. Relax and repeat. Do not bounce. Do not dip the head forward.

Side Stretch

Sit with the feet apart and toes pointed straight ahead. Knees should be slightly bent. Place one hand on the hip and extend the other arm up over the head. Slowly bend to the side toward the hand on the hip. Hold for 10 seconds and relax. Repeat in the opposite direction.

Upper Leg Stretch

From a standing position, bend the left knee, grasping the ankle. Stretch the upper leg by pulling on the leg while leaning slightly forward. Relax and change legs.

Grasshopper Stretch

Assume a position with the hands and feet on the floor. Move one leg forward until the knee is over the ankle. The other knee should be on the floor. Stretch slowly by lowering the hips. Hold for 10 seconds. Switch legs.

Squat

Squat down, keeping the feet flat and the toes pointed slightly out. Place the elbows inside the knees. Hold for 30 seconds, stand up, and repeat.

Skill-Development Activities (20 minutes)

Jumping Crossed Double Ropes

Arrange children in groups of 8 to 10, each group with two long jump ropes.

1. Two ropes are crossed and turned so that both strike the ground simultaneously.
2. The jumper jumps in with both ropes being turned toward him or her ("front door") and jumps several times.
3. After achieving some skill, the jumper tries running in from the other side ("back door").
4. The children should establish a rotation system for jumping and turning.

Jogging

Mark a large oval area with cones.

1. Have the children jog for 8 to 10 minutes.
2. Encourage the children to run as far as possible, but walking is permitted if they tire.
3. Cool down by walking two laps.

Concluding Activities (5 minutes)

Physical Fitness Concept

Arrange children in information formation.

1. Review the following concept: *Everyone has some fat, but too much fat is unhealthy. Obesity is bad for your health. Obesity is when you have too much body fat. Fat is also called adipose tissue.*
2. Discuss obesity. *Everyone has a certain number of fat cells. There are also muscle cells, bone cells, blood cells, and nerve cells in the body. Bodies are made up of billions of tiny cells that you cannot see. You can become fat, or obese, when your fat cells grow larger or when the number of fat cells increases. One of the causes of fat cells getting larger, or sometimes the*

number of fat cells increasing, is eating more food than your body needs. Sometimes the body also stores excessive fat because its chemistry is upset, but this is rare. Such a condition requires a doctor's care. Most people who have too much fat eat more than their bodies need. The food we eat provides our bodies with energy. The amount of energy in the food is usually measured in calories. One pound of fat is equal to 3,500 calories. So when you take in more calories than you use, the extra calories are stored. If your activity level stays the same (if you use the same amount of energy) and you eat 3,500 extra calories you will gain one pound of body fat. This can be done a little at a time; if you ate one extra piece of cake that has 100 calories each day for 35 days, you could gain one pound (100 × 35 = 3,500 calories).

Henry's Problem

Arrange children in cooperative groups of four to six.

1. Ask each group to help Henry solve his problem. He is 15 pounds overweight and he wants to lost weight.
2. Think of as many suggestions as you can that Henry might try.

FITNESS

LESSON 27
ROPE JUMPING AND JOGGING

Student Objectives

- Explain how exercise helps you lose fat.
- Practice rope jumping.
- Jump rope for five minutes.

Equipment

- One short rope (8 feet long) for each child
- Six to eight long jump ropes (12 to 16 feet long)
- Cones to mark jogging course

Warm-Up Activities (5 minutes)

Individual Stretching Activities IV

See Grades 6-8: Fitness, Lesson 26, page 64.

Skill-Development Activities (20 minutes)

Jumping Crossed Double Ropes

See Grades 6-8: Fitness, Lesson 26, page 65.

Five-Minute Jump

Arrange children in teams of six. Each child has an individual jump rope.

1. The object of the activity is for all but one team member to be jumping at all times.
2. One person can be resting, but if a second person tires and stops, the first jumper must start again.
3. Continue taking turns jumping and resting for five minutes.

Cooperative Jogging

Mark a large oval area with cones. Arrange children in cooperative groups of six to eight.

1. Have the children jog for 8 or 10 minutes with each person counting the number of laps completed.
2. Each student reports the number completed, and the total for each group is calculated. The group with more total laps completed wins for the day.
3. This is a run-walk, but children are encouraged to run as far as possible.
4. Cool down by walking two laps.

Concluding Activities (5 minutes)

Physical Fitness Concept

Arrange children in information formation.

1. Introduce the following concept: *Exercise increases leanness and decreases fat.*

2. Discuss how exercise helps you lose weight. *Many people think that the best way to lose weight is to diet. Though it is true that to lose weight you have to use more calories than you eat and that you may be eating more calories than you need, most diets require that you eat fewer servings and calories each day than are recommended. Some diets limit the types of food to one or two of the food groups. This is usually unhealthy. Also, when a person only restricts calories and doesn't exercise, the body weight lost will be both fat and lean tissue. This means that the person will be losing muscle! A person who exercises burns more calories and loses mainly fat tissue.*

3. Tell the children: *Youngsters should probably not diet. If a child needs to lose fat, exercise and a well-balanced diet are recommended. Adolescents need 2,000 to 2,400 calories each day. Eating a balanced diet of 2,400 calories each day with increased exercise should reduce a person's amount of fat in a healthy way. And a lean person is generally healthier than a fat one.*

Ways to Increase Activity

Arrange children in cooperative groups of four to six.

1. Review the guidelines for cooperative group work.

   All students must participate in the discussion.

   Students must respect others.

2. Present the following question for the groups to discuss. *What are some ways a person who wants to lose weight can increase the amount of activity he or she gets?* (Walk to school instead or riding, plan an exercise program, or use the stairs rather than the elevator.)

FITNESS

LESSON 28
CHINESE ROPE JUMPING

Student Objectives

- Explain that the body burns calories during and after exercise.
- Practice Chinese rope jumping.
- Jog for 8 to 10 minutes.

Equipment

- 8 to 10 Chinese jump ropes (8- to 10-foot lengths of half-inch-wide elastic, each length sewn into a circle)
- Cones to mark jogging course

Warm-Up Activities (5 minutes)

Individual Stretching Activities IV

See Grades 6-8: Fitness, Lesson 26, page 64.

Skill-Development Activities (20 minutes)

Chinese Jump Rope: Basic Jumping

Arrange children in groups of three or four.

1. Two children stand facing each other with the Chinese jump rope stretched around their legs.
2. One of the other children performs stunts while jumping into, between, and out of the rope.
3. Describe and demonstrate Basic Jumping.
4. The jumper stands with the right ankle against the left side of the rope.
5. The jumper jumps and lands with the right foot between the ropes, then jumps again, returning to starting position.
6. The jumper stands near the rope with the right foot hooked under the left rope, jumps lifting the left rope with the right foot so it crosses over the right rope, and lands with the right foot between the two ropes.
7. The jumper then jumps again, returning to starting position.
8. Practice Basic Jumping. Rotate so that each child has a chance to practice.

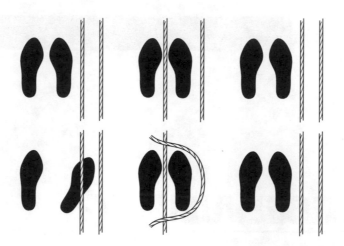

Cooperative Jogging

See Grades 6-8: Fitness, Lesson 27, page 67. Cool down by walking two laps.

Concluding Activities (5 minutes)

Physical Fitness Concept

Arrange children in information formation.

1. Introduce the following concept: *With an exercise program you burn more calories during and after a workout.*

2. Explain that exercise requires energy and uses calories. *Strenuous exercise increases the number of calories burned. This increase continues even after you stop exercising; you will burn more calories for several hours after you stop the exercise. This helps you stay lean, and for the person who needs to lose weight, exercise makes it easier to lose without becoming discouraged.*

3. Tell the children *when a person's activity levels are high, he or she doesn't seem to get as hungry and therefore doesn't eat as much. This is also helpful for someone who needs to lose weight. Exercise requires energy. So when you exercise, you are using calories. The extra energy needed because of the vigorous movement can make it much easier for a person to lose extra weight or maintain a desirable weight.*

Ways to Burn Calories After School

Arrange children in cooperative groups of four to six. Present the following question for the groups to discuss. *What are some ways to increase your activity level after school each day?* (Take a bike ride, mow the yard, walk to the park, go roller skating, play sports, or rake leaves.)

FITNESS

LESSON 29
CHINESE JUMP ROPE AND FITNESS STUNTS

Student Objectives

- Explain how to figure a training heart rate range.
- Perform Chinese jump rope steps.
- Perform fitness stunts.

Equipment

- 8 to 10 Chinese jump ropes (8-to 10-foot lengths of half-inch-wide elastic, each length sewn into a circle)

Warm-Up Activities (5 minutes)

Individual Stretching Activities IV

See Grades 6-8: Fitness, Lesson 26, page 64.

Skill-Development Activities (20 minutes)

Chinese Jump Rope

See Grades 6-8: Fitness, Lesson 28, page 69. Review and practice the basic steps.

Intermediate Jumping With a Chinese Jump Rope: Two-Foot Jump

Arrange the children in groups of three or four.

1. Describe and demonstrate the Two-Foot Jump.
   - *Stand facing the rope.*
   - *Place both feet under the rope and jump across to the other side of the rope. Take the rope across with your feet (start on the right side of the rope and jump to the left side). Then turn to your right.*
   - *Jump so that the rope springs back to its original position and you land with one foot on each side of the rope.*
2. Practice the Two-Foot Jump.

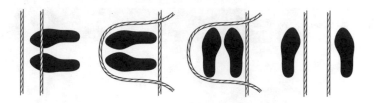

Intermediate Jumping With a Chinese Jump Rope: Twist Jumping

Arrange the children in groups of three or four.

1. Describe and demonstrate Twist Jumping.
    *   *Stand with one foot on each side of the rope.*
    *   *Slide your feet close together and turn around so you are facing the opposite direction. The rope will be wrapped around your ankles.*
    *   *Jump up so the rope springs back to its original position and you land with one foot on each side of the rope.*
2. Practice Twist Jumping.

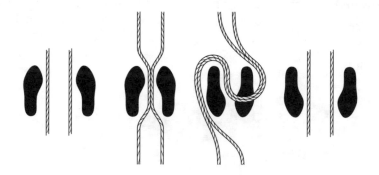

Fitness Stunts

Arrange children in six relay lines and mark two lines about 10 yards apart.

1. Describe and demonstrate the stunts.
2. Have children perform the stunts several times.

Seal Walk

Get into a push-up position with the weight on your hands and toes. Keep your back and legs straight. Walk forward with your hands, dragging your legs and toes.

Crab Walk

Support your weight on your hands and feet with your stomach facing the sky. Walk forward, keeping your back as straight as possible.

Rabbit Walk

Start in a squat position with your hands on the ground. Reach forward with the hands, supporting your body weight. Jump both feet toward the hands. Continue to move forward.

All Fours Walk

Support your weight on your hands and feet. Move on all fours, keeping the head up.

Measuring Worm

Get into a push-up position with the weight on your hands and toes. Keeping the knees stiff, walk the feet up as close as possible to the hands. Return to starting position by inching forward with the hands. Continue walking, first the feet and then the hands.

Concluding Activities (5 minutes)

Physical Fitness Concept

Arrange children in information formation.

1. Review and discuss the following concept: *Cardiorespiratory endurance increases when you exercise within a training heart rate range. Cardiorespiratory endurance is the ability of the heart and lungs to supply oxygen to the working muscles. Training heart rate range is the range of heart rates high enough during exercise to make gains in cardiorespiratory endurance, but not too high; in other words, the intensity is high enough but not so high that it is dangerous.*

2. Continue discussing cardiorespiratory endurance and its development. *Developing cardiorespiratory endurance depends on four things: frequency, which means that you must exercise frequently enough; intensity, which means that the exercise must be hard enough; time, which means that you must exercise for a long enough time; and style, which means the kind of exercise that you do. You can remember this by remembering FITS:*

    Frequency—you must exercise at least three times a week.

    Intensity—you must exercise within your training heart rate range. This is 75% to 90% of your maximal heart rate; maximal heart rate is the fastest your heart can beat.

    Time—you must exercise for at least 20 minutes each time.

    Style—the exercise must be an aerobic activity.

Figuring Target Heart Rate Range

Arrange children in cooperative groups of four to six.

1. Give each group a card or sheet of paper with the following formulas:

    Training heart rate = 220 – age $\times$ .75 (lower end)

    Training heart rate = 220 – age $\times$ .90 (upper end)

2. For a 12-year old, the range would be

    220 – 12 = 208 $\times$ .75 = 156 (lower end)

    220 – 12 = 208 $\times$ .90 = 187 (upper end)

3. The training heart rate range for a 12-year-old is between 156 and 187 beats per minute.

4. Each student should figure his or her own training heart rate range.

5. Remind the students that everyone in the cooperative group must understand the formula and how to figure it out before the group is successful.

FITNESS

LESSON 30
FITNESS STUNTS AND GAMES

Student Objectives

- Explain the health benefits of physical activity.
- Perform fitness stunts.
- Participate in fitness games.

Equipment

- Parachute

Warm-Up Activities (5 minutes)

Individual Stretching Activities IV

See Grades 6-8: Fitness, Lesson 26, page 64.

Skill-Development Activities (20 minutes)

Fitness Stunts

See Grades 6-8: Fitness, Lesson 29, page 72.

Fitness Games

Describe the following fitness games.

Fitness Tag

Arrange children in a scatter formation.

1. Select one student to be It.
2. On the signal to start, the It tries to tag a player. The player who is tagged becomes It.
3. Players are "safe" from a tag if they are in a push-up position. The maximum amount of time a player can be in the "safe" position is 10 seconds.
4. Variation: Players are safe when they are balanced on one foot, in a crab position, doing sit-ups, etc.

Parachute Fitness Game

Arrange children around the outside of a parachute that is spread out on the ground.

1. Perform the following fitness activities while holding on to the parachute:

   Jog in place.

   Jump or hop in place.

   Slide to the right eight counts and back to the left eight counts.

   Sit down and perform eight sit-ups.

2. Repeat from the beginning.

Cool Down With Exchange Positions

Assign numbers to the children around the parachute.

1. Students should hold the parachute with the left hand and circle counterclockwise.

2. On a signal, the odd-numbered students release the parachute and move forward to take the place of the next odd-numbered player in front of them.

3. Repeat with even-numbered players moving. Use walking, skipping, and galloping.

Concluding Activities (5 minutes)

Physical Fitness Concept

Arrange children in information formation.

1. Review the following concept: *There are many health benefits of physical activity.*

2. Discuss the benefits of physical activity. *Individuals who exercise tend to*

   feel better about themselves (i.e., have a better self-concept);

   be less prone to obesity, heart disease, and high blood pressure; and

   be better able to cope with stressful situations.

3. Continue the discussion by explaining that there are some things that exercise cannot do:

   Increase intellectual ability.

   Improve your reading scores.

   Change your personality.

4. Rearrange children in cooperative groups of five or six.

5. Ask each group to describe a fit and an unfit person.

GAMES AND SPORTS

The games and sports program is designed to develop competence in specific movement patterns and skills so that students can perform these skills in more real game situations. These skills are refined by practicing game-like drills and lead-up activities. The conditions for practicing these skills and techniques are gradually changed to match those expected in actual performance. While competition is an important part of the program, students are encouraged to set individual goals for skill improvement, rather than striving to perform better than others. Many cooperative learning activities are incorporated so that students can work together to solve movement problems without thinking about winning and losing.

UNIT ORGANIZATION

This section contains 40 lesson plans designed to provide instruction and practice in individual and team sports. The sports selected for inclusion at this level are tennis, soccer, basketball, softball, volleyball, track and field, and football. Some of the sports are recommended as one-week units (e.g., tennis), while others are planned for a two-week period. The lessons are numbered from 1 through 40, but there are also additional activities in the final lesson for many of the sports. This additional information can be used to supplement the earlier lessons.

Each lesson begins with a warm-up activity that you select from the previous games and activities. The warm-up should take about five minutes. This is followed by a skill-development activity that will take about 20 minutes. This time is spent refining specific skills in game-like drills and participating in games for individual

and team sports. Each lesson has a concluding activity that often gets students involved in a question-and-answer session designed to reinforce information about the skill or game.

LESSON DESCRIPTIONS

The games and sports warm-up section describes two circuits that can be used numerous times throughout the school year. Suggestions are provided for increasing the intensity as the students advance. You can use the activities exactly as described, or you can replace some of the exercises with activities that you have used before and the students like. In addition to the circuit training activities, there are several active games suggested for warming up. Some of the games are simply running relays, but others, such as the Softball Relay, are designed with a specific sport in mind. Finally, there is an individual stretching routine that includes flexibility exercises and ends with a jog in place.

Lessons 1 through 5 introduce tennis and provide partner practice activities for the Forehand and Backhand Groundstrokes. The groundstrokes are practiced with partners and in cooperative groups. Students are encouraged to observe their teammates and provide feedback about their technique.

Lessons 6 through 10 present drills and activities for soccer. Dribbling, Punting, and Goal Kicking are practiced with partners and in simple competitive games. Lesson 10 contains a review activity and a description of additional skills and games. Depending on the grade level you are working with, you can choose from these activities or continue practicing the skills presented in

Lessons 6 through 10. A modified soccer game is also described in Lesson 10.

Lessons 11 through 18 focus on basketball. The first three lessons (11-13) address basic ballhandling and shooting. Students are provided with opportunities to participate in organized drills, as well as group cooperative and competitive activities, and they are encouraged to evaluate the skill performance of a partner. Lesson 14 describes a basketball station learning activity that can be used for several days. Students work individually and progress at their own rates. Lessons 15 through 18 continue with the station learning format, but introduce cooperative learning. A modified basketball game is also described in this section.

Lessons 19 through 23 present the basic skills of softball. Throwing, Catching, and Fielding Ground Balls are practiced with partners. Batting, Hitting, and Base Running are practiced in small groups. Several modified games that provide maximum opportunities for participation are presented. Lesson 23 offers additional practice activities, a skill development station learning plan, and rules for simplified softball. These can be used to supplement or enhance the unit lessons.

Volleyball is presented in Lessons 24 through 28. The lessons focus on the skills of Serving, Spiking, Blocking, and Bumping. Lesson 28 offers review activities and simplified rules if additional lessons are needed.

Lessons 29 through 36 focus on track and field activities. Hurdling, the Triple Jump, the Scissors method of high jumping, and the Sprint Start for the dash are introduced and practiced in the first four lessons. Lessons 33 through 36 provide suggestions for a station learning activity that can be continued for several days. Tips for organizing a track and field meet are provided if additional lessons are needed.

Football skills and games are presented in Lessons 37 through 40. Skill-development activities include drills for Punting, Blocking, and Ball Exchange. Also, the technique is described for the Three-Point and Four-Point Stances. At the conclusion of Lesson 40, simplified football rules are outlined so that modified games can be introduced.

TEACHING TIPS AND LESSON MODIFICATIONS

In the middle grades (sixth to eighth) the emphasis shifts from a range of movement patterns and basic skills to specific skills related to traditional games and sports. Skills and techniques should be gradually changed to match those expected in game play. Teachers should work to assist students as they refine skills in game-like drills. It is important to note that if you have older students who have not had formal work on the fundamental skills, remedial practice is needed. Students who are not proficient in fundamental patterns are likely to have trouble with specialized skills.

There are several useful ways for teachers to modify skills and activities to adjust the difficulty level. One effective way is to change the complexity of the skill by increasing or decreasing the number of skills performed simultaneously, or changing the environmental conditions for performance. For example, running and ball dribbling each become more difficult when performed simultaneously. If students are having trouble, they should develop competency in stationary dribbling before progressing to a running dribble. When practicing football passing, students can perform first from a stationary base and then from a moving base. They can throw toward a stationary target first and then aim for a moving target. A very effective way to vary the complexity of sports skills is to adjust the height or size of the equipment. You can use lower basketball goals, smaller balls, lower nets, shorter rackets, and smaller courts and fields. The size and weight of the object to be thrown, kicked, or hit can be increased or decreased according to the skill level of the students. The size of the target to be hit and the size of the striking surface of a bat or racket can be made larger or smaller. As students participate in drills and games, it is our goal to improve and refine the quality of complex sports skills. As competency increases, more specialized participation and competitive involvement are emphasized.

Sports and games activities offer many opportunities to involve students in decision making. The student in grades six through eight is able to understand and apply the movement concepts and principles needed to detect, analyze, and correct errors in his or her own performance and the performance of classmates. Students should be able to identify the critical elements of the various sports skills and to assess a partner's performance and provide appropriate feedback. Many cooperative learning activities should be incorporated so that students can work together to solve movement problems.

Students can be asked to design new games using the skills and techniques introduced in the sports and games lessons. For example, when practicing football or soccer skills with a partner, students can be asked to make up a game using a ball, two hoops, several cones, and a rope. When students gain more experience, they can expand the game to include four to six players on each team.

Table S4.1: Unit Plan for Grades 6-8: Games and Sports

Week 5: tennis	Week 6: soccer	Week 8: football
Monday: warm-up, grip, ups and downs Tuesday: warm-up, forehand Wednesday: warm-up, drop and hit, group rally Thursday: warm-up, backhand Friday: warm-up, rally, sidewalk tennis	Monday: warm-up, dribbling Tuesday: warm-up, dribbling, keep-away Wednesday: warm-up, punting Thursday: warm-up, goal kicking, line soccer Friday: warm-up, review, short game	Monday: warm-up, punting, kickover Tuesday: warm-up, blocking, kickoff Wednesday: warm-up, three- and four-point stances, fourth down Thursday: warm-up, exchanges, relay Friday: warm-up, placekicking, game
Week 12: basketball	**Week 13: basketball**	**Week 22: volleyball**
Monday: warm-up, dribbling, flag dribble Tuesday: warm-up, lay-up contest Wednesday: warm-up, jump shot contest Thursday: warm-up, stations Friday: warm-up, stations	Monday: warm-up, cooperative learning Tuesday: warm-up, cooperative learning Wednesday: warm-up, cooperative learning Thursday: warm-up, modified game Friday: warm-up, modified game	Monday: warm-up, serve Tuesday: warm-up, spike Wednesday: warm-up, block, spike Thursday: warm-up, bump, three-pass Friday: warm-up, set and spike, three-pass
Week 23: softball	**Week 35: track and field**	**Week 36: track and field**
Monday: warm-up, throwing, catching, fielding Tuesday: warm-up, base running, base relay Wednesday: warm-up, batting, pepper Thursday: warm-up, batting, base running Friday: warm-up, fungo, line up	Monday: warm-up, hurdling Tuesday: warm-up, triple jump Wednesday: warm-up, scissors Thursday: warm-up, sprint start Friday: warm-up, stations	Monday: warm-up, stations Tuesday: warm-up, stations Wednesday: warm-up, stations Thursday: warm-up, track meet Friday: warm-up, track meet

Note: This is one example of how games and sports can be incorporated into a curriculum plan that corresponds to the yearly plan presented in the introduction of this book. Modifications can be made to accommodate your individual needs.

WARM-UPS

Circuit Training

Divide the students into six groups, and assign each group to one of the six stations.

1. On the *go* signal, the students exercise at their stations for 20 seconds, counting the number of repetitions.

2. Call *stop* after 20 seconds; the students stop and change stations. Allow 15 seconds for the children to rotate to new stations.

3. The children complete as many repetitions of the exercise as possible at each station.

4. The time at each station can be increased each week as shown in the table. Fifteen seconds is allowed initially for children to rotate to the next station and prepare to exercise.

	Time at each station	Time to move between stations
Week 1	20 s	15 s
Week 2	25 s	15 s
Week 3	30 s	10 s
Week 4	35 s	5 s

Circuit 1

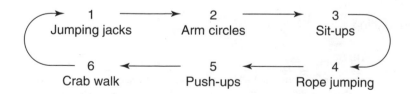

Jumping Jacks

Standing with feet together and hands at sides, the student bounces up and lands with feet apart while moving the arms overhead and clapping hands above the head and then jumps back to starting position.

Arm Circles

Standing with feet comfortably apart and arms at sides, the student circles arms forward and backward.

Sit-Ups

The student lies supine with arms folded across chest, hands placed on shoulders, knees bent, and raises the body until the arms touch the thighs, and then returns to starting position.

Rope Jumping

The student jumps with a short jump rope using a Two-Foot Single Step (one jump for each turn of the rope).

Push-Ups

Beginning in a kneeling front support position with back straight, the student lowers chin and chest to the ground, keeping back straight, and then returns to starting position.

Crab Walk

Assuming a back support position with knees bent and body straight, the student walks on hands and feet from Line A to Line B, and then back to Line A, continuing until time is up.

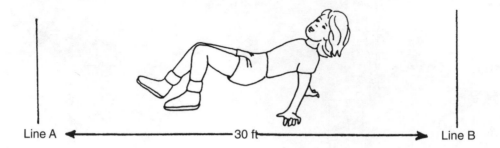

Line A ◄———————— 30 ft ————————► Line B

Circuit 2

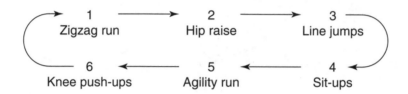

1 Zigzag run → 2 Hip raise → 3 Line jumps
6 Knee push-ups ← 5 Agility run ← 4 Sit-ups

Zigzag Run

Cones are arranged in a zigzag fashion. The student runs around the cones and then straight back to the starting line. One point is scored for each cone the runner passes.

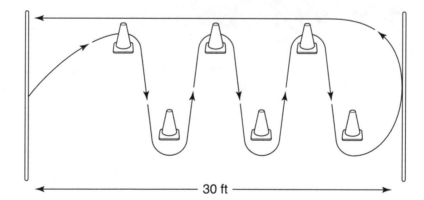

◄———————— 30 ft ————————►

Hip Raise

Sitting with upper body supported by arms, the student lifts trunk until the body is straight and then returns to sitting position. One point is scored for each Hip Raise.

Line Jumps

Two lines are marked on the ground about 12 inches apart. Standing on the outside of one line with feet together, the student jumps sideways over both lines and then jumps back to starting position. One point is scored for each jump.

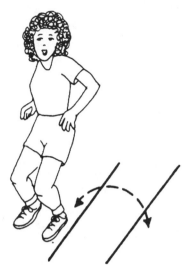

Sit-Ups

One point is scored for each Sit-Up.

Agility Run

Two lines are marked about 10 feet apart. Beginning at the starting line, the student runs, touches the second line, turns around, runs back, touches the starting line, and continues running back and forth, touching each line. One point is scored for each time a line is touched.

Starting line   Return line

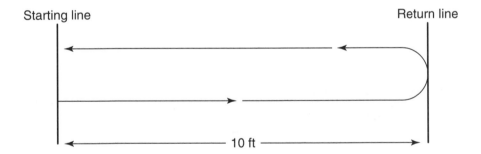

10 ft

Push-Ups

One point is scored each time the chin and chest touch the ground. The push-ups are done from the hands-and-knees position.

Games

Sprint Relay

Arrange the children in groups of five or six. Mark a starting line and a return line, 20 yards apart, and line up the groups single file behind the starting line.

1. On the signal, Player 1 runs to the return line, runs back to the starting line, touches the hand of Player 2, and goes to the end of the line.

2. Player 2 runs, and so on, until all the students in the group have had a turn.

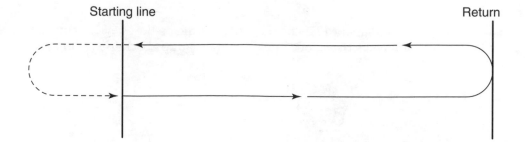

Shuttle Relay

Arrange the students in teams of six, and line up half of each team behind the starting line and the other half behind the return line.

1. On each team, Player 1 runs from the starting line to the return line to touch the hand of Player 2 and then goes to the end of that line.

2. Player 2 then runs to the starting line to touch the hand of Player 3, and so on.

3. Players will end up on the line opposite from where they started.

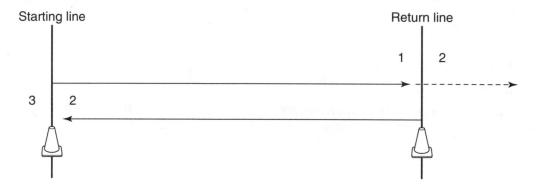

Zigzag Relay

Arrange the students in groups of five or six. For each group, arrange a zigzag course of cones laid about eight feet apart from one another between two lines.

1. Have the groups line up single file behind the starting line.

2. On a signal, Player 1 runs around the cones to the return line and then runs straight back to the starting line to touch the hand of Player 2, who then runs the course and returns to tag Player 3. This continues until all players have completed the race and are back in their original places.

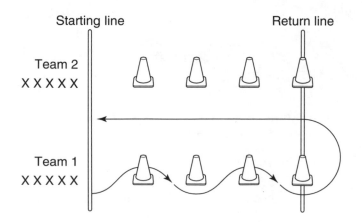

Rescue Relay

Arrange the students in groups of five or six. Mark a starting line and a return line. Player 1 starts on the starting line and the other players line up behind the return line.

1. On the signal, Player 1 runs and gets Player 2, and holding hands they both return to the starting line.

2. Player 2 then runs back for Player 3, and so on until all players are behind the starting line.

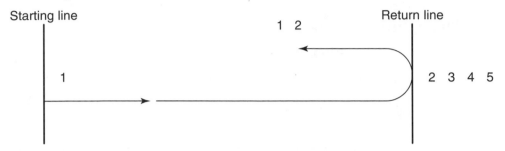

Softball Relay

Arrange the students in four groups. Using a regulation softball diamond, place each group at one of the bases or at home plate.

1. Player 1 from each team runs in a counterclockwise direction touching all the bases and returns to touch the hand of Player 2, who then starts off to run around the bases.

2. Player 1 goes to the end of the line. This continues until all team members have run around the bases.

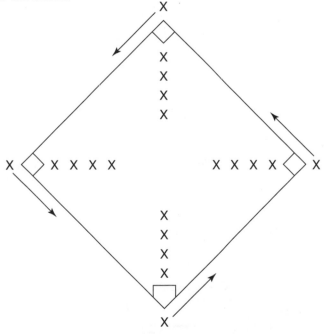

Fetch and Pass Relay

Arrange the students in relay teams of five or six. Each team lines up behind the starting line across from a hoop that is on the floor with a football inside it.

1. Player 1 runs to the hoop and stands in it, picks up the football, and while standing in the hoop, passes the ball to Player 2, who passes it back to Player 1.

2. Player 1 puts the ball down in the hoop, runs back to the starting line, and touches hands with Player 2, who then repeats the actions of Player 1.

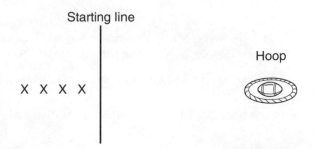

Starting line

Hoop

Running and Sliding Drill

Arrange the students at different starting points around a basketball court, two or three at each cone.

1. In single file, the students run in a zigzag fashion around the cones on the court.
2. The drill is completed three times: running forward, running backward, and sliding sideways.

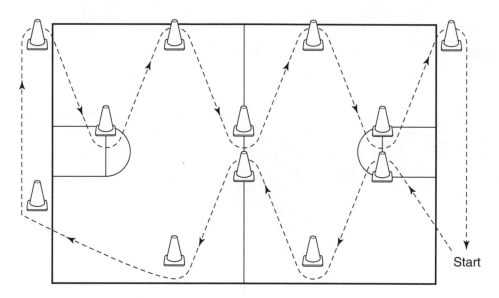

Start

Individual Stretching Exercises

Arrange the students in scatter formation. The students perform the following stretching activities.

Toe Touch

Sitting with legs straight and feet together, the student reaches toward the toes, lowers the chin to the knees, holds for five seconds, relaxes, and repeats several times.

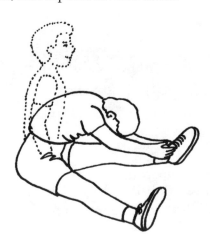

Body Bend

Standing with feet shoulder width apart and arms by the sides, the student bends down to the right as far as possible and holds for five seconds, returns to starting position, bends to the left, holds, and repeats several times to the right and to the left.

Trunk Twister

Standing with feet shoulder width apart and hands clasped in front of the chin (arms horizontal), the student rotates slowly to the right and left, holding each position for five seconds, repeating several times.

Forward Lunge

Standing with feet together and hands on hips, the student lunges forward with the right leg, keeping the left leg straight. The right knee should form a right angle. The student holds the lunge position for five seconds, returns to starting position, and lunges with the left leg forward. This is repeated several times with the right and left legs.

Running in Place

The student runs in place 20 steps.

GRADES 6-8

LESSON 1
TENNIS

Student Objectives

- Demonstrate the Eastern Forehand Grip.
- Work cooperatively with a group to improve scores on Ups and Downs.

Equipment

- One wooden paddle or short tennis racket for each child
- One tennis ball for each child
- Six stopwatches
- Jump ropes and cones for warm-up activities

Warm-Up Activities (5 minutes)

Circuit 1 or Circuit 2

Arrange the children into six groups and assign each group to one of the six stations. See Grades 6-8: Games and Sports, Warm-Ups, page 80.

1. On the "go" signal, the students exercise at their stations for 20 seconds, counting the number of repetitions.
2. Call "stop" after 20 seconds; the students stop and change stations. Allow students 15 seconds to rotate to new stations.
3. The children complete as many repetitions as possible of the exercise at each station.

Skill-Development Activities (20 minutes)

Forehand Grip

Arrange the children in scatter formation. Each has a tennis ball and a racket or paddle.

1. Describe and demonstrate the Forehand Grip: *The paddle is held so that it is perpendicular to the floor, gripped as though one were shaking hands with it.*
2. Present the following individual activities with students using the Forehand Grip (and hitting on the front side unless instructed otherwise):

   Dribble the ball five times while standing still. Use your dominant and then your nondominant hand.

   Dribble the ball five times while moving forward (backward, sideways). Use your right hand and then your left hand.

   Hit the ball into the air, let it bounce, and catch it on the racket. Don't hit it too high.

Hit the ball into the air five times. Use your right and then your left hand.

Walk different directions while hitting the ball into the air. Use your right and left hands.

Hit the ball up and then turn the paddle and hit it the second time with the other side. Use your right and left hands.

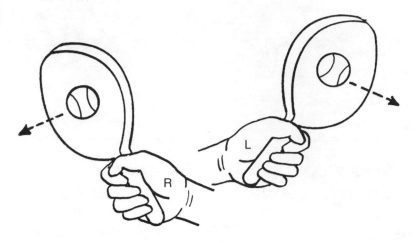

Concluding Activities (5 minutes)

Timed Ups and Downs

Arrange the children in groups of six, in scatter formation, each with a racket or paddle and a tennis ball.

1. One student from each group serves as the timer and times students for one minute while they hit as many upward and downward hits as possible using the forehand side of the racket.

2. The timer serves as a teacher and observes the hitters to make sure they are using the handshake grip. He or she provides feedback to the students when needed.

3. The students count the number of hits they complete in one minute.

4. Repeat several times, allowing each student an opportunity to be the leader.

LESSON 2
TENNIS

Student Objectives

- Demonstrate the correct technique for the Forehand Groundstroke.
- State two important things to remember about the arm when you perform the Forehand Groundstroke.

Equipment

- One paddle or racket and one tennis ball for every two children
- Materials for marking crosses and footprints
- Jump ropes and cones for warm-up activities

Warm-Up Activities (5 minutes)

Circuit Training

See Grades 6-8: Games and Sports, Warm-Ups, page 80.

Skill-Development Activities (20 minutes)

Forehand Groundstroke

Arrange the children in pairs and assign each pair to a cross on the floor. Mark footprints at each cross. Each set of partners has a racket or paddle and a tennis ball.

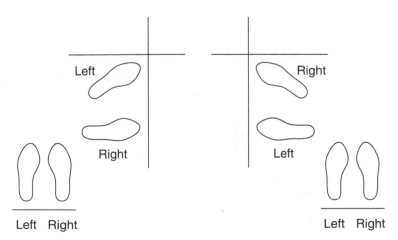

Court markings for practice of forehand groundstroke

1. The paddle or racket is held in the right hand (forehand grip).

2. Turning on the right foot to place it on the right footprint marker, while swinging the racket back, the student steps forward with the left foot to the left foot mark and swings the racket forward, level with the wrist.

3. Follow through is in the direction the ball is to go. The elbow and wrist are kept straight. (These instructions are for right-handed players. For left-handed players, reverse the actions.)

4. Describe the court markings for the footwork (right- and left-handed).

5. Have the students practice the following tasks with partners:

   With your partner go to a cross. Without a ball, take turns practicing the step pattern and swing, using the markings on the cross.

   Take turns tossing balls to your partner; the ball should bounce once and come up so your partner can hit it without moving. Toss five times and then exchange places and repeat.

   When your partner can hit from a stationary position, toss the ball slightly farther away so that she or he must take a step or two to get to it before striking. You should back up slightly for this.

   Repeat.

Right-handed

Left-handed

Cooperative Practice

Arrange the children in groups of four and assign each group to a practice area.

1. Players in each group are to help each other with the correct technique: grip; turn, step, swing; keeping the elbow and wrist straight.
2. The goal of the activity is for each player in the group to demonstrate the technique.
3. Children are encouraged to help each other.

Concluding Activities (5 minutes)

Forehand Groundstroke

Continue groundstroke practice in groups of four, but have each group of students count their number of successful hits.

Question and Answer

Arrange the children in information formation. Ask the children the following questions:

What should you remember about your grip for the Forehand Groundstroke?

What should you remember about your arm when you practice the Forehand Groundstroke?

What are some ways that you helped others in your group be successful?

What is one thing you do to help yourself be more successful?

GAMES AND SPORTS

LESSON 3
TENNIS

Student Objectives

- Hit the ball, using correct technique, back and forth with a partner five consecutive times without making an error.
- Work cooperatively in a group practice activity.

Equipment

- One paddle or racket and one tennis ball for every child
- Materials for marking crosses and footprints
- Jump ropes and cones for warm-up activities

Warm-Up Activities (5 minutes)

Circuit Training

Increase the time at each station. See Grades 6-8: Games and Sports, Warm-Ups, page 80.

Skill-Development Activities (20 minutes)

Self-Drop and Hit

Arrange the children in partners at crosses marked on the floor. Each child has a racket or paddle and a tennis ball.

1. Describe the Self-Drop and Hit.
   - The student drops the ball in the circle while pivoting and swinging the racket back.
   - Keeping eyes on the ball, the student steps forward and, as the ball bounces waist high, hits it, keeping the elbow and wrist straight.
2. Demonstrate the Self-Drop and Hit.
3. Have the students practice in pairs at the crosses.
4. Have one child stand at least 10 feet from the other to catch or retrieve the balls.
5. Have the students switch places after five hits and repeat.

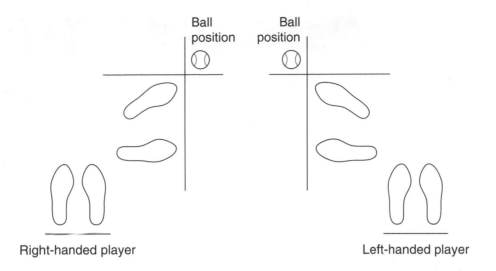

Right-handed player   Left-handed player

Cooperative Practice

Arrange the children in groups of four and assign each group to a practice area. Players in each group are to help each other with the correct technique: grip; turn, step, swing; keeping the elbow and wrist straight; and hitting waist high.

Concluding Activities (5 minutes)

Group Rally

Keep the same groups of four; starting with a self-drop by one of the players, the group rallies back and forth.

1. A rally is a continuous series of hits between players.
2. Two students stand on one line facing the other two students, who are 10 feet away.
3. Each group counts the number of successful hits.
4. After 10 successful hits in a series, increase the distance to 12, 14, and 16 feet.

LESSON 4
TENNIS

Student Objectives

- Demonstrate the Backhand Grip and the correct technique for the Backhand Groundstroke.
- State one important thing to remember about the Backhand Groundstroke.

Equipment

- One paddle or racket and one tennis ball for each child
- Materials for marking crosses and footprints
- Jump ropes and cones for warm-up activities

Warm-Up Activities (5 minutes)

Circuit I

Increase the time at each station. See Grades 6-8: Games and Sports, Warm-Ups, page 80.

Skill-Development Activities (20 minutes)

Backhand Grip

Arrange the children in scatter formation. Each child has a racket or paddle and a tennis ball.

   1. Describe and demonstrate the Backhand Grip.
- The racket is held perpendicular to the ground.
- The hand is rotated to the left until the first knuckle is on top and lined up with the edge of the racket, and then the racket is turned approximately an eighth of a turn. (For left-handed players, reverse the instructions.)

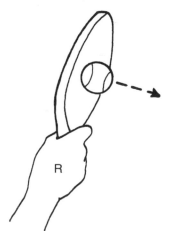
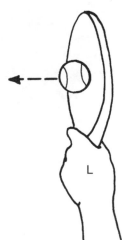

2. Practice the Backhand Grip.

3. Have the children take the Backhand Grip, change to the Forehand Grip, and then return to the Backhand Grip. Repeat.

Backhand Groundstroke

Arrange the children in pairs at the court markings.

1. Describe the Backhand Groundstroke (including how to use the footprints at the crosses).

    - *Standing facing the target holding the racket with a Backhand Grip, turn to the left, placing your left foot on the left marker; and at the same time swing the racket straight back across in front of the body.*

    - *Stepping forward, place your right foot on the right foot marker while swinging the racket forward, keeping your arm and wrist straight. (For left-handed players, reverse instructions.)*

2. Demonstrate the Backhand Groundstroke (right- and left-handed).

3. Have the children practice the following tasks using the Backhand Groundstroke:

    With your partner go to a cross. Without a ball, take turns practicing the step pattern and swing, using the markings for the Backhand Groundstroke. This stroke is like drawing a sword from a scabbard. Reach across your body, pretend the racket is a sword, and shift the sword to a position in front of the body. Observe your partner to see if the movement looks like reaching and pulling a sword.

    Take turns tossing balls to your partner to hit. Toss five times and then exchange places. When your partner is successful at hitting five in a row, toss the ball so she or he has to move a step or two before striking; this means the tosser must back up slightly. Repeat.

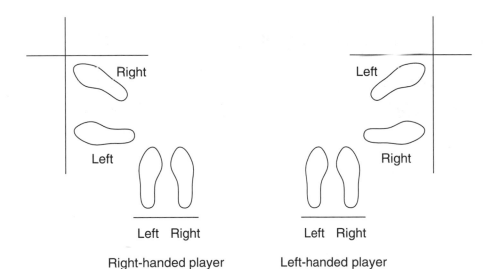

Right-handed player   Left-handed player

Court markings for practice of backhand groundstroke

Right-handed player

Left-handed player

Concluding Activities (5 minutes)

Backhand Groundstroke

Continue the same activity, but have each pair of students count their number of successful Backhand Groundstrokes.

GAMES AND SPORTS

LESSON 5
TENNIS

Student Objectives

- Rally with a partner five consecutive times without an error.

Equipment

- One paddle or racket for each child
- One tennis ball for every two children
- Materials for making nets or marking lines
- Jump ropes and cones for warm-up activities

Warm-Up Activities (5 minutes)

Circuit Training

Increase the time at each station. See Grades 6-8: Games and Sports, Warm-Ups, page 80.

Skill-Development Activities (10 minutes)

Forehand and Backhand Groundstrokes

Arrange the children in pairs. Each pair has a tennis ball, and each child has a paddle or racket.

1. One partner tosses the ball underhand five times to the partner's forehand and then repeats, tossing to the backhand.
2. Partners then exchange places.
3. Mark lines for nets and have partners stand on opposite sides of the lines, about 10 feet from each other.
4. Using both Forehand and Backhand Groundstrokes, partners rally for as long as possible.

Concluding Activities (15 minutes)

Sidewalk Tennis

Arrange the children in pairs, each pair at a line on the ground or at a net. Each pair has a tennis ball, and each child has a paddle or racket.

1. One player drops the ball and starts a rally over a line or net with a partner. Partners count the number of consecutive hits.
2. After five minutes the pair with the greatest number wins.
3. Have the children rotate to new partners and play again.

LESSON 6
SOCCER

Student Objectives

- Demonstrate the correct technique for the soccer Dribble.
- Evaluate the technique of a partner and provide the partner with feedback.
- State two important things to remember about the soccer Dribble.

Equipment

- One soccer ball for every two children
- Jump ropes and cones for warm-up activities

Warm-Up Activities (5 minutes)

Circuit Training

Increase the time at each station. See Grades 6-8: Games and Sports, Warm-Ups, page 80.

Skill-Development Activities (15 minutes)

Dribbling

Arrange the children in pairs, with the children in each pair facing each other from about 20 yards apart. Each pair has a soccer ball.

1. Describe and demonstrate Dribbling.

   - Dribbling involves moving the ball with short running kicks. The skill is used to elude defensive players or to advance the ball to set up a scoring attempt.
   - Tap the ball with the inside of the foot, using alternate feet and keeping the ball close for good control. You can use both the inside and outside of the foot.

2. Ask the students to perform the following tasks:

   Practice Dribbling to your partner, who will dribble back to the other end. Repeat several times.

   Practice Dribbling around the field with your partner (any direction); each partner should dribble the ball a few yards and then pass to the other partner.

   Observe your partner to see if he or she is using alternate feet and keeping the ball close for good control. Remind your partner to use both the inside and outside of the foot.

Concluding Activities (10 minutes)

Circle Dribble

Arrange the children into teams of six to eight players, with each team in a 30-foot circle with a soccer ball in the center. Assign each player a number.

1. When a number is called, the player with that number runs to the center and dribbles the ball back out through his or her place and around the outside of the circle as fast as possible.
2. The player finishes by placing the ball back in the center and sitting in place.
3. The person finishing first among all the teams scores one point for his or her team. The team with the most points at the end of the playing time wins.

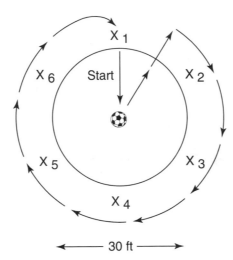

Question and Answer

Arrange the children in information formation. Ask the students the following questions:

What should you remember about the soccer Dribble?

When in a game would you use the Dribble?

What helps you the most to be successful in your practice?

LESSON 7
SOCCER

Student Objectives

- Maintain possession of the soccer ball while Dribbling around an obstacle.

Equipment

- 1 soccer ball for every 2 children
- 35 cones for marking the field
- Jump ropes and cones for warm-up activities

Warm-Up Activities (5 minutes)

Circuit Training

Increase the time at each station. See Grades 6-8: Games and Sports, Warm-Ups, page 80.

Skill-Development Activities (20 minutes)

Dribbling Practice

Arrange the children in groups of four, facing a line of cones, each group with a soccer ball.

1. The students practice Dribbling around cones.
2. Have them go as quickly as they can while maintaining control of the ball. Repeat several times.

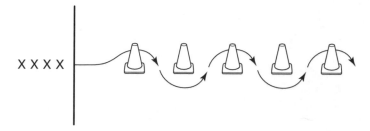

Arrange cones so that each group of four has a goal.

3. The students practice Dribbling and kicking toward a goal area in a one-on-one or two-on-two situation.
4. The child with the ball dribbles toward the goal marked by two cones and tries to kick the ball through; the other partner attempts to block the kick.

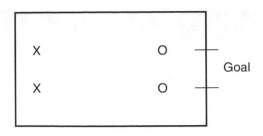

Concluding Activities (5 minutes)

Soccer Keep-Away

Arrange the children in teams of four to six, with two teams on each field. The fields can be any size and marked out with cones; 30 × 50 feet is appropriate. Each field has a soccer ball. The team with the ball dribbles or passes the ball to keep it away from the other team.

LESSON 8
SOCCER

Student Objectives

- Demonstrate the correct technique for the soccer Punt.
- Evaluate the technique of a partner and provide the partner with feedback.
- State two important things to remember about the soccer Punt.

Equipment

- 1 soccer ball for every 2 children
- One 20-foot rope for goal (mounted on standards so it is at least 10 feet high)
- 12 hoops
- Chalk, flour, tape, or cones to mark lines
- Jump ropes and cones for warm-up activities

Warm-Up Activities (5 minutes)

Circuit Training

Increase the time at each station. See Grades 6-8: Games and Sports, Warm-Ups, page 80.

Skill-Development Activities (20 minutes)

Punt

Arrange the children in pairs, each pair with a soccer ball.

1. Describe and demonstrate the Punt.
   - The Punt is used only by the goalkeepers.
   - Hold the ball in both hands, about waist high over the kicking leg, take a short step with the kicking foot and a full step with the nonkicking foot, and swing the kicking foot forward to contact the ball.

2. Have the children practice at different distances with partners.

3. Tell the children: *Observe your partner to see if he or she is starting with the ball waist high over the kicking leg, taking two steps before kicking the ball, and following through with the kicking foot after contact.*

4. Start them at 20 feet and after some success move them farther apart (e.g., 30 or 40 feet).

5. Arrange the children into groups of six with each group on a punting line facing three target hoops on the ground.

6. The students practice punting for accuracy, attempting to kick the ball so it first hits the ground inside the hoop.

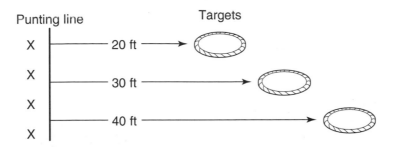

Concluding Activities (5 minutes)

Punt Over

Mark out a 20 × 40-foot field with goal posts made with rope at one end. Arrange the children in teams of four to six with all teams standing on the 20-foot line facing the goal. Each team has a soccer ball.

1. Beginning at the 20-foot line, the first player on each team attempts to Punt the ball over the goal post.

2. One point is scored for each successful kick.

3. After every player has kicked at the 20-foot line, move to the 30-foot line, where a successful kick is two points. The 40-foot kick is three points.

4. The team with the most points at the end of the playing time wins.

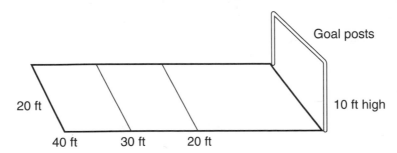

Question and Answer

Arrange the children in information formation. Ask the children the following questions:

What should you remember about the soccer Punt?

What problems did you have today?

What helped you the most to be successful?

What did your partner say or do that helped you?

GAMES AND SPORTS

LESSON 9
SOCCER

Student Objectives

- Show increased skill in Goal Kicking.

Equipment

- 1 soccer ball for every 6 children
- 10 cones to mark goals
- Chalk, flour, tape, or cones to mark lines
- Jump ropes and cones for warm-up activities

Warm-Up Activities (5 minutes)

Circuit Training

Increase the time at each station. See Grades 6-8: Games and Sports, Warm-Ups, page 80.

Skill-Development Activities (15 minutes)

Goal Kicking

Arrange the children in groups of six at a playing area, each group with a soccer ball.

1. The students practice Goal Kicking from a stationary position with a goalie defending; have them start with a 20-foot wide goal and a kicking line 30 feet away.
2. Gradually decrease the size of the goal and increase the distance to the kicking line.
3. Rotate students from kicker to goalie to ball chaser. Repeat.

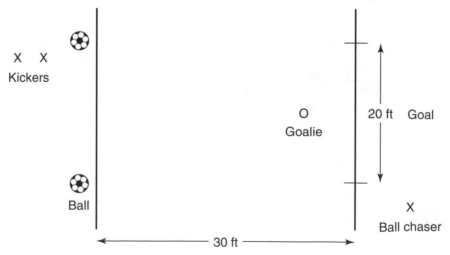

Concluding Activities (10 minutes)

Line Soccer

Arrange the children into teams of six, each team with a soccer ball, with two teams assigned to each playing area. The children on each team are numbered from 1 to 6. Each playing area is marked by two parallel lines 30 feet apart. The teams line up opposite each other behind the lines.

1. Call a number from 1 to 6 to identify active players. The players with that number attempt to dribble and kick the ball below shoulder level over the opposing team's line.

2. The line players act as goalies and can use their hands to pick up the ball and throw it to an active player.

3. Only active players can score. A player stays active, and thus can score, until a new number is called or a score is made.

4. Variations:

    Increase the size of the playing area.

    Call more than one number at a time.

    Use a square formation and have four teams.

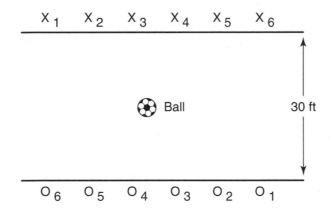

GAMES AND SPORTS

LESSON 10
SOCCER

Student Objectives

- Show increased skill in controlling the ball while Dribbling and Passing.

Equipment

- One soccer ball for every nine children
- Chalk, flour, tape, or cones to mark field lines
- Jump ropes and cones for warm-up activities

Warm-Up Activities (5 minutes)

Circuit Training

Increase the time at each station. See Grades 6-8: Games and Sports, Warm-Ups, page 80.

Skill-Development Activities (15 minutes)

Basic Skills

Arrange the children in groups of nine, each group with a soccer ball, with each group assigned to a playing area.

1. Describe and demonstrate the drill. The children practice Dribbling, Passing, and Goal Kicking using this drill.

   - Three children dribble the ball and pass among themselves from the dribbling line to the kicking line.
   - At the kicking line, one child attempts a goal and the goalie attempts to block the kick.
   - The ball chasers retrieve the ball, and the goalie and ball chasers rotate to become the next three children waiting a turn; the three who just attempted a goal become the goalie and the ball chasers.

2. Start with a 20-foot wide goal, a kicking line 30 feet away, and a dribbling line 60 feet away. Distance can be adjusted according to skill level.

3. Have the children practice the drill.

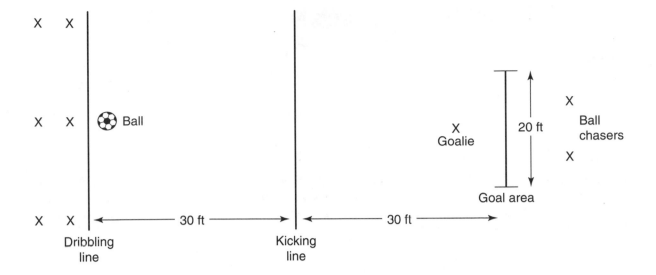

Concluding Activities (10 minutes)

Short Field Game

Mark out fields 30 × 60 feet with a 10-foot goal marked at each end. Arrange the children into teams of four, with two teams assigned to each field and one soccer ball per field. Each team is assigned to half of the field.

1. Team A kicks off from the center and attempts to score through Team B's goal.
2. Team B tries to intercept and score through Team A's goal.
3. Each time a goal is scored the ball is returned to the center.
4. Teams alternate taking the kickoff.
5. Touching the ball or committing a personal foul (pushing another player) result in a free kick for the opposing side.
6. A free kick is one that is taken from a line 20 feet from the goal. Only one opponent can defend against the kick. All other players must stand back.
7. When a ball goes over the sideline, it is thrown in by the nonviolating team.

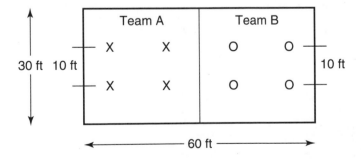

ADDITIONAL ACTIVITIES FOR GRADES 6-8: SOCCER

Presented below are skill-development ideas and skill rules for a soccer unit. For a longer period or for additional lessons, devise group activities that allow students to practice these activities and to practice playing by these rules.

Juggling

The ball is kept off the ground by being tapped alternately with any body part except the arms and hands. Tell the students: *See how many times you can tap the ball up to keep the sequence going. Find a partner and see how many times you can juggle back and forth. The ball may bounce once as it is passed from one player to another.*

Heading

Heading is used to change the ball's direction of flight. Standing in a forward stride position with eyes on the ball, the student propels his or her body forward from the waist, striking the ball with the forehead. The neck should be kept tense. Follow through is in a forward direction. Tell the students: *With a partner, toss the ball for each other to head it.*

Additional Games for Soccer

Dribble Relay

Players are in groups of four or five in a relay line formation.

1. Player 1 from each team dribbles the ball to the return line, turns, and dribbles the ball back to the starting line.

2. Player 2 takes the ball and dribbles, and so on.

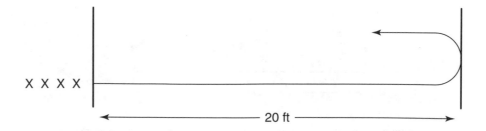

X X X X

20 ft

3. Here are some variations to this game:

Dribble to the line, turn, and pass the ball back to the next player.

Dribble around in a square area rather than in a line.

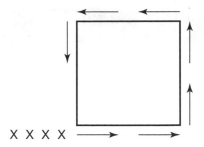

Modified Soccer

Players: Six per team, one goalkeeper (in front of goal), two halfbacks (midfield), and three forwards (near center line). Field: A large area (100 × 50 feet) with a 20-foot goal at each end and a circle on the center line. A semicircle approximately 36 feet in diameter is marked as a goal circle. (These dimensions are all suggestions. Larger or smaller fields can be used.)

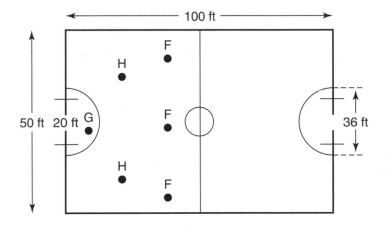

1. The game begins with a pass from the center circle by the team winning the coin flip.
2. The kicking team attempts to pass the ball among teammates toward the opposite goal.
3. A goal is scored by kicking the ball through the goal past the goalkeeper.
4. Defenders try to intercept the ball and move it toward the opposite goal.
5. The ball cannot be touched with the hands, except by the goalkeeper.
6. When the ball is kicked out-of-bounds, the opposing team begins play with a throw-in.
7. Personal fouls result in a free kick for the opposing team, taken at the spot of the foul.
8. Personal fouls by the defense in the semicircle result in a penalty kick taken from a point on the goal circle. Only the goalkeeper is allowed to defend.
9. If the ball goes out-of-bounds over the end line without a defending player touching it, the goalkeeper is awarded a kick. If the ball goes out-of-bounds over the end line but is last touched by a defender, a corner kick is awarded the attacking team.
10. As an alternative, play without a goalkeeper, but with three halfbacks and three forwards. This increases the scoring and excitement of the game. Goal kicks must be taken outside the semicircle.

LESSON 11
BASKETBALL

Student Objectives

- Show increased control of the ball while moving.
- Explain how the Speed Dribble is different from the Stationary Dribble.

Equipment

- 1 basketball or large ball for each child
- 12 cones
- 1 flag-football belt for each child

Warm-Up Activities (5 minutes)

Running and Sliding Drill

Arrange the children at different starting points around a basketball court, with two or three at each cone.

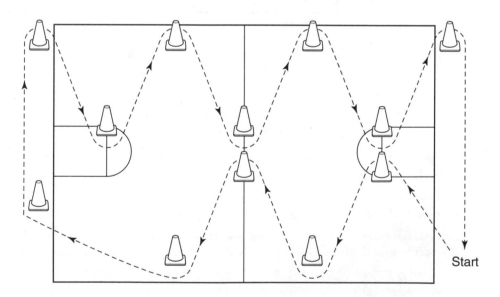

Start

1. In single file, students run in a zigzag fashion around the cones on the court.
2. Have them complete the drill three times: running forward, running backward, and sliding sideways.

Skill-Development Activities (15 minutes)

Dribbling and Ball Control

Arrange the children in scatter formation, each with a ball.

1. Describe and demonstrate Dribbling: Dribbling is a way to move the ball down the court, break for a basket, or move to get away from an opponent. The ball is controlled by the fingers. The knees are bent, and the body is flexed over the ball. The dribbler should not look at the ball, but keep his or her eyes beyond the ball.

2. Have the children practice Stationary Dribbling using the right hand, the left hand, and alternate hands.

3. Have the children practice Dribbling at different levels, under the legs, and behind the back.

4. Indicate a direction with hand signals and have the children practice Dribbling while moving. The students watch for direction signals and dribble forward, backward, right, and left.

5. Have the children practice Waist Circles, Leg Circles, Double Leg Circles, Figure 8, and Quick Hands in a stationary position. See Grades 4-5: Games and Sports, Lesson 18.

Speed Dribble

Arrange the children in pairs in scatter formation, each pair with a ball.

1. Describe and demonstrate the Speed Dribble: The Speed Dribble is used when a player needs to move the ball rapidly down the court. The technique is identical to that of the Stationary Dribble except that the ball is bounced waist high out in front of the body. The player runs quickly while controlling the ball.

2. Taking turns with a partner, the students practice the Speed Dribble across the court and back with the following variations:

   Dribble with your right hand (your left hand, alternate hands).

   Dribble around obstacles.

   Dribble with your partner guarding you.

Leg Circles With a Walk

Arrange the children in scatter formation. Each child has a ball.

1. Describe and demonstrate Leg Circles With a Walk: A walk is added to the right and left leg circles. Each time the leg is placed forward, the ball is circled around the calf.

2. Have the students practice Leg Circles With a Walk by having them walk between 5 and 10 steps and return to starting position.

Concluding Activities (10 minutes)

Flag Dribble

Arrange the children in teams of 4 to 10, with two teams on a court. Courts are hard surfaced and can be any size according to the number of players. Each player wears a flag-football belt and has a ball. The two teams on each court each should wear different colors of flags.

1. The object of the game is to eliminate the players on the opposing team while avoiding being eliminated. A player can be eliminated by losing control of the ball, by having her or his flag pulled, or by going out-of-bounds.

2. After a period of time, the team with more players remaining in the game wins.

3. Players who are eliminated practice Speed Dribbling around the outside of the court until the game starts over.

Question and Answer

Arrange the children in information formation. Ask the children the following questions:

When would you use the Speed Dribble in basketball?

How is the Speed Dribble different from the Stationary Dribble?

What helped you the most to be successful with the Speed Dribble?

What should you remember when you practice the Dribble?

GAMES AND SPORTS

LESSON 12
BASKETBALL

Student Objectives

- Demonstrate the correct technique for the Lay-Up.
- Evaluate the technique of a partner, and provide the partner with feedback.
- State two important things to remember about the Lay-Up.

Equipment

- 1 basketball for every 2 students
- 12 cones

Warm-Up Activities (5 minutes)

Running and Sliding Drill

See Grades 6-8: Games and Sports, Warm-Ups, page 86.

Skill-Development Activities (15 minutes)

Lay-Up

Arrange the children in scatter formation with partners, each pair with a basketball.

1. Describe and demonstrate the Lay-Up.

   - The Lay-Up is a shot taken at the end of a dribble or after receiving a pass from a teammate while running toward the goal.
   - The backboard should be approached from a 45-degree angle if possible, although the Lay-Up can also be done from the front of the basket.
   - The ball is held with the shooting hand and is supported with the nonshooting hand.
   - The ball is pushed against the target spot on the backboard as the body is lifted up by jumping from the foot opposite from the shooting arm. Raising the knee on the shooting side helps the player gain height.
   - The ball is released at the top of the jump.

2. Have the children practice the Lay-Up with partners in scatter formation.

3. Each child should observe his or her partner to determine if he or she is jumping from the foot opposite from the shooting arm as the ball is being released. Tell the students: *Take three steps and then shoot the ball toward your partner.*

4. For a right-handed player, the step pattern will be left, right, left, and jump. Tell the students: *Observe your partner to see if this step pattern is used and if the jump is from the foot opposite from the shooting arm. Add a dribble to your Lay-Up Shot.*

5. Arrange the children in four groups and assign each group to a basketball goal.

6. The children practice Lay-Up Shots from the right, left, and front of the goal.

Shoot

Left

Right

Left

Concluding Activities (10 minutes)

Lay-Up Contest

Arrange the children in teams of four to six players. Line the teams up at the half-court line with two teams facing each goal. Each team has a basketball.

1. On a signal the first player on each team dribbles toward the goal and shoots a Lay-Up Shot.

2. The player continues shooting until she or he scores a goal.

3. After scoring, the player dribbles back to midcourt. The first player arriving back at midcourt after scoring a goal is awarded one point.

4. The team with more points after every player has had a turn wins. The game may be repeated any number of times.

5. Variation: Specify that the shot must be taken with the dominant or the nondominant hand.

Question and Answer

Arrange the children in information formation. Ask the children the following questions:

When would you use the Lay-Up Shot?

What should you remember about the technique?

What did you have the most problems with today?

How did your partner help you to be successful?

LESSON 13
BASKETBALL

Student Objectives

- Show developmental progress toward being able to perform the technique for the Jump Shot.
- Evaluate the technique of a partner, and provide the partner with feedback.

Equipment

- 1 basketball for every student
- Tape, cones, or other materials for marking shooting lines
- 12 cones

Warm-Up Activities (5 minutes)

Running and Sliding Drill

See Grades 6-8: Games and Sports, Warm-Ups, page 86.

Skill-Development Activities (20 minutes)

Jump Shot

Arrange the children in information formation. Describe and demonstrate the Jump Shot.

- The Jump Shot is a one-hand set shot combined with a jump.
- The ball is held with the shooting hand behind and under the ball; it is supported by the palm of the other hand.
- The jump is straight up, and the ball is held over the head and released at the height of the jump.

Jump Shot for Distance

Arrange the children in four groups and assign each group to a goal. Mark lines 6, 8, 10, and 12 feet from the basket. Each child has a basketball.

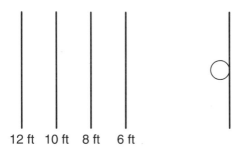

12 ft   10 ft   8 ft   6 ft

1. Have the children practice Jump Shots, beginning at a six-foot distance.
2. After making at least three goals at one distance, students move to the next farther shooting line.
3. Have them repeat at all distances.
4. Rearrange the children with partners in scatter formation, each pair with a basketball. Have the students perform the following tasks:

    Practice the jump shooting technique, shooting the ball toward your partner, who catches the ball.

    Observe your partner to see if the jump is straight up and the ball is released over the head at the height of the jump.

    Dribble three or four steps and then jump up and shoot.

Concluding Activities (5 minutes)

Shooting Contest

Arrange the children in teams of four to six players. Assign two teams to each half of a basketball court. Mark shooting lines 6, 8, 10, and 12 feet from the goals. Each team has a basketball.

1. Players at each goal take turns shooting. The player can choose the type of shot (Jump Shot or One-Hand Set Shot) and the distance.
2. Use the following point system:
   - One-Hand Set Shot

     6 feet = 1 point

     8 feet = 3 points

     10 feet = 5 points

     12 feet = 7 points

- Jump Shot

    6 feet = 2 points

    8 feet = 4 points

    10 feet = 6 points

    12 feet = 8 points

3. After all players have taken at least one shot, the team with the most points is declared the winner.

LESSON 14
BASKETBALL

Student Objectives

- Show improved skill in ball handling, Passing and Catching, Dribbling, and Free Throw shooting

Equipment

- One basketball for every two students
- Cones for basketball stations

Warm-Up Activities (5 minutes)

Running and Sliding Drill

See Grades 6-8: Games and Sports, Warm-Ups, page 86.

Skill-Development Activities (25 minutes)

Basketball Stations

Arrange the children in four groups with each group assigned to a station.

1. Have the children learn the activity to be performed at each station.
2. Rotate the children to new stations every four minutes.

Station 1: Passing and Catching

1. Review the techniques for the Chest Pass, the One-Handed Pass, and the Bounce Pass.
2. Form groups of three. Each group is provided with a 12-foot square.
3. Players 1 and 2 pass the ball using the Chest Pass, the One-Handed Pass, or the Bounce Pass. You can specify the type of pass, and you can adjust the size of the area.
4. Player 3 attempts to intercept the ball.
5. Player 3 becomes a thrower after intercepting the ball. If there is an extra player at the station, she or he can rotate in after an interception.

Chest Pass: The ball is held with fingers spread and the thumbs on the back of the ball, pointed toward each other. Elbows are bent and close to the body. With feet in a forward stride position and weight on the back foot, the ball is released with an equal forward push of both arms. Weight is shifted forward and the wrists snap as the ball is released. Follow through is with arms extended toward the receiver. Receive the ball at chest level.

One-Handed Pass: The ball is held in a baseball-like throwing position above the shoulder and slightly behind the head. The free arm is placed on the ball for balance. With the foot opposite of the throwing

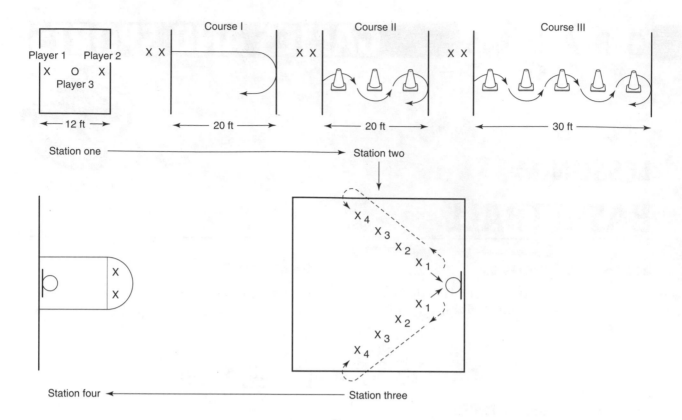

hand forward, weight is shifted to the front foot and the ball is pushed toward the target. The throwing arm should follow through.

Bounce Pass: Either the Chest Pass or the One-Handed Pass can be adapted to a bounce pass by bouncing the ball to the receiver. The ball should be bounced slightly past the halfway mark between the thrower and the receiver.

Station 2: Dribbling

In small groups, students take turns Dribbling, progressing to more difficult Dribbling courses.

Station 3: Lay-Ups

Establish two groups, and assign each group to one side of the goal. Player 1 from each team dribbles the ball toward the basket, shoots a Lay-Up shot, catches the ball, and passes it to the next player on his or her team. After all players have had several turns, teams change sides and repeat.

Station 4: Free Throw Shooting

Review the technique for the One-Hand Set Shot.

One-Hand Set Shot: The ball is held with the shooting hand behind and under the ball. The ball is supported by the palm of the other hand. The knees should be slightly flexed, in preparation for a shot. The arms and legs straighten to shoot the ball up toward the goal. The shooting hand should follow through. Eyes should be on the target.

Using the One-Hand Set Shot, students shoot free throws, keeping records of the number made out of 10 attempts. Each student attempts to improve his or her score.

Concluding Activities

None.

LESSONS 15 TO 18
BASKETBALL

Student Objectives

- Show improved skill in ball handling, Passing and Catching, Dribbling, and Free Throw Shooting.
- Work successfully in a cooperative learning group.

Equipment

- One basketball for every two students
- 12 cones

Warm-Up Activities (5 minutes)

Running and Sliding Drill

See Grades 6-8: Games and Sports, Warm-Ups, page 86.

Skill-Development Activities (25 minutes)

Cooperative Learning Groups

Continue practice at the four basketball stations. Rotate the children every six minutes.

1. Review the guidelines for cooperative group work (see Grades 6-8: Organization, Lesson 2, page 7).
2. Discuss that in group work cooperative effort is important.

   Each student is responsible for his or her own work and the work of the team. The group is not successful unless all students can demonstrate the correct technique for each basketball skill.

   Students must help each other. Observe others in your group and make helpful comments.

   It is important that each student try hard.

3. The goal for this activity is for all students in each group to be able to demonstrate the technique for Passing (Chest Pass, One-Handed Pass, Bounce Pass); Dribbling; Lay-Up Shot; and One-Hand Set Shot (Free Throw).

Concluding Activities

None.

ADDITIONAL ACTIVITIES FOR GRADES 6-8: BASKETBALL

Presented in this section are skill rules for a basketball unit. For a longer period or for additional lessons, devise group activities that allow students to practice playing by these rules.

Modified Basketball

Players: Five per team. A team consists of two forwards, two guards, and one center.

1. The game is divided into four quarters of six minutes each.
2. The ball is put into play at the beginning of a quarter by a jump ball.
3. A jump ball is also used when two players of opposing sides tie up the ball.
4. After a successful free throw or field goal, the ball is put into play by the opposing team at the end line.
5. If the ball goes out-of-bounds, it is put into play by a player of the opposing team at the spot where it went out. A field goal is two points and a free throw is one point.

Infractions

Rule infractions are of two kinds: violations and fouls. Violations are those infractions that do not involve other players, and the ball is awarded to the opponents. Fouls can be personal or technical. Personal fouls involve contact between players. Technical fouls are a result of game-procedure infractions. Free throws are awarded according to the nature of the foul. Examples of violations, personal fouls, and technical fouls are:

Violations
- Running with the ball
- Kicking the ball
- Failure to keep the ball in bounds
- Palming the ball (not clearly pushing the ball)
- Double dribbling (a second series of dribbling without another player handling the ball)

Personal Fouls
- Charging
- Pushing
- Tripping
- Holding
- Unnecessary roughness (e.g., a vicious act toward opponent)

Technical Fouls
- Too many timeouts
- Delay of game
- Poor conduct (e.g., undesirable language or gesture)

LESSON 19
SOFTBALL

Student Objectives

- Demonstrate the correct technique for Fielding a Ground Ball.
- Evaluate the technique of a partner, and provide the partner with feedback.
- State two important things to remember about Fielding a Ground Ball.

Equipment

- One softball for every two children
- One jump rope for each child

Warm-Up Activities (5 minutes)

Rope Jumping

Arrange the children in scatter formation, each with a jump rope. The students jump rope slowly for five minutes.

Skill-Development Activities (20 minutes)

Throwing

Arrange the children with partners in scatter formation. Each pair has a softball. The student should show opposition in stepping, good body rotation with hips opening in the direction of the throw in advance of the upper body, and good forearm lag.

Catching

Arrange the children in two lines, 20 feet apart, facing each other.

1. Designate each child's partner as the person directly opposite him or her.
2. The catch should be made with hands and fingers in cupped position. The hands and arms go toward the body as the ball arrives, and the body adjusts to the ball.
3. The eyes should follow the ball into the hands.
4. Have the students practice Throwing and Catching, beginning at 20 feet apart. After they make five successful throws, have them move farther apart.
5. Children should observe each other. Tell the children: *Observe your partner to see if he or she is stepping in opposition and using good body rotation.*

Fielding a Ground Ball

Arrange the students in a scatter formation with partners.

1. Describe and demonstrate Fielding a Ground Ball.

    - The fingers should be positioned close to the ground and pointed downward. The feet are placed shoulder width apart. The knees and waist are bent to bring the body low to the ground.

    - Move directly in line with the ball and place the foot opposite your throwing arm slightly forward, watching the ball as it approaches. As the ball makes contact, cover it with the opposite hand.

    - You should move into throwing position as quickly as possible.

2. Have the children practice fielding with a partner (have partners begin about 15 feet apart from each other); one partner rolls the ball toward the other partner, who fields it and throws it back as quickly as possible. After five turns, partners exchange duties.

3. Children should observe each other for points in technique.

4. Variations:

    Roll the ball so that your partner must move to the right or left to successfully field it.

    Roll two or three balls in rapid succession, causing the fielder to react quickly.

    Throw a bouncing ball for your partner to field.

Concluding Activities (5 minutes)

Chicken

Arrange the children in two teams on facing lines (20 feet apart) as in the figure. (There can be any number on teams; simply extend the lines.) Each player is paired off with a partner standing directly across on the other line, and each set of partners has a softball.

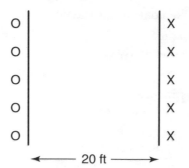

1. Each player attempts to roll the ball between the feet of his or her partner.
2. One point is awarded to the team of the player who rolls the ball for each ball that is not fielded by the partner.
3. The team with more points at the end of a designated time period wins.
4. The ball must be rolled underhand and must bounce at least twice before getting to the partner.
5. Variation: The ball can be rolled slightly to either side to make the partner change position.

Question and Answer

Arrange the children in information formation. Ask them the following questions:

What are some important things to remember when you field a ground ball?

After fielding the ball why is it important to move into throwing position as quickly as possible?

What are some of the reasons you had trouble with fielding?

How did your partner help you?

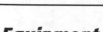

LESSON 20
SOFTBALL

Student Objectives

- Run the bases, using a mature running pattern, without slowing down, while touching each base.

Equipment

- Four bats
- Four home plates
- Four sets of bases (3 per set, for a total of 12)
- One jump rope for each student

Warm-Up Activities (5 minutes)

Rope Jumping

See Grades 6-8: Games and Sports, Lesson 19, page 125.

Skill-Development Activities (15 minutes)

Base Running

Arrange the children into four groups and have them gather near a base-running area.

1. Describe and demonstrate Base Running.
   - The first step toward first base should be taken with the rear foot. The runner should run straight through first base on any balls playable at first base.
   - If the run is to continue to second base, the runner should swing outward five or six feet to the right of the base, approximately two-thirds of the distance between the bases. The runner should touch the inside corner of each base with either foot.
2. Assign each group to an area marked with a home plate and first base 20 feet away.
3. Taking turns, each student swings the bat, drops it, and runs through first base. Repeat several times.

Take the first step with your back foot.

Run straight through first base.

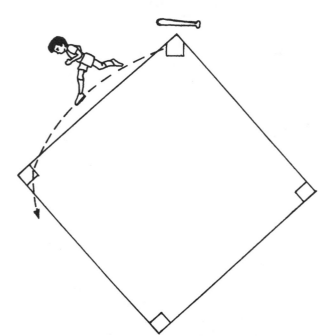

Swing outward two-thirds of the
distance between the bases.

Touch the inside section of the base.

Concluding Activities (10 minutes)

Around-the-Bases Relay

Arrange the children into four teams of five to seven players, and assign each team to a base. Use a standard softball diamond, with 60 feet between bases.

1. The teams line up, one at each of the bases and one at home plate.
2. On the start signal, the first player on each team runs one complete circuit around the bases.

3. When the first player touches her or his team's home base, the next player begins to run. The first team to have all players complete one circuit wins.

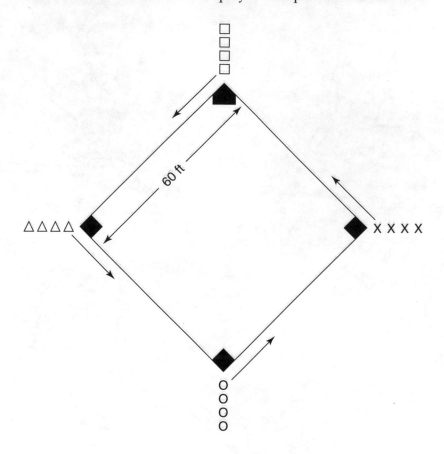

LESSON 21
SOFTBALL

Student Objectives

- Hit a ball pitched by a pitcher, using correct technique.
- State two important things to remember about Batting.

Equipment

- Four bats
- One softball for each child
- One jump rope for each child

Warm-Up Activities (5 minutes)

Rope Jumping

See Grades 6-8: Games and Sports, Lesson 19, page 125.

Skill-Development Activities (20 minutes)

Hitting a Pitched Ball

Arrange the children in information formation. Describe and demonstrate Hitting a Pitched Ball.

- The feet should be comfortably apart with the front of the body facing the plate. The knees are bent and the eyes should be on the pitcher, with the bat shoulder high and slightly behind the back foot.
- The batter should watch the ball until it makes contact with the bat. The swing should begin with a stride toward the ball with the front foot.
- The ball should be contacted in front of the forward hip.

Batting

Arrange the children in four groups, each with one batter and the other teammates as fielders standing 20 feet away.

1. Have the students practice Batting.
2. The fielders line up side by side facing the batter.
3. Taking turns, the fielders pitch balls to the batter, who hits back to the fielders. The

batter must change position slightly for each different pitcher.

4. Rotate positions after five successful hits (the batter becomes number 5, 5 goes to 4, and 1 becomes batter).

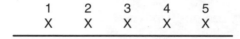

```
1     2     3     4     5
X     X     X     X     X
_____


            X
          Batter
```

Concluding Activities (5 minutes)

Circle Team Pepper

Arrange the children in teams of six to eight. Each team forms a 30-foot circle with one member in the center with a bat. Each circle has a softball.

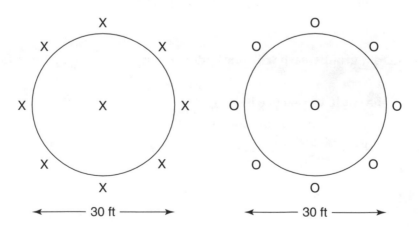

1. One at a time, team members pitch to the center player, who hits the ball to the person on the thrower's left.
2. Continue this procedure around the circle. The team finishing first wins.
3. Repeat several times.
4. Variation: Use the bunt.

Question and Answer

Arrange the children in information formation. Ask the children the following questions:

What should you remember about batting?

Why is it important to shift the weight forward when starting the forward swing with the bat?

What happens when you swing and hit the ball too quickly (i.e., too far in front of the body)?

What happens when you swing too late?

LESSON 22
SOFTBALL

Student Objectives

- Hit a pitched ball using correct technique, drop the bat, and run through first base.

Equipment

- 1 bat and 1 softball for every 4 children
- 1 home plate for every 4 children
- 12 bases

Warm-Up Activities (5 minutes)

Softball Relay

Repeat the relay two or three times, declaring a winner each time. See Grades 6-8: Games and Sports, Warm-Ups, page 85.

Skill-Development Activities (15 minutes)

Batting and Base Running

Arrange the children in groups of four and assign each group to an area marked with a home plate and one base 60 feet away. Each group has a bat and a softball.

1. The students practice Batting and Base Running.
2. Taking turns, one player pitches, one bats, and two field. The batter hits the ball, drops the bat, and runs through first base.
3. Players then rotate with the pitcher becoming the batter, one fielder becoming the pitcher, and the batter becoming a fielder.
4. See Grades 6-8: Games and Sports, Lessons 20 and 21, pages 128 and 131 for descriptions of Base Running and Batting, respectively.

Concluding Activities (10 minutes)

Home Run

Arrange the children in teams of six to eight players, with two teams assigned to a regulation softball field with three extra bases 10 feet past the normal bases. Each field has a bat and a softball.

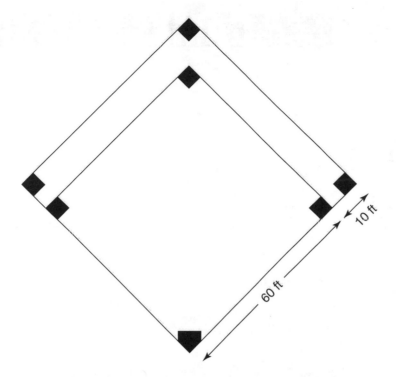

1. The pitcher is a member of the batting team. The opposing team spreads out in the field.

2. Taking turns, a batter hits a pitched ball (on a maximum of two pitches) and runs around the inside bases to home plate.

3. The fielders catch the ball and throw it around the outside bases to first, second, third, and home, trying to get the ball home before the runner reaches home.

4. If the ball reaches home plate before the runner, the runner is out. If the runner reaches home plate before the ball, the batting team scores a point.

5. After all players on a team have batted, teams exchange places. The team with the most points wins.

LESSON 23
SOFTBALL

Student Objectives

- The students hit balls they have pitched to themselves.

Equipment

- 4 bats and 4 softballs
- 4 home plates
- 12 bases

Warm-Up Activities (5 minutes)

Softball Relay

See Grades 6-8: Games and Sports, Warm-Ups, page 85.

Skill-Development Activities (15 minutes)

Fungo Hitting

Arrange the children in four groups and assign each group to a field marked with normal positions. Each group has a bat and a softball.

1. Have the students practice Fungo Hitting (hitting a ball you toss up to yourself).
2. Each batter tosses and hits 10 balls to players in the field, who throw the ball back to a catcher standing near the batter.
3. After 10 hits, the batter becomes a fielder, the catcher becomes the batter, and one of the fielders becomes the catcher.

Concluding Activities (10 minutes)

Line Up

Arrange teams of six to eight players with two teams assigned to each playing area. Each playing area is two lines 60 feet apart. One team is on each line, with at least 10 feet between each player. Each team has a bat, and each play area has a softball.

1. A player on one team Fungo Hits a ground ball, attempting to send it through the opposing team's line.
2. The fielders (the members of the opposing team) attempt to field the ball. After each hit, batting rotates from team to team and from player to player.

3. One point is scored for each ball driven through the opposing fielders. Ground balls must bounce before the line of the opposite team.

4. If there is a great variation in the players' ability to hit and field, students may need to be grouped into games by skill level.

ADDITIONAL ACTIVITIES FOR GRADES 6-8: SOFTBALL

Presented below are skill rules for a softball unit. For a longer period or for additional lessons, devise group activities that allow students to practice playing by these rules.

Skill Development Stations

Arrange students in four groups with each group assigned to a station.

1. Have the children practice the activities at each station.

2. The children should rotate to new stations every four or five minutes.

Station 1: Batting

Form groups of three and practice each of the following activities.

Students take turns batting from a batting tee, with one hitting and the other students fielding.

Students take turns hitting pitched balls, with one student pitching, one hitting, and the other student fielding the ball.

Station 2: Pitching

Students practice pitching at various size targets from various distances.

Students practice pitching to a batter.

Station 3: Fielding Ground Balls

Students practice fielding balls rolled by a partner from various distances and directions.

Students practice fielding balls hit by a batter.

Station 4: Base Running

Taking turns, students are timed running from home to first base.

Taking turns, students are timed running around the bases.

Lead-Up Games

Softball Toss Ball

Players: 6 to 12 on a team. Field: Softball diamond, any size.

1. Regular softball rules are used, except that the batter stands in the batter's box and throws the ball into the field rather than batting it.

2. No stealing is allowed, and a foul ball constitutes an out.

Three-Pitch Softball

Players: Six to nine on a team. Field: Softball field, any size. The rules of softball apply with the following exceptions.

1. The team at bat must provide its own pitcher.

2. The pitcher is allowed to pitch only three balls to each batter, and each is called a strike.

3. The pitcher is not allowed to touch the batted ball.

4. Stealing and bunting are not allowed.

Simplified Softball Rules

Strike

A strike is a pitched ball that crosses home plate between the shoulders and knees of the batter. The batter is called out after three strikes or if a foul tip on the third strike is caught by the catcher. A strike is called when the batter swings and misses a ball or when a foul ball is hit and not caught on the fly.

Fair and Foul Ball

A fair ball in the infield is one that is touched or settles on or within the boundary lines. A fair ball in the outfield is one that is touched or first lands on or within the boundary lines. A foul ball in the infield is one that is touched or settles outside the boundary lines. A foul ball in the outfield is one that is touched or first lands outside the boundary lines.

Fly Ball

A fly ball, if caught, is an out (both fair and foul). A foul fly must be hit so that it goes higher than the head of the batter; otherwise, it is a foul tip. A foul tip counts as a strike.

Base Running

When a batter hits the ball and runs to first base, those on the bases ahead may be forced to run also. If only first and third bases are occupied, the runner at first is forced to second, but the runner on third has a choice whether or not to run.

When a fly ball is hit and likely to be caught, runners should wait on the bases. The runners can advance after the ball is caught.

A runner can overrun first base without being tagged. If the runner on second or third is touched with the ball while he or she is off the base, it is ruled an out.

LESSON 24
VOLLEYBALL

Student Objectives

- Serve a volleyball into the opponent's court from behind the baseline.
- State two important things to remember about the Underhand Serve and the Overhead Serve.

Equipment

- One volleyball for every two children
- Two volleyball courts with nets
- Materials for marking lines

Warm-Up Activities (5 minutes)

Rescue Relay

Arrange the students in groups of five or six. Mark a starting and a return line, 60 feet apart, for relays.

1. For each group, Player 1 stands at the starting line and the other players line up behind the return line.
2. On a signal, Player 1 runs to get Player 2, and holding hands they return to the starting line. Player 2 then runs back for Player 3, and so on.
3. The team whose players all finish running first wins.
4. Repeat the relay two or three times, declaring a winner each time.

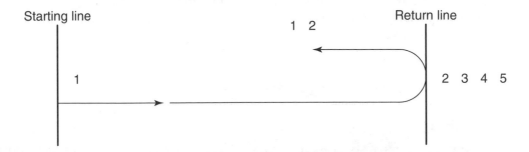

Skill-Development Activities (20 minutes)

Underhand Serve

Arrange the children in pairs, with partners facing each other from opposite ends of the volleyball court. Divide the court into scoring zones. Each set of partners has a volleyball.

1. Describe the Underhand Serve: *Holding the ball in front of you about waist high, swing the serving hand and arm downward and back and then forward in an underhand arc, hitting the ball on the heel of the hand. The ball should go over the net and deep into the other court. The ball is contacted just below the center of gravity.*

2. Demonstrate the Underhand Serve.

3. Standing behind their respective baselines and opposite one another, partners practice serving a regulation volleyball. Pairs of students can rotate on and off the court to practice.

4. Encourage the students to serve the ball deep and to keep score for each server. (Score is determined by landing area.)

Net

X	3	1	2		X
X	3	1	2		X
X	3	1	2		X
X	3	1	2		X

Overhead Serve

1. Describe and demonstrate the Overhead Serve.

   - For a right-handed serve, begin with the left foot forward and the left side of the body slightly toward the net. The weight is on both feet.

   - The ball should be tossed about three or four feet overhead, and as the ball is tossed the weight shifts back.

   - As the ball drops, the weight is shifted forward, and the ball is contacted directly over the head and slightly in front of the body.

   - The heel of the hand strikes the ball in the center (the hand remains open). There is slight follow through in the direction of flight.

2. Using the same formation as for the Underhand Serve, have the students practice the Overhead Serve.

Concluding Activities (5 minutes)

Target Serve

Arrange the children on teams of six to eight, with two teams and one volleyball at each court. Teams stand behind opposite baselines facing each other.

1. A player on one team serves the ball into the other team's court.

2. If the ball lands (on its first hit) in a zone marked "3," the player scores for her or his team. A player on the other team then serves back.

3. A game consists of each player on each team taking one Underhand and one Overhead Serve.

4. Two points are awarded for an Overhead Serve that hits in the target area, and one point is awarded for an Underhand Serve that hits in the target area.

Question and Answer

Arrange the children in information formation. Ask the children the following questions:

What should you remember about the Underhand Serve and the Overhead Serve?

Why is it important to shift the weight forward as the ball is contacted?

What happens when you toss the ball so that it goes too far behind you?

LESSON 25
VOLLEYBALL

Student Objectives

- Demonstrate the correct technique for the Spike.
- Evaluate the technique of a striker using a criteria sheet.

Equipment

- One volleyball for every two children
- Two volleyball courts with nets
- Materials for marking lines
- A made-up criteria sheet for every group of three children (optional)

Warm-Up Activities (5 minutes)

Rescue Relay

Arrange the students in groups of five or six. Mark a starting line and a return line, 60 feet apart, for relays. See Grades 6-8: Games and Sports, Lesson 24, page 139.

Skill-Development Activities (15 minutes)

Spike

Arrange the children in information formation.

1. Describe and demonstrate the Spike.

    - *A three-step approach is used. On the final step the feet come together, and you jump up into the air.*

    - *While in the air, you hit the ball with an overhand striking action using an open hand.*

2. Arrange the children along the sideline of the volleyball court.

3. Have the students practice the approach and jump. Have half of the students step, step, step, close, and jump several times while moving across the floor.

4. Repeat with the other half of the students.

Peer Teaching

Arrange the children in groups of three. Establish a rotation system for each group, with one tosser, one spiker, and one observer.

1. The students practice spiking the ball to the floor so that it rebounds onto a wall and back; one player should toss the ball into the air for the second player to spike.

2. The third player is the observer and is provided a criteria sheet (optional), which lists the following major points in technique to look for:

    Three-step approach

    Jump up

    Overhead strike with open hand

3. After several trials the players rotate.

Concluding Activities (10 minutes)

Spike for Points

Arrange the children into teams of four to six players with two teams and one volleyball per court. Each court is an area on the volleyball court with a net six feet high. Teams line up on opposite sides of the net.

1. One player tosses the ball to the spiker, who attempts to spike the ball successfully. A successful spike scores one point.

2. Students rotate with each spike (tosser to returner, returner to the end of the spiking line, spiker to tosser). The team with the most points wins.

LESSON 26
VOLLEYBALL

Student Objectives

- Demonstrate the correct technique for the Block.

Equipment

- 1 volleyball for every 6 children
- 2 volleyball courts with nets
- 12 cones

Warm-Up Activities (5 minutes)

Zigzag Relay

Arrange the students in groups of five or six in relay teams. For each group, lay out a zigzag course with cones about eight feet apart from one another between two lines. Teams line up behind the starting line.

1. On a signal, Player 1 runs around the cones to the return line and back to the starting line to touch the hand of Player 2.
2. Each player runs in turn. The first team through scores a point.
3. Repeat several times.

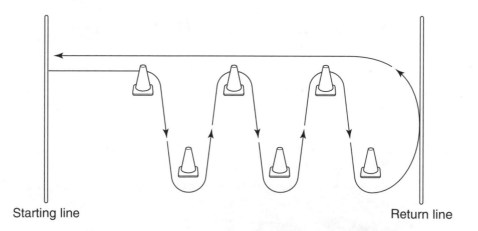

Starting line   Return line

Skill-Development Activities (15 minutes)

Block

Arrange the children in information formation.

1. Describe and demonstrate the Block.
   - The blocker should move into position to block a spike at the net.

- After getting into position, the blocker assumes a deep crouch position.
- From this position the blocker jumps up high, extending the arms and hands over the net.
- When contacting the ball, the wrists are flexed, deflecting the ball into the opponent's court.

2. Arrange the children in groups for the blocking drill.

3. Players take positions along the net (both sides of the net can be used) and practice jumping for the Block.

4. Repeat the drill, having the students slide to the right and to the left before the jump.

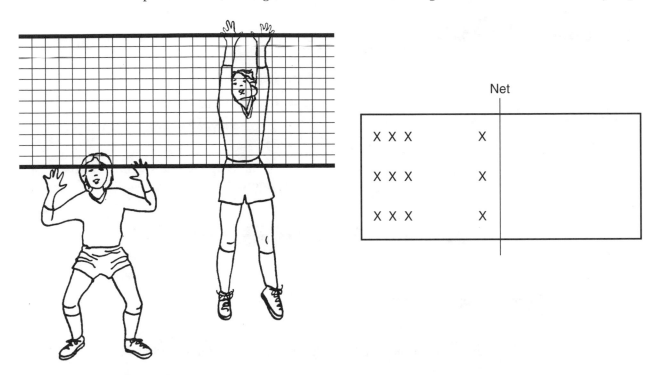

Concluding Activities (10 minutes)

Spike and Block

Arrange six to eight children on each team. Each court is an area on a volleyball court with a net six feet high. Give each court a volleyball.

1. One player from Team A tosses the ball to the spiker, who attempts to successfully spike the ball.

2. One player from Team B attempts to block the spike.

3. A spike that is not blocked scores one point. A successful block also scores one point.

4. When all offensive players have had a chance to spike, teams exchange duties (spikers become blockers).

5. The team with the highest number of points after every person has had a chance to spike and block wins.

LESSON 27
VOLLEYBALL

Student Objectives

- In three attempts, Bump a ball thrown by a partner to a setter standing by the net.
- Evaluate the technique of a player practicing the Bump.

Equipment

- One volleyball for every three children
- Two volleyball courts with nets
- 12 cones
- A made-up criteria sheet for every group of four children (optional)

Warm-Up Activities (5 minutes)

Zigzag Relay

See Grades 6-8: Games and Sports, Warm-Ups, page 84.

Skill-Development Activities (15 minutes)

Bump

Arrange the children in groups of four, with three or four groups per court. Each group has a volleyball.

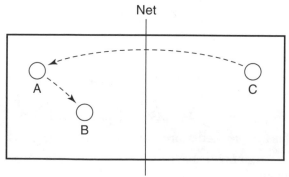

1. Describe and demonstrate the Bump: The Bump is done underhand with the forearms close together. The ball should go in an arc, slightly higher than the net and toward Player B at the net.

2. Drill: Player C tosses the ball over the net to Player A. Player A takes a receiving position and bumps the ball to Player B standing by the net. The fourth player ob-

serves the three hitters and provides feedback. A criteria sheet is provided with the major points to look for in the Bump (optional):

> Feet shoulder width apart and knees bent
>
> Hands clasped together so that forearms are parallel
>
> Elbows locked
>
> Legs extended as ball is contacted

3. Players rotate after 10 trials.
4. Have the students practice the Bump.

Concluding Activities (10 minutes)

Three-Pass Volleyball

Arrange the children into teams of six with two teams and one volleyball per court. Use regular volleyball courts with the nets set six feet high.

1. Regular volleyball rules are used, except that a team loses a point or serve if the ball is not hit three times on a side.
2. If the ball goes over the net on the first or second hit, a point or side out is awarded.
3. The first team to get 15 points wins.
4. Encourage use of the bump pass.
5. If there are extra children, have them practice the bump on the sidelines while waiting to rotate into the game.

LESSON 28
VOLLEYBALL

Student Objectives

- Increase accuracy in Setting the ball.

Equipment

- One volleyball for every two children
- Two volleyball courts with nets
- 12 cones

Warm-Up Activities (5 minutes)

Zigzag Relay

Arrange the children in relay teams. See Grades 6-8: Games and Sports, Warm-Ups, page 84.

Skill-Development Activities (15 minutes)

Setting and Spiking

Arrange the children in groups of three with four or five groups per court. Each group has a volleyball. The nets should be six feet high.

1. Have the students practice Setting to a spiker.
2. Player A tosses the ball to Player B, who is the setter.
3. Player B sets the ball to Player C, who spikes it over the net.
4. After five sets, the players rotate.
5. See Grades 6-8: Games and Sports, Lesson 25, "Spike," page 142.

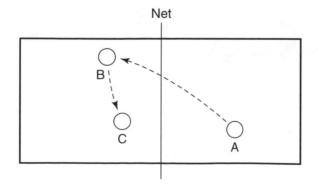

Three-Pass Volleyball

Emphasize Bumping, Setting, and Spiking as the three hits. See Grades 6-8: Games and Sports, Lessons 27, 28, and 25, respectively, pages 146, 148, and 142.

ADDITIONAL ACTIVITIES FOR GRADES 6-8: VOLLEYBALL

Presented below are skill rules for a volleyball unit. For a longer period or for additional lessons, devise group activities that allow students to practice playing by these rules.

Simplified Volleyball Rules

1. Official rules specify a court 30 × 60 feet, divided by a net (eight feet high for men and seven and one half feet for women) and a center line. For a middle school age group, a lower net is recommended (six or seven feet). A team is composed of right, center, and left net players and right, center, and left back players.

2. The ball is put into play by the right back player from behind the back line of the court. The right back player continues to serve until the serving team fails to return the ball legally, or until a serving fault is committed. When a team becomes the serving team, each person rotates one position in a clockwise direction, making the right front player the next server.

3. Only the serving team can score. The server has only one chance to serve the ball over the net. If the ball fails to go over, touches the net, or lands out-of-bounds, a side out is called and the serve goes to the opposing team. Any ball that touches a player is considered to be in bounds.

4. A team must return the ball over the net with three touches or less, or a violation is called, which causes the loss of a point or a serve (side out). Other violations are hitting the ball twice in succession, touching the net, stepping over the center line, or letting the ball rest in the hands during the hit.

5. The first team scoring 15 points wins the game if the team has at least 2 points more than the opponents. If there is not a 2-point difference, play continues until one team wins by 2 points.

LESSON 29
TRACK AND FIELD

Student Objectives

- Demonstrate the correct technique for running over hurdles.
- Evaluate the technique of others, and provide them with feedback.
- State two important things to remember about Hurdling.

Equipment

- One hurdle (16 to 18 inches high), made of cones and dowel rods, for each group of three children

Warm-Up Activities (5 minutes)

Individual Stretching Exercises

Arrange the children in scatter formation. See Grades 6-8: Games and Sports, Warm-Ups, page 86 for a description of the exercises.

1. Students perform the following exercises: Toe Touch, Body Bend, Trunk Twister, and Forward Lunge.
2. Have them run in place 20 steps between exercises.

Skill-Development Activities (20 minutes)

Hurdling

Arrange the children in information formation.

1. Describe and demonstrate Hurdling.
   - The runner should run toward the hurdle, lifting the knee of the lead leg high. The lead foot is extended so that it passes over the hurdle.
   - The trailing knee is pulled out to the side and over the hurdle.
   - The arm opposite the lead foot is extended forward for balance.
   - The lead foot snaps down after it clears the hurdle, and the trailing leg follows through in front of the body to continue the run.
2. Arrange the children in groups of three with one hurdle per group.
3. Have the students practice running over a hurdle placed about 20 yards from a starting line.

4. Children should observe each other for points in technique. Tell the children: *Observe players in your group to see if they are lifting the lead knee high enough to get over the hurdle.*

5. Arrange the children in groups of nine by combining groups of three and their hurdles.

6. Have the students practice running over three hurdles placed at about 25-foot intervals.

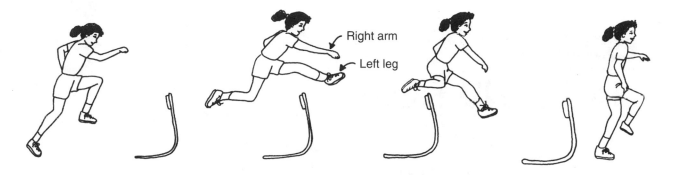

Concluding Activities (5 minutes)

Hurdle Relay

Arrange the children in relay formation in groups of five to seven. Each group is at a starting line facing three hurdles.

1. Each runner strides over the three hurdles, touches the finish line, and runs around the outside of the hurdles back to the starting line.

2. When runner 1 reaches the starting line, runner 2 begins.

3. The first group whose runners complete all the hurdles wins.

4. Repeat the relay several times, declaring a winner each time.

Question and Answer

Arrange the children in information formation. Ask the children the following questions:

What are some important things to remember about Hurdling?

What did you have the most trouble with today?

What did you do that helped you the most?

GAMES AND SPORTS

LESSON 30
TRACK AND FIELD

Student Objectives

- Demonstrate the technique for the Triple Jump.

Equipment

- Six tumbling mats
- Six measuring tapes
- Six starting boards

Warm-Up Activities (5 minutes)

Individual Stretching Exercises

See Grades 6-8: Games and Sports, Lesson 29, page 150.

Skill-Development Activities (20 minutes)

Triple Jump

Arrange the children in information formation.

1. Describe and demonstrate the Triple Jump.

   - The Triple Jump, or hop-step-and-jump, begins with a run similar to that for the Long Jump.
   - The takeoff from the starting board is with one foot. The jumper lands on the same foot for the hop.
   - The hop is followed with a step and a jump; you land on both feet.

2. Arrange the children in six groups, one group at each mat. Mark a starting board approximately 10 to 12 feet away.

3. Have the children practice running to the takeoff line and completing the hop-step-and-jump onto the mat. Repeat several times.

4. Set up jumping areas with starting lines at various distances.

5. Assign children to areas according to their proficiency levels.

6. Mark the mats with measuring strips to determine distance.

7. Have the children practice the Triple Jump on the mats a couple of times.

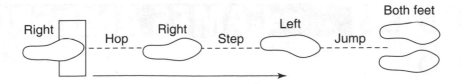

Right · · · Hop · · · Right · · · Step · · · Left · · · Jump · · · Both feet

Concluding Activities (5 minutes)

Triple Jump Event

Each child gets five jumps and records the best distance.

LESSON 31

TRACK AND FIELD

Student Objectives

- Demonstrate the technique for the Scissors method of high jumping.
- Observe the technique of others, and provide them with feedback.

Equipment

- One portable High Jump bar with a tumbling mat for each five or six children

Warm-Up Activities (5 minutes)

Individual Stretching Exercises

See Grades 6-8: Games and Sports, Lesson 29, page 150.

Skill-Development Activities (20 minutes)

Scissors Jump

Arrange the children in information formation.

1. Describe and demonstrate the Scissors Jump.
   - The jumper approaches the bar at a slight angle of 15 to 20 degrees.
   - When the bar is reached, the outside foot is planted and the inside foot is lifted over the bar. The rear leg follows in the same manner.
   - The legs should be straight for jumping to prevent touching the bar. The landing should be on the leading foot with the knees bent.
2. Arrange five or six children at each high bar and landing mat for practice. The bar should be placed at a height where all children can be successful. The emphasis should be on technique rather than height.
3. Have the students practice the Scissors Jump. Repeat several times. Gradually increase the height.
4. Children are encouraged to observe and help each other.

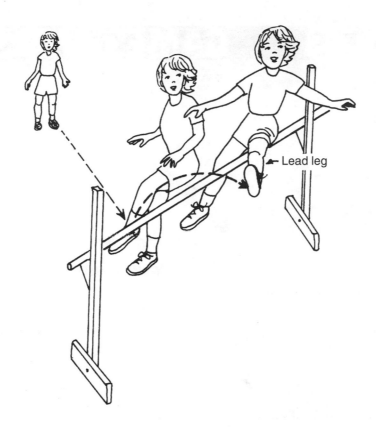

Lead leg

Concluding Activities (5 minutes)

High Jump Event

Each child gets five jumps and records the best height.

GRADES 6-8

GAMES AND SPORTS

LESSON 32
TRACK AND FIELD

Student Objectives

- Improve technique in the Sprint Start for the 50-Yard Dash.

Equipment

- Chalk, flour, cones, or other material to mark lines
- Six to eight stopwatches

Warm-Up Activities (5 minutes)

Individual Stretching Exercises

See Grades 6-8: Games and Sports, Lesson 29, page 150.

Skill-Development Activities (20 minutes)

Sprint Start

Arrange the children in information formation.

1. Describe and demonstrate the Sprint Start.
   - The front foot is placed 12 to 18 inches behind the starting line. The rear foot is placed 12 to 18 inches behind the front foot. The hands are placed just behind the starting line with thumb and forefinger making a V for support. This position is assumed on, "To your marks."
   - On "set," the back and rear end are raised so they are parallel to the ground.
   - On "go," the runner runs as fast as possible for several steps.
2. Arrange the children in groups of three.
3. Have two children in each group practice the Sprint Start while the third child serves as the starter.
4. Have children in each group rotate until each child has had 10 tries.

Concluding Activities (5 minutes)

50-Yard Dash

Arrange the children in groups of six at the starting line. Mark a finish line 50 yards away.

1. Four children run the dash, one serves as the starter, and one serves as the timer for each round.
2. Have them rotate responsibilities.

GAMES AND SPORTS

LESSONS 33 TO 36
TRACK AND FIELD

Student Objectives

- Work toward improved performance in the 50-Yard Dash, the High Jump, the Hurdles, and the Triple Jump by using a circuit for a week.

Equipment

- Six hurdles (16 to 18 inches high)
- Jumping pit or tumbling mats, standards, and bar for High Jump
- Two tumbling mats for Triple Jump
- Two measuring tapes
- Two starting boards
- One stopwatch
- Materials for marking lines

Warm-Up Activities (5 minutes)

Individual Stretching Exercises

See Grades 6-8: Games and Sports, Lesson 29, page 150.

Skill-Development Activities (25 minutes)

Track and Field Stations

Arrange the children in four groups with one group at each activity station. The children stay at each station for six minutes.

Station 1: 50-Yard Dash

Assign one student to be the starter and another to be the timer. The starter stands at the starting line, and the timer stands at the finish line with the stopwatch. On "go" the starter lowers his or her arm from an overhead position so that the timer can both see and hear the signal. The timer starts the watch and times the runner to the finish line. Each student has at least one turn to run the dash, as well as an opportunity to start and time.

Station 2: High Jump

Each student uses a short run up to the bar and jumps using a Scissors Jump. Vary the height of the bar for the different skill levels of the children. Record the highest jump for each child.

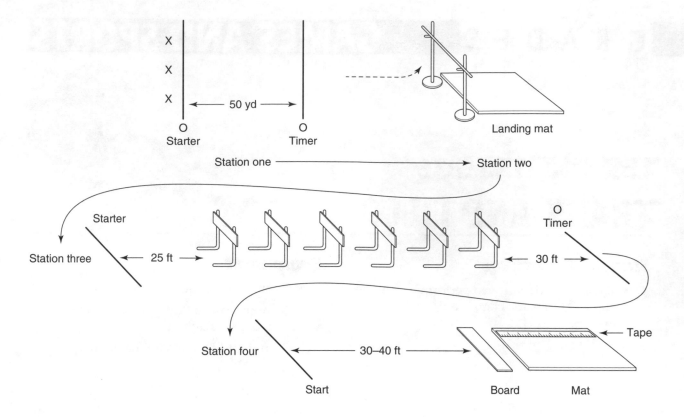

Station 3: Hurdles

Assign one student to be the starter and another student to be the timer. Set up five hurdles at 25-foot intervals, with a longer distance from the last hurdle to the finish line. The children take turns sprinting over the hurdles, timing, and starting.

Station 4: Triple Jump

Each student runs from the starting line and performs the hop-step-and-jump onto a tumbling mat from the starting board. The distance is measured by the students with a tape.

Concluding Activities

None.

ADDITIONAL ACTIVITIES FOR GRADES 6-8: TRACK AND FIELD

Presented below are skill-development ideas for a track and field unit, to be used for a longer period or for additional lessons. Organize a track and field meet in which students will compete. The meet can last for two or three days.

- Include any number of events.
- Organize students into teams for competition.
- Let each student decide which events he or she will participate in.
- Students can be limited to two individual events and one relay.
- Select starters and timers.
- Award points (5, 3, 1) for first, second, and third place winners in each event. The points achieved by individual winners contribute to a team total. Determine a winning team.

LESSON 37
FOOTBALL

Student Objectives

- Demonstrate the correct technique for Punting.
- State two important things to remember about Punting.

Equipment

- One junior football for every two children
- Materials for marking playing areas

Warm-Up Activities (5 minutes)

Sprint Relay

Arrange the children in relay teams of five or six players. Mark a starting line and a return line 20 yards apart, and line up the teams single file behind the starting line.

1. On the start signal, the first player on each team runs to the return line, steps beyond it, and returns to the starting line.
2. The second player may start when the first player recrosses the starting line.
3. Repeat the relay two or three times, declaring a winner each time.

Skill-Development Activities (15 minutes)

Punting

Arrange the children in information formation.

1. Describe and demonstrate Punting.
   - The ball is held out in front of the kicking foot, slightly above waist height. The hand corresponding to the kicking foot is placed under the ball at its center. The opposite hand is placed toward the front and to the side of the ball.
   - The kicker should stand with the nonkicking foot slightly ahead of the kicking foot.
   - A step forward is taken with the kicking foot, followed by a step forward with the nonkicking foot.
   - The kicking foot swings forward, contacting the ball at about knee height on the instep and slightly to the outside of the foot.
   - The toe is pointed and the body leans away.

- The dropping of the ball is timed so that the ball arrives at knee level when the kicking foot arrives to contact the ball.

2. Arrange the children in pairs in scatter formation. Partners should be about 20 yards apart from each other.

3. Have partners practice Punting and receiving the punt. Increase the distance after five successful punts.

4. Have partners punt as far as possible.

Concluding Activities (10 minutes)

Kickover

Arrange six to eight children per team with two teams facing each other in a playing area 40 × 60 yards. Each playing area has a football.

1. Players attempt to kick the ball over the opponent's goal line without it being caught.

2. Play is started by a player kicking the ball from about 20 feet in front of her or his team's own goal line.

3. If the ball is caught on the fly by an opposing player, the catcher is allowed to take five steps forward before kicking the ball. If the ball is not caught, it is kicked from the point where it was first touched.

4. When a player catches a ball behind the goal line, she or he brings the ball to the goal line, takes five steps, and then kicks.

5. One point is scored for the kicking team for each uncaught ball that is kicked over the opponent's goal line.

Question and Answer

Arrange the children in information formation. Ask the children the following questions:

When do you use a Punt in football?

How can you make sure that you kick the ball straight ahead instead of off to the right or left?

What did you have trouble with today?

What helped you the most to be successful?

LESSON 38
FOOTBALL

Student Objectives

- Demonstrate the correct Blocking position.
- State two important things to remember about Blocking.

Equipment

- One junior football for every five children
- One flag-football flag for each child
- Materials for marking field lines

Warm-Up Activities (5 minutes)

Shuttle Relay

Arrange the students in relay teams of five to six players; line up half of each team behind the starting line and the other half behind the return line.

1. Player 1 on each team runs to the return line and hands off the football to Player 2. Player 2 runs back to the starting line and hands the ball to the next player. The relay continues until all players have run.

2. Repeat several times, and declare a winner each time.

Skill-Development Activities (15 minutes)

Blocking

Arrange the children in information formation.

1. Describe and demonstrate Blocking.
   - A block involves getting the body in front of the opposing player to block the pathway of that player. The blocker cannot use the hands or push (contact) with the shoulders or hips.
   - The blocker's elbows should be out, with the hands held over the chest. Contact is light.
   - This is not an aggressive block; rather, the blocker is simply trying to stay between the defensive player and his or her destination.

2. Arrange the children in groups of five. Two are offensive players, two are defensive players, and one is the quarterback.

3. Two defensive players stand about eight yards back and, on a signal, attempt to move through two offensive players to touch the quarterback, who has the ball.

4. The offensive players block the pathway to the quarterback.

5. Have the students practice several times and then rotate positions and repeat.

Concluding Activities (10 minutes)

Kickoff

Arrange the children in teams of six to eight players with two teams per field. The fields are 30 × 60 yards. Each player wears a flag-football flag, and each field has one football.

1. One team kicks off with a Punt from midfield.

2. The player receiving the ball returns it as far as possible until her or his flag is pulled by a member of the other team.

3. The ball carrier may use a lateral pass (a pass made backward or sideways) but not a forward pass.

4. When the runner's flag is pulled, the ball is dead.

5. The receiving team kicks off from midfield and the action is repeated.

6. Record the yards gained each play. The team gaining more yards wins. Repeat several times.

Question and Answer

Arrange the children in information formation. Ask the children the following questions:

What is the goal of a blocker?

How can a blocker use his or her hands?

What helped you to be successful in Blocking the pathways of defensive players?

LESSON 39
FOOTBALL

Student Objectives

- Demonstrate the Three-Point Stance and the Four-Point Stance.
- Describe the techniques for the Three-Point Stance and the Four-Point Stance.

Equipment

- One junior football for each game
- One flag-football flag for each child
- Materials for marking field lines
- One large hoop for every five or six children

Warm-Up Activities (5 minutes)

Fetch and Pass Relay

Arrange the children in relay teams of five or six players. Each group lines up behind the starting line across from a hoop that is on the floor with a football inside it.

1. Player 1 runs to the hoop, picks up the football, and while standing in the hoop passes the ball to Player 2, who passes it back to Player 1.
2. Player 1 puts the ball down in the hoop and runs back and touches the hand of Player 2, who then repeats the actions of Player 1.

Skill-Development Activities (15 minutes)

Three-Point and Four-Point Stances

Arrange the children in information formation.

1. Describe and demonstrate the Three-Point and Four-Point Stances.
   - The basic stance assumed before the ball is put in play is with the feet shoulder width apart, one foot slightly ahead, knees bent, and weight slightly forward and resting on one or both hands.
   - In the Three-Point Stance the knuckles of the hand on the side of the foot that is back are placed on the ground.
   - In the Four-Point Stance, both hands are in contact with the ground.
2. Arrange the children in relay teams of five or six players. Line up the teams behind a starting line opposite a return line 10 yards away.
3. On the signal *"down,"* the first person in each line assumes a Three-Point or Four-Point Stance.

4. On the signal *"run,"* those players run forward to the return line and sit down. The drill continues with the second players.

5. When all players have had a turn, repeat the game going in the opposite direction.

Three-point stance

Four-point stance

Concluding Activities (10 minutes)

Fourth Down

Arrange the children in teams of six to eight with two teams and one football per field. Fields are 30 × 60 yards. Each player wears a flag-football flag.

1. The purpose of the game is to score a touchdown in one play.

2. The team with the ball may throw the ball from any point on the field any number of times in order to score during a single down.

3. Players line up in an offensive formation (center and four other players in a line), and play starts at midfield with a player centering the ball to a player in the backfield.

4. The player receiving the ball may run or pass. If a pass is thrown, the receiver of the pass may run or pass.

5. The player first receiving the ball from the center has 10 seconds before having to run or pass.

6. During this time period the defensive players are not allowed to rush.

7. To down a runner or a pass receiver, the player's flag is pulled.

8. If a player is downed, the ball goes to the other team at that spot.

9. For an incomplete pass, the ball is given to the other team at the spot where it was thrown.

10. After each touchdown, the ball is returned to midfield. Each touchdown counts six points.

Question and Answer

Arrange the children in information formation. Ask the children the following questions:

What are the points in technique that you want to remember when practicing the Three-Point Stance?

How is the Four-Point Stance different?

When do you use the Three-Point Stance? Four-Point Stance?

GAMES AND SPORTS

LESSON 40
FOOTBALL

Student Objectives

- Successfully execute a Ball Exchange.

Equipment

- One junior football for every six children
- Materials for marking field lines

Warm-Up Activities (5 minutes)

Fetch and Pass Relay

See Grades 6-8: Games and Sports, Warm-Ups, page 85.

Skill-Development Activities (20 minutes)

Ball Exchange

Arrange the children in information formation.

1. Describe and demonstrate the Ball Exchange.
   - In a Ball Exchange, a player starts running in one direction and gives the ball to a player going the opposite direction.
   - The player making the exchange holds the ball in both hands until the receiver is approximately six feet away.
   - The ball is then shifted to the hand on the side of the receiver. The receiver bends the arm nearest the exchange player, putting it in front of the chest with the palm down. The receiver's other hand should be waist high, with palms up.
   - The exchange player places (not throws) the ball between the receiver's hands. The receiver holds on to it and assumes a normal carrying position.
2. Arrange the children in groups of six. Give each group a football and line them up in shuttle formation (half of each group at each line) in single file behind two lines that are five yards apart.
3. Player 1 walks with the ball to Player 2 and hands it off.
4. Player 2 walks and hands it off to Player 3, and so on.
5. Teammates continue exchanging the ball back and forth. Emphasize that correct technique is important.

6. After several practice trials, the distance is increased between the lines, and players jog.

7. Continue until the children can run 20 yards and hand off successfully.

Concluding Activities (5 minutes)

Ball Exchange Relay

Arrange the children in relay teams of five or six players. Players on each team form two lines 20 yards apart, and each team has a football.

1. On each team Player 1 runs and hands the ball off using a good exchange to Player 2, who runs back and hands off to Player 3.

2. Continue until all players on a team have run. Repeat several times.

ADDITIONAL ACTIVITIES FOR GRADES 6-8: FOOTBALL

Presented below are skill rules for a football unit. For a longer period or for additional lessons, devise group activities that allow students to practice playing by these rules.

Skills

Place-Kicking

One student holds the ball on the ground, endpoint up, with the index finger while the kicker runs toward the ball and makes contact with the instep. The kicker should follow through in the direction of the kick. Have the students practice Place-Kicking in groups of three with a kicker, a holder, and a retriever. Rotate positions.

Simplified Football Rules

A team consists of six to nine players. For a six- or seven-player team, four players must be on the line of scrimmage. Teams with eight or nine players must place five players on the line. Each player has two flags.

Depending on the length of the period, you can set the number of plays in a game. Twenty-five plays might constitute one half of a game. A touchdown is six points, and the extra point is one point. A safety is worth two points.

A safety occurs any time an offensive player with the ball has his or her flag pulled during a play behind his or her own goal line. The point after a touchdown is attempted from three feet from the goal. A play is allowed for the extra point, which can be a pass or a run.

The game begins with a kickoff from the goal line. All players on the kicking team must be behind the goal line. Players on the receiving team must be 10 yards away from the goal line for the kickoff. The field is divided into three zones of 10 yards each. If the kickoff does not cover at least one zone, a second try is given. If the second try is unsuccessful, the opposing team is given the ball at midfield. A punt is used for the kickoff.

A team has four downs to move the ball to the next zone. If successful, they get four more downs to move to the next zone or to score. Balls landing on lines dividing zones are considered to be in the next zone.

The line of scrimmage is the place on the field where the ball is centered. All forward passes must be made from behind the line of scrimmage.

Any player is eligible to receive a pass. All punts must be announced. The team with the ball has 30 seconds to plan plays in a huddle.

A player may block only by positioning her or his body in the pathway of the opponent. Blockers must remain on their feet. The ball is dead when a fumble occurs. The first player touching the ball recovers the fumble.

A touchback occurs any time the ball is kicked over the end line by the offensive team, or when a defensive player intercepts the ball behind his or her own goal line and chooses not to run. The ball is put into play at the nearest zone line.

Physical tackling is not permitted. A player is considered downed when one flag is pulled.

A penalty of five yards is awarded for the following rule infractions:

- Too much time in the huddle
- Offside or crossing the line of scrimmage before the ball is centered
- Failure to announce a punt
- Adjusting flags in a way to make it difficult to pull them
- Passing in front of the line of scrimmage

A penalty of 15 yards is awarded for the following rule infractions:

- Poor conduct
- Holding or tripping
- Illegal tackling

G R A D E S 6-8 RHYTHMIC ACTIVITIES

The rhythmic program offers opportunities to practice traditional and novel dance steps and to participate in both structured and creative rhythmic dances. Basic locomotor and nonloco-motor skills are combined into complex sequences and practiced in novelty, folk, and square dance activities. The quality of movement is refined as more difficult steps are introduced. While traditional dance forms are important, students are encouraged to invent their own rhythmic sequences. Creative expression is a major goal of the program at this age.

UNIT ORGANIZATION

The 24 lessons in this section present traditional folk dance steps with procedures for incorporating the steps into dances. Also included in this section are descriptions of the basic and advanced steps for Tinikling, a folk dance from the Philippine Islands. Detailed instructions and teaching suggestions are provided for the dance, which is done with two 8-foot bamboo poles placed and manipulated on two crossbars. Several different routines are described and with some practice the children can create their own. Finally, a series of jump rope lessons is presented; this offers students opportunities to perform structured routines and to compose their own sequences.

Several of the lessons can be used for more than one day, and at times, review sessions can combine the dances introduced during the various rhythmic activity units. Each lesson begins with a warm-up activity that is selected from the rhythmic activity warm-up section. As you use these activities, numerous ways to modify and extend them will come to mind. The warm-up

should take about 5 minutes and is followed by the 15- or 20-minute skill-development phase. The skill-development activities focus on traditional dance steps and novelty rhythmic sequences. The concluding activities are designed for additional practice.

LESSON DESCRIPTIONS

The rhythmic activity warm-up section includes a follow-the-leader activity that can be modified and used repeatedly. The Move and Stop warm-up requires students to travel using various locomotor skills and to stop on a signal. Rhythmic Patterns With Ropes allow opportunities for students to move to 3/4 and 4/4 tempos and can be adapted to use different locomotor skills and different pieces of equipment, such as wands or ropes. Rhythmic Rope Jumping and Rhythm Steps offer excellent practice for jump rope and the dance steps that are introduced earlier. Finally, an active folk dance, Seven Jumps, is an excellent choice for a rhythmic warm-up; other folk and novelty dances can be used as well.

Lessons 1 through 5 introduce and provide practice for the Polka, the Schottische, and the Step Hop. Several traditional folk dances using these steps are presented. Lessons 6, 7, and 8 are devoted to the Grapevine, which is used in many traditional dances and can also be used in creative assignments and country dance routines. A Three-Step Turn replaces the Grapevine step in Lesson 9 and is used in country line dance. Lesson 10 introduces the Two-Step, which is then used in Cotton-Eyed Joe. Lessons 11 through 19 focus on Tinikling steps and routines. The basic tinikling step and accompanying rhythm are introduced in Lessons 11 and 12. Lessons 13, 14, and 15 describe Two Steps In, Straddle, and Turning, which are all variations of the Basic Tinikling Step. These steps are combined into routines by the students during the concluding activities. Two new formations, line and square, are offered in Lesson 16 and opportunities are provided for practice.

Lesson 17 introduces the Two-Foot and the Crossover Steps, which are advanced skills. This lesson focuses on combining steps into a routine. The basic 3/4 Tinikling rhythm is adjusted to a 4/4 time in Lesson 18. This modification offers opportunities to use alternate music, which can be selected by the students with your approval. Lesson 19 describes a station learning plan for the practice of Tinikling skills, which can be continued for several days. These stations provide practice for the basic step in traditional and alternative formations. It includes complex variations using 3/4 and 4/4 time and offers opportunities for creative expression.

Lessons 20 through 24 are devoted to rope jumping. The simple and complex steps described in these lessons will take some time to learn, especially if students have not mastered the basic One- and Two-Foot Single and Double Jump patterns. Lesson 20 introduces the basic Double Jump patterns and describes the Hustle and Grapevine steps and variations.

During the concluding activity, students are asked to work in cooperative groups to create a routine using the steps presented in the lessons. These activities can be extended over four or five days, depending on the skill level of the class. Lesson 21 continues with additional variations, including Single Jump patterns, the Scissors, and the Schottische. Students are asked again to create a routine, but this time using the single pattern steps. Two complex jumping skills, Double Under and 360 Turn are the focus of Lesson 23.

RHYTHMIC ACTIVITY TERMINOLOGY

Polka. Hop, step, step, step or hop, step, close, step.

Schottische. Step, step, step, hop.

Two-Step. Step, close, step; step, close, step.

Grapevine. Step to right with right foot, step behind right foot with left foot, step to right

with right foot, lift or swing left foot. Repeat to the left. (Step, back, step, lift).

Rhythm. Variations in rhythm indicate a range or combinations of accented and unaccented beats.

Tempo. Variations in tempo reflect changes in the speed of the movement.

Direction. Movements can be varied by moving forward, backward, up, or down.

Level. Movements can be varied by performing at low, medium, or high levels.

Pathways. Movements can be performed in straight, curved, or circular pathways.

Relationships. Different relationships are reflected when students move alone, with a partner, or in a group.

TEACHING TIPS AND LESSON MODIFICATIONS

It is important that students experience rhythmic activities, but at this level they do not always show an appreciation and enthusiasm for learning folk and square dances. There are many ways teachers can help students understand the significance of the dance program and enjoy learning the basic steps and formations. One suggestion is to challenge students to explore variations of steps and movements that are familiar to them. This can be done individually with changes in tempo, direction, level, and pathways. After some involvement in these beginning level activities, students will begin to show enthusiasm for developing skill in the more traditional steps and formations.

Most of the rhythmic activities can be performed in lines or in circles without partners; this approach is recommended if students are not comfortable with the couple holds and formations. Gradually, more emphasis can be placed on group dances and partner relationships. Cooperative learning activities provide opportunities to observe and appreciate the rhythmic movement of others, and this is recommended for this age group. It is important, however, to follow closely the rules established for cooperative learning.

Throughout the rhythmic activity units, students should be challenged to combine steps previously learned into novel sequences. This can be done with dance steps, Tinikling steps, or jump rope skills. Students can be asked to invent individual and group patterns using tempo, directions, floor patterns, and relationships to provide variations.

Teachers are encouraged to go beyond the ideas presented in these lessons. There are many traditional folk, social, and square dances that are appropriate for this age group. As skill and confidence increases, students can suggest alternative music and additional novelty and fad dance patterns.

Table RA4.1: Unit Plan for Grades 6-8: Rhythmic Activities

Week 7: dance steps	Week 11: folk dances	Week 18: tinikling
Monday: move and stop, Polka Tuesday: move and stop, challenges, face-to-face Wednesday: warm-up, heel-toe, Polka, Schottische Thursday: warm-up, two-step tasks, Jessie Polka Friday: rhythm steps, heel-toe, Pattycake Polka	Monday: rhythm steps, step touch, Grapevine Tuesday: follow leader, Hora Wednesday: follow leader, freeze Thursday: follow leader, three-step turn, freeze Friday: two-step, Cotton-eyed Joe	Monday: rhythmic ropes, basic tinikling Tuesday: rhythmic ropes, pole striking, basic step Wednesday: warm-up, two steps in, straddle step Thursday: warm-up, two steps in, straddle step Friday: warm-up, practice steps
Week 19: tinikling	**Week 24: advanced tinikling**	**Week 34: rope jumping**
Monday: warm-up, turning step Tuesday: warm-up, line, square Wednesday: warm-up, two-foot step, crossover Thursday: warm-up, practice steps Friday: warm-up, practice steps	Monday: warm-up, 4/4 steps Tuesday: warm-up, 4/4 steps Wednesday: warm-up, stations Thursday: warm-up, stations Friday: warm-up, stations	Monday: warm-up, two-foot, one-foot, Hustle, Grapevine Tuesday: warm-up, singles one-two, straddle, scissors, Schottische Wednesday: warm-up, side hits, swing turn Thursday: warm-up, double under, 360 turn Friday: warm-up, rope stations

Note: This table provides a suggested plan for the incorporation of rhythmic activities into the yearly curriculum. There are other arrangements that are appropriate, and teachers are encouraged to arrange the lessons according to their students' own interests and needs.

WARM-UPS

Follow the Leader

Arrange the children in groups of three to five and designate a leader for each group.

1. Select a rhythmic dance step.
2. The group moves around the area to music, following the pathway of the leader. Encourage leaders to make curved pathways. Change leaders often.
3. This activity can also be done with rope-jumping steps: the leader selects a sequence of jumping skills to perform, and the group imitates the actions of the leader.

Move and Stop

Arrange the children in scatter formation.

1. On a signal, the children travel freely throughout the space.
2. Children freeze when a drumbeat begins, and they start again on the signal.
3. Have them try sliding, galloping, skipping, or hopping.

Rhythmic Patterns With Ropes

Arrange the children in scatter formation, each with a short jump rope laid out to form a circle.

1. The children jump in and out of the circle with a 3/4 rhythm (two jumps in and one jump out) and continue jumping to a drumbeat, maintaining an even tempo.
2. Have them try one jump in and two jumps out. Repeat, using hops rather than jumps.
3. Variation: Have them use 4/4 rhythm. This could include two jumps in and two jumps out, three jumps in and one jump out, or one jump in and three jumps out.

Rhythmic Rope Jumping

The students jump rope continuously to music, using any combination of steps.

Rhythm Steps

Arrange the children in scatter formation.

1. The children travel freely around the area to music using a rhythmic step (e.g., skip, gallop, Step-Hop, or Tinikling).
2. Encourage movement in various directions and along a variety of pathways. This activity can be done individually or with a partner.

Seven Jumps

Arrange the children in a circle.

1. The children Step-Hop around the circle to music.
2. When the music stops, make a tone sound. The children touch their right knees to the floor on the tone and then stand and prepare to Step-Hop when the music resumes.
3. Each time the music stops include an additional tone, indicating that the children should touch an additional body part to the floor, in the following order: right knee, left elbow, right elbow, head, head covered with arms, stomach.

LESSON 1
DANCE STEPS

Student Objectives

- Slide, leading with both the right foot and the left foot.
- Perform the Polka step from a slide.
- Define the step pattern for the Polka step.

Equipment

- Music: "Jessie Polka" from *Basic Dance Tempos*, Honor Your Partner Records, LP 501A; Folkraft 1093, 1071. (*Note:* Any Polka music can be used.)

Warm-Up Activities (5 minutes)

Move and Stop

Arrange the children in scatter formation. See Grades 6-8: Rhythmic Activities, Warm-Ups, page 172.

1. On a signal, the children slide freely throughout the space.
2. The children freeze when a drumbeat begins, and they start again on a signal.
3. Have them slide, leading with the left foot and then with the right foot.
4. Have them make curved pathways.

Skill-Development Activities (20 minutes)

Polka

Arrange the children in a large circle, facing in.

1. Describe and demonstrate the Polka step.
2. Tell the children: *Listen to Polka music and clap to the beat. Slide to the right eight steps. Slide to the left eight steps.*

Single circle,
facing in

3. Have the children continue practicing eight right and eight left slides until the change in direction can be done smoothly.
4. Repeat the sequence with four slides right and four slides left.
5. Repeat with two slides right and two slides left.
6. Have the children practice sliding to the right again (counterclockwise). At any point during the slide have them turn to face the outside of the circle, continuing to slide counterclockwise.
7. Have them turn back to face the center of the circle.
8. Have the children practice sliding eight steps facing in and eight steps facing out.
9. Have them practice the Polka step. They hop on the right foot, step on the left foot, close the right foot to the left foot, step on the left foot. *Hop, step, step, step: or hop, step, close, step.* The steps can be performed moving sideways or forward.
10. Have the children practice the Polka step moving sideways: one step (hop, step, close, step) to the right and one step to the left (hop, step, close, step).

Concluding Activities (5 minutes)

Polka

Have the children Polka freely around the room to the music.

Question and Answer

Arrange the children in information formation. Ask the children the following questions:

How are the Polka step and the slide alike?

What steps do you combine to perform the Polka step?

Is the Polka performed in an even or an uneven rhythm?

LESSON 2
RHYTHMIC STEPS

Student Objectives

- Gallop, leading with both the right foot and the left foot.
- Perform a Polka step from a gallop.

Equipment

- Music: "Jessie Polka" from Basic Dance Tempos, Honor Your Partner Records, LP 501A; Folkraft 1093, 1071. (*Note:* Any polka music can be used.)

Warm-Up Activities (5 minutes)

Move and Stop

Use the gallop. See Grades 6-8: Rhythmic Activities, Warm-Ups, page 172. Have the children gallop with the right foot leading and then with the left foot leading, making straight and curved pathways.

Skill-Development Activities (20 minutes)

Rhythm Challenges

Arrange the children in a large circle facing counterclockwise.

1. Ask the children to do the following challenges:

   Listen to Polka music and clap to the beat.

   Gallop forward eight steps with your right foot leading.

   Gallop forward eight steps with your left foot leading.

2. Have the children continue practicing eight steps with the right foot leading and eight steps with the left foot leading until the change can be done smoothly.

3. Have them repeat the sequence using four gallops with the right foot and four gallops with the left foot.

4. Repeat, using two gallops and finally one gallop with the right and left feet. Tell the children: *Hop, step, close, step.* (A Polka is a gallop plus a hop.)

Face-to-Face Polka

Arrange the children with partners in scatter formation.

1. Describe and demonstrate the Face-to-Face Polka.

2. Facing each other with hands joined, partners Polka; one partner begins on the right foot and the other partner begins on the left foot.

3. Partners can Polka forward or backward using the hop-gallop movement (hop, step, close, step).

4. Have the students practice the Face-to-Face Polka forward and backward (one partner moves forward while the other moves backward, and then they reverse).

5. Repeat moving sideways. Tell the children: *Hop, step, close, step; hop-turn, step, close, step.* To Polka sideways, a half turn is added on each hop.

6. Have the students practice the Face-to-Face Polka to music, forward, backward, and sideways.

Face-to-Face, Back-to-Back Polka

Arrange the children with partners in scatter formation.

1. Describe and demonstrate the Face-to-Face, Back-to-Back Polka.

2. Standing beside each other with inside hands joined, partners face each other and, beginning on the inside foot, take a Polka step (hop, step, close, step); they then take a second Polka step in a back-to-back position.

3. Have them continue, alternating Face-to-Face and Back-to-Back.

4. Have the children practice.

Concluding Activities (5 minutes)

Face-to-Face, Back-to-Back Polka

Partners perform the Face-to-Face, Back-to-Back Polka, moving freely around the room to music.

LESSON 3
FOLK DANCE

Student Objectives

- Combine the Heel-Toe Polka Step, Schottische, and Step-Hop in the Weggis Dance.
- Demonstrate Skater's Position with a partner.

Equipment

- One drum
- Music: "Weggis Dance," Folkcraft 1160; HLP 4029 (Hoctor Records)
- Music: "Jessie Polka" from *Basic Dance Tempos*, Honor Your Partner Records, LP 501A; Folkraft 1093, 1071

Warm-Up Activities (5 minutes)

Polka

Arrange the children in scatter formation and have them listen to "Jessie Polka." See Grades 6-8: Rhythmic Activities, Lesson 1, page 174.

1. The children Polka (hop, step, close, step), moving freely around the area.
2. Have them change directions several times.

Skill-Development Activities (20 minutes)

Heel-Toe Polka Step

Place the children in a double circle, facing counterclockwise. Each pair should be placed in Skater's Position.

1. Demonstrate Heel-Toe Polka Steps, beginning with the left foot. The student places the left heel forward, touches the toe of the left foot back in place, and takes a Polka step beginning with a hop on the right foot. *Heel, toe, hop, step, close, step.*
2. Have the students practice the Heel-Toe step with the left foot. *Heel, toe, Polka.*
3. Have them repeat the step on the right foot.
4. Have the students practice four Heel-Toe Polka Steps to a drumbeat.

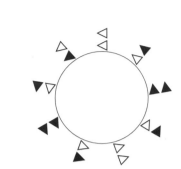

Double circle, facing counterclockwise

Skater's position

Schottische

Arrange the children in a double circle, facing counterclockwise. Inside hands should be joined.

1. Say to the children: *Step, step, step, hop. Practice one Schottische step away from your partner and one Schottische step back to your partner.*
2. Have the children combine the Schottische steps with four turning Step-Hops.

Weggis Dance

Arrange the children in a double circle, facing counterclockwise. Inside hands should be joined.

Part I

The children take four Heel-Toe Polka Steps forward, beginning with the left foot.

Part II

The children take one Schottische step away from their partners, beginning on the outside foot. They repeat, moving back to the partner. In Shoulder-Waist Position, they take four turning Step-Hops with their partner. They hold eight counts for the interlude.

Part III

Repeat Parts I and II.

Shoulder-waist position

Concluding Activities (5 minutes)

Weggis Dance

The children perform the entire sequence to the music.

LESSON 4
DANCE STEPS

Student Objectives

- Perform a rhythmic sequence using the Two-Step.
- With a partner demonstrate the Varsouvienne Position.
- Combine the Heel-Toe Polka Step and the Two-Step to perform the Jessie Polka.

Equipment

- Music: "Two-Step Music" from *American Folk Dances*, KIM 3040, 3050
- Music: "Jessie Polka," Folkraft 1093, 1071

Warm-Up Activities (5 minutes)

Two-Step

Arrange the children in scatter formation.

1. The Two-Step goes as follows: step left, close right, step left, step right, close left, step right. Say to the children: *Step, close, step; step, close, step.*

2. Have the children listen to "Two-Step Music" as they Two-Step freely around the area to the music.

Skill-Development Activities (20 minutes)

Two-Step Tasks

Arrange the children in pairs in a double circle, facing counterclockwise.

Double circle, facing counterclockwise

Ask the children to do the following tasks:

Do eight Two-Steps forward.

Do Two-Steps in an individual circle (turning away from your partner).

Repeat with four more Two-Steps in an individual circle with your partner.

Varsouvienne Position

Continue with children in pairs in a double circle, facing counterclockwise.

1. Describe and demonstrate the Varsouvienne Position.

   • Partner 1 stands slightly to the left of and behind Partner 2.

   • Partners hold left hands in front and right hands over Partner 2's right shoulder.

2. Have the children practice the Varsouvienne Position with partners.

3. Have them repeat the position with different partners.

Varsouvienne position

Jessie Polka

Arrange the children in a double circle, facing counterclockwise. Partners should be in Varsouvienne position.

1. Describe and demonstrate Part I.

   Part I: Place left heel forward and return left foot to place, putting weight on the left foot.

   Place right toe back, touch in place, touch right heel forward, and return to place, putting weight on the right foot.

   Place left heel forward, and bring left toe across in front of right.

   Count 1: Left heel forward.

   Count 2: Return to place, putting weight on left foot.

   Count 3: Right toe behind.

Count 4: Touch right toe in place.

Count 5: Touch right heel forward.

Count 6: Return right foot to place, putting weight on it.

Count 7: Left heel forward.

Count 8: Left toe across in front of right, keeping weight on right.

2. Have the students practice Part I. Say to the students: *Heel, step, toe, touch, heel, step, cross.*

3. Describe and demonstrate Part II.

    Part II: Beginning with the left foot, take four Two-Steps counterclockwise.

4. Have the students practice Part II.

Concluding Activities (5 minutes)

Jessie Polka

The students perform the entire sequence to the music.

LESSON 5
FOLK DANCE

Student Objectives

- Combine the Heel-Toe and the slide in the Pattycake Polka.

Equipment

- Music: "Pattycake Polka," Folkcraft 1260; HLP 4001 (Hoctor Records); Lloyd Shaw E-12, 228

Warm-Up Activities (5 minutes)

Rhythm Steps

Arrange the children in scatter formation and have them listen to "Pattycake Polka."

1. The children travel freely around the room using the slide, the gallop, or the Polka step.
2. Students can choose a step but must change steps on the teacher's cue. Have them change steps often.

Skill-Development Activities (20 minutes)

Heel-Toe

Arrange the children in a double circle, partners facing each other, one partner in the inner circle and the other in the outer circle.

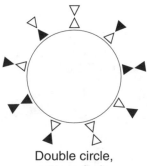

Double circle,
partners facing

1. Describe and demonstrate the Heel-Toe: The student places one foot out to the side with the heel down and toe up and then returns the foot to its original position with toe down and heel up.
2. Have the children practice the Heel-Toe.

Pattycake Polka

Continue with the children in a double circle, partners facing each other, one partner in the inner circle and the other in the outer circle.

1. Describe and demonstrate Parts I and II of the Pattycake Polka.

   Part I: The student does two Heel-Toe steps with the lead foot (the foot toward the counterclockwise direction).

   Part II: The student does four slides counterclockwise.

2. Have the students practice Parts I and II.
3. Have them practice Parts I and II to music.
4. Describe and demonstrate Parts III and IV.

   Part III: The student does two Heel-Toe steps with the foot that is toward the clockwise direction.

   Part IV: The student does four slides clockwise.

5. Have the students practice Parts III and IV.
6. Have them practice Parts I-IV to music.
7. Describe and demonstrate Parts V and VI.

   Part V: The student claps his or her own thigh three times, his or her own hands three times, the partner's right hand three times, and the partner's left hand three times.

   Part VI: Partners hook right elbows and walk around once with six steps.

8. Have the students practice Parts V and VI.
9. Have them practice Parts I-VI to music.
10. Describe and demonstrate Part VII.

    Part VII: The partner with his or her back to the center of the circle walks two steps to the left to a new partner.

11. Have the students practice Part VII.

Concluding Activities (5 minutes)

Pattycake Polka

The students perform the entire sequence with music.

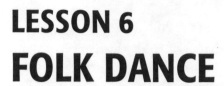

LESSON 6

FOLK DANCE

Student Objectives

- Work in a cooperative learning group to learn to Step Touch to music.
- Work in a cooperative learning group to learn to perform the Grapevine step to music.
- Combine the Grapevine and the Step Touch in Alley Cat.

Equipment

- Music: "Alley Cat" from *All-Time Favorite Dances*, KIM 9126 (or Columbia CL-2400; Atlantic 13113)

Warm-Up Activities (5 minutes)

Rhythm Steps

Arrange the children in scatter formation and have them listen to "Alley Cat." See Grades 6-8: Rhythmic Activities, Warm-Ups, page 173.

1. Using the gallop or the slide, the children travel freely around the area.
2. Have them change steps often.

Skill-Development Activities (20 minutes)

Step Touch

Arrange the children in groups of five or six, and assign each group to a practice area. Explain and demonstrate Step Touch:

- With weight on the right foot, the child touches the left toe back and in place (two counts).
- Repeat, touching the left toe to the side and in place (two counts).
- On the last touch, put the weight on the left foot and repeat the touches with the right foot (back, in place, side, in place).

Review Guidelines for Cooperative Learning

Arrange children in information formation. Tell the children:

> *Each student is responsible for his or her own work and the work of the team. The group is not successful unless all students accomplish the goal.*

Students must help each other.

Each student must try hard.

1. The goal of this activity is for all students in the group to be able to perform the Step Touch sequence to the music.
2. Listen to the music "Alley Cat" and practice the Step Touch in groups.

Grapevine

Arrange the children in two or three lines facing forward.

1. Explain and demonstrate the Grapevine to the students: The child steps to the right with the right foot; brings the left foot behind and steps on it; steps to the right again with the right foot; and brings the left foot in front, lifting the left knee across in front of the right knee while balancing on the right foot. The step takes four counts: step, back, step, lift.
2. Repeat the demonstration, beginning with the left foot moving to the left.
3. Rearrange the children into cooperative groups. Practice the Grapevine to music.

Alley Cat

Arrange the children in two or three lines facing forward. Explain and demonstrate Alley Cat.

Part I: Grapevine step to the right beginning with the right foot.

Grapevine step to the left beginning with the left foot.

Part II: Touch the right toe back, and then in place.

Repeat (right back, right in place).

Touch the left toe back, and then in place.

Repeat (left back, left in place).

Part III: Lift the right foot, with knee bent, across in front of the body.

Touch the right foot in place.

Lift the right foot, with knee bent, across in front of the body.

Touch the right foot in place, putting the weight on the right foot.

Repeat with the left foot (left lift, touch in place, left lift, touch and put weight on it).

Part IV: Lift the right foot, with knee bent, across in front of the body.

Touch the right foot in place, putting the weight on the right foot.

Lift the left foot, with knee bent, across in front of the body.

Touch the left foot in place, putting the weight on the left foot.

Jump and clap hands once.

Turn one-quarter turn to the right.

Repeat the routine above three times, making a quarter turn each time until a full circle is made.

Concluding Activities (5 minutes)

Alley Cat

The students perform the entire sequence with music.

LESSON 7
FOLK DANCE

Student Objectives

- Combine stepping and the step swing to perform the Hora.
- Perform variations of the Hora.

Equipment

- Music: "Jessie Polka," Folkraft 1093, 1071 (or other Polka music)
- Music: "Hora" from *All-Time Favorite Dances*, KIM 9126

Warm-Up Activities (5 minutes)

Follow the Leader

Arrange the children in groups of four with a leader for each group.

1. Have the children listen to "Jessie Polka " or other polka music.
2. Using the gallop, slide, or Polka, the group moves around the area, following the pathway of the leader. The leader selects the step and the pathways, and the group imitates and follows.

Skill-Development Activities (20 minutes)

Hora

Arrange the children in a circle, partners facing in.

1. Describe and demonstrate the sequence.

   Part I: Step right on the right foot.

   The left foot crosses behind the right foot.

   Step right on the right foot.

   Hop on the right foot and swing the left foot forward.

   Hop on the left foot and swing the right foot forward.

   (The cues will be step, back, step swing, step swing.)

   Part II: Repeat the sequence moving right in the circle until the music ends.

2. Have the children practice the sequence with music.

3. Variation: The circle can change to a line with the lead person winding in and out through raised arms. Practice the variation.

Concluding Activities (5 minutes)

Hora

The students perform the variation with music.

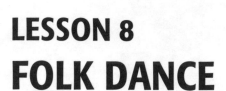
LESSON 8
FOLK DANCE

Student Objectives

- Work in a cooperative learning group to learn the steps to the Freeze.
- Perform the step pattern for the Freeze.

Equipment

- Music: "The Freeze" from *Cowboy Swing*, Melody House (MH-C35 Cassette)
- Music: "Polka" from *Cowboy Two-Step*, Melody House (MH-C35 Cassette)

Warm-Up Activities (5 minutes)

Follow the Leader

Arrange the children in groups of four, each group with a leader, and have them listen to polka music. Using the Polka step, groups move to the music following the leaders. Change leaders often.

Skill-Development Activities (15 minutes)

Freeze

Arrange the children in groups of five or six, and assign each group to a practice area.

1. Describe and demonstrate Parts I, II, and III of the Freeze.

    Part I: The students do one Grapevine to the right and one Grapevine to the left (step, back, step, lift).

    Part II: The students take three steps backward, starting with the right foot.

    Part III: The students touch the left heel to the front, twice. On the second touch, they put weight on the left foot and pivot a quarter turn to the left.

2. Have students repeat the entire sequence.

Review Guidelines for Cooperative Learning

Arrange the children in information formation. Tell the students:

> *Each student is responsible for his or her own work and the work of the team. The group is not successful unless all students accomplish the goal.*
>
> *Students must help each other.*
>
> *Each student must try hard.*

1. The goal of this activity is for all students in the group to be able to perform the Freeze sequence to the music.
2. Listen to the Freeze music and practice the step sequence in groups.
3. Perform the sequence to music.

Concluding Activities (10 minutes)

Freeze

Arrange the children in groups of 4 to 10.

1. Select one group to perform the sequence.
2. As this group finishes the sequence, they point to another group, who then performs the sequence.
3. This continues until all groups have done the Freeze.
4. When the last group finishes, all groups do the Freeze together.

LESSON 9
FOLK DANCE

Student Objectives

- Substitute a Three-Step Turn for the Grapevine Step in the Freeze.

Equipment

- Music: "Hora" from *All-Time Favorite Dances*, KIM 9126
- Music: "The Freeze" from *Cowboy Swing*, Melody House (MH-C35 Cassette)

Warm-Up Activities (5 minutes)

Follow the Leader

Arrange the children in groups of four to six, each group with a lead dancer. Perform the Hora, with each lead dancer deciding on a pathway to follow.

Skill-Development Activities (20 minutes)

Three-Step Turn

Arrange the children in two lines facing the music.

1. Describe and demonstrate the Three-Step Turn: The child steps right on the right foot, spinning counterclockwise to face the opposite direction, steps on the left foot, continues the spin counterclockwise around to face the original direction, steps on the right foot, and lifts the left foot across in front of the body.

2. Have the children practice the Three-Step Turn to the right. Tell the children: *Right, left, right, lift. With each Three-Step Turn you should make a complete circle.*

3. Have them repeat the turn to the left. Say to the students: *Left, right, left, lift.*

4. Repeat, alternating left and right.

Freeze Variation

Arrange the children in two lines facing the music.

1. Describe and demonstrate Parts I, II, and III of the Freeze Variation.

   Part I: The children do a Three-Step Turn to the right.

   Part II: The children do a Three-Step Turn to the left.

Part III: The children touch the left heel to the front two times. On the second touch, have them put weight on the left foot and pivot a quarter turn to the left. Repeat the entire sequence.

2. Have the children practice Parts I, II, and III.

3. Perform the entire sequence to music.

Concluding Activities (5 minutes)

Freeze

Arrange the children in groups of 4 to 10.

1. Allow the children to select the formation (lines, partners, circle, etc.) for their groups.

2. Have them perform the Freeze (see Grades 6-8: Rhythmic Activities, Lesson 8, page 190) and the Freeze Variation alternately to music.

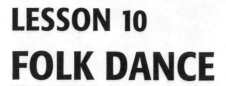

LESSON 10
FOLK DANCE

Student Objectives

- Combine the Step-Close-Step in an uneven rhythm to perform the Two-Step.
- Combine the Two-Step and the right and left leg swings in Cotton-Eyed Joe.

Equipment

- Music: "Cowboy Two Step" from *Cowboy Two-Step*, Melody House (MH-C35 Cassette)
- Music: "Cotton-Eyed Joe" from *All-Time Favorite Dances*, KIM 9126

Warm-Up Activities (5 minutes)

Two-Step

Arrange the children in scatter formation, with partners.

1. Say to the children: *The Two-Step goes as follows: step left, close right, step left, step right, close left, step. Step, close, step; step, close, step.* See Grades 6-8: Rhythmic Activities, Lesson 4, page 181.

2. The children Two-Step freely around the room to the "Cowboy Two-Step." When the music stops, they find partners, join hands, and skip in a circle.

3. They Two-Step freely again when the music resumes.

Skill-Development Activities (20 minutes)

Cotton-Eyed Joe

Arrange the children in scatter formation.

1. Describe and demonstrate Parts I through VIII of Cotton-Eyed Joe.

   Part I: Lift the right foot out and around the left foot, keeping weight on the left foot. (This is a brushing motion, with the ball of the foot brushing the floor as it crosses the left foot and returns to starting position.)

   Part II: Extend the right foot out in front of the left foot (a kicking motion).

   Part III: Take three small steps backward (right, left, right).

   Part IV: Lift the left foot out and around the right foot, keeping weight on the right foot.

   Part V: Extend the left foot out in front of the right foot.

Part VI: Take three small steps backward (left, right, left).

Part VII: Repeat Parts I through VI.

Part VIII: Take eight Two-Steps forward.

2. The children practice Parts I through VIII. Say to the children: *Brush right, kick right, step back 2, 3. Brush left, kick left, step back 2, 3.*

3. Have them practice the Two-Step to music.

4. Have them practice the entire sequence to music.

Concluding Activities (5 minutes)

Cotton-Eyed Joe

Arrange the children in several long lines, standing shoulder to shoulder, each with arms around the waist or shoulders of the next child. The children perform Cotton-Eyed Joe in lines.

LESSON 11
TINIKLING

Student Objectives

- Perform the Basic Tinikling Step.

Equipment

- One short jump rope for each child
- Record: "Tinikling," Kimbo (KEA 8095, 9015)
- Six to eight sets of bamboo poles (8 to 12 feet)

Warm-Up Activities (5 minutes)

Rhythmic Patterns With Ropes

Arrange the children in scatter formation with their jump ropes in circles on the ground.

1. The children jump in and out of the circles in a 3/4 rhythm. For example, two jumps in and one jump out.
2. The children continue jumping rhythmically to a drumbeat. Have them try one jump in and two jumps out.

Skill-Development Activities (20 minutes)

Basic Tinikling Step

Arrange the children in groups of four in scatter formation. Each group has a set of Tinikling poles.

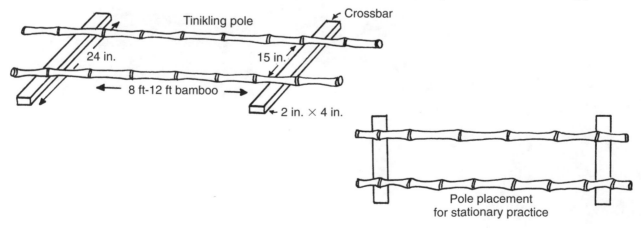

Tinikling pole
Crossbar
24 in.
15 in.
← 8 ft-12 ft bamboo →
2 in. × 4 in.
Pole placement
for stationary practice

1. Have the children listen to Tinikling music, clapping and counting the 3/4 time.
2. The children in each group begin by standing with right sides to the poles.
3. Describe and demonstrate Counts 1 to 3.

    Count 1: Step in place with the left foot (the foot away from the pole).

    Count 2: Step with the right foot between the poles.

    Count 3. Step with the left foot between the poles (lift up right foot).

4. Arrange the sticks on the floor and practice with the sticks stationary. In each group all students practice at the same time.
5. Have the children practice Counts 1 to 3. Say to the children: *Step left, right between, left between.*
6. Describe and demonstrate Counts 4 to 6.

    Count 4: Step with the right foot out to the right of the poles.

    Count 5: Step with the left foot between the poles.

    Count 6: Step with the right foot between the poles (lift up left foot).

    Count 7: Step with the left foot to the left side of the poles. (Count 7 becomes Count 1 for the second step.)

7. Have the children practice all the counts. Say to the children: *Step left, right between, left between, right out, left between, right between, left out.*
8. Have the children repeat the basic Tinikling steps, Counts 1 to 6.

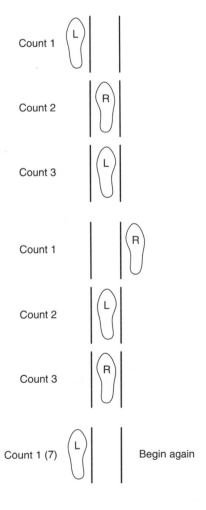

Concluding Activities (5 minutes)

Basic Tinikling Step

The students perform the Basic Tinikling Step, one child in each group at a time, to music; on the seventh count, the second child enters while the first child exits. Repeat until each child in each group has had several turns.

LESSON 12
TINIKLING

Student Objectives

- Strike the Tinikling poles with the beat of the music.

Equipment

- A short jump rope for every child
- Music: "Tinikling," Kimbo (KEA 8095, 9015)
- One set of Tinikling poles for each group of four children

Warm-Up Activities (5 minutes)

Rhythmic Patterns With Ropes

The students jump rope to the Tinikling music. See Grades 6-8: Rhythmic Activities, Warm-Ups, page 172.

Skill-Development Activities (20 minutes)

Tinikling Rhythm

Arrange the children in groups of four, in scatter formation. Each group has a set of poles placed in the stationary practice formation (see Grades 6-8, Rhythmic Activities, Lesson 11, page 196).

1. Select two children in each group to sit at opposite ends of the poles.
2. Have the children listen to "Tinikling" and clap the rhythm (1, 2, 3; 1, 2, 3).
3. Have them practice clapping on Count 1 and snapping their fingers on Counts 2 and 3 (clap, snap, snap).

Striking the Tinikling Poles

A striker sits at each end of the set of poles, with crossbars.

1. The strikers hit the poles together on Count 1 and on the crossbars (approximately 15 inches apart) on Counts 2 and 3.
2. Continue with the 3/4 rhythm (together, out, out or together, apart, apart).
3. With two children practicing at each set of poles, have the students practice striking the Tinikling poles to the music.
4. The other children in the group should clap the rhythm. During the striking practice there are no dancers.

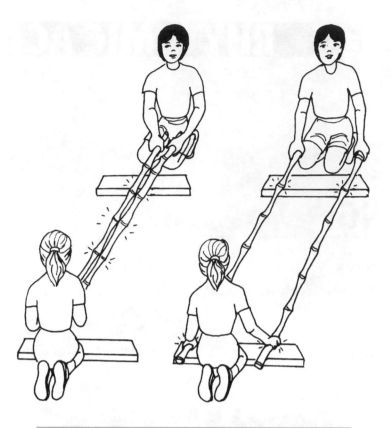

Concluding Activities (5 minutes)

Basic Tinikling Step

Arrange the children in groups of four in scatter formation. Each group has a set of Tinikling poles.

1. The students perform the Basic Tinikling Step with the music and the poles striking.
2. One student practices the step and two children strike the poles. The children take turns within groups.
3. The dancer begins with his or her right side to the poles.
4. On Count 1, the poles are closed (striking together). This is when the dancer steps in place with the left foot.
5. Steps 2 and 3 are done inside the poles as the poles are striking the crossbars.
6. As the poles close again on Count 1, the dancer steps with the right foot out to the right of the poles.
7. Continue with in, in, out; in, in, out as the poles are apart for two counts and together for one count. See Grades 6-8, Rhythmic Activities, Lesson 11, page 196.

LESSONS 13 AND 14
TINIKLING

Student Objectives

- Perform at least one simple variation of the Basic Tinikling Step.

Equipment

- Music: "Tinikling," Kimbo (KEA 8095, 9015)
- One set of Tinikling poles for each group of four students

Warm-Up Activities (5 minutes)

Basic Tinikling Step

Arrange the children in scatter formation. See Grades 6-8: Rhythmic Activities, Lesson 11, page 196. The children practice the Basic Tinikling Step in place to the music without the poles. As they perform the step, they try to take turns.

Skill-Development Activities (20 minutes)

Two Steps In

Arrange the children in groups of four in scatter formation. Each group has a set of poles. The students begin with their right sides to the poles.

1. Describe and demonstrate Two Steps In. Use the cues: *out, in, in.*

    Count 1: Step in place with the left foot.

    Count 2: Step with the right foot between the poles.

    Count 3: Hop (rebound) on the right foot between the poles.

    Count 4: Step to the left with the left foot (return to starting position).

2. Within their groups, arrange the children with their right sides to the set of stationary poles.

3. Have the students practice Two Steps In with the poles stationary.

4. Assign two children in each group to strike the poles. Rotate so that each child has a chance to strike the poles and practice the step.

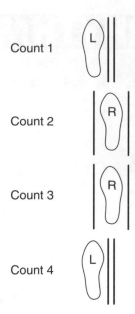

Count 1

Count 2

Count 3

Count 4

Straddle Step

The students begin with their right sides to the poles.

1. Describe and demonstrate the Straddle Step.

   Count 1: Straddle the poles.

   Count 2: Jump between the poles with both feet.

   Count 3: Jump a second time between the poles with both feet.

2. Within their groups, arrange the children with their right sides to the set of stationary poles.

3. Have the children practice the Straddle Step with the poles stationary.

4. Assign two children in each group to strike the poles. Rotate so that each child has a chance to strike the poles and practice the steps.

5. Have the children practice the step, striking the poles to music.

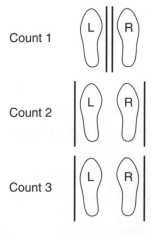

Count 1

Count 2

Count 3

Concluding Activities (5 minutes)

Tinikling

Have the children combine the Basic Tinikling Step and one variation from this lesson into a routine while striking poles to music. See Grades 6-8: Rhythmic Activities, Lessons 11 and 12, pages 196 and 199.

RHYTHMIC ACTIVITIES

LESSON 15
TINIKLING

Student Objectives

- Perform a turning variation of the Basic Tinikling Step.

Equipment

- Record: "Tinikling," Kimbo (KEA 8095, 9015)
- One set of Tinikling poles for each group of four children

Warm-Up Activities (5 minutes)

Tinikling Steps

Arrange the children in scatter formation. See Grades 6-8: Rhythmic Activities, Lessons 11 to 14, pages 196, 199, 201, and 202. Moving freely about the area without the Tinikling poles, the children practice any of the Tinikling steps learned (Basic Tinikling Step, Two Steps In, or Straddle Step).

Skill-Development Activities (20 minutes)

Turning Step

Arrange the children in groups of four in scatter formation. Each group has a set of poles. The students start with their right sides to the poles.

1. Describe and demonstrate the Turning Step.

   Count 1: Step in place with the left foot.

   Counts 2 and 3: Complete the Basic Tinikling Step (right in, left in).

   Count 1: Step to the right with the right foot outside of the poles.

   Counts 2 and 3: Take two walking steps forward to make a half turn (the right side is now in toward the poles).

   Count 1: Start the traditional step again with a step in place with the left foot.

   Counts 2 and 3: Complete the traditional step.

   Count 1: Step out on the original side of the poles (where the practice started).

   Counts 2 and 3: Repeat the turn back to the original position.

2. Say to the students: *Begin with the traditional step for Counts 1, 2, and 3; step out on your right foot, turning right for two more steps; step on your left foot and repeat the traditional step again, but now you will be facing the opposite direction.*

3. Have the students practice the Turning Step with poles stationary. Say to the students: *Traditional 1, 2, 3; out right, turn, turn; traditional 1, 2, 3.*

4. Have the students practice to music, striking the poles.

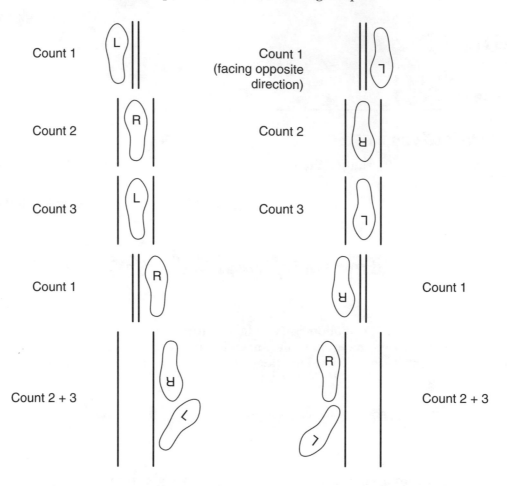

Concluding Activities (5 minutes)

Turning Step

The students perform the turning variation to music.

GRADES 6-8

RHYTHMIC ACTIVITIES

LESSON 16

TINIKLING

Student Objectives

- Perform the Basic Tinikling Step using at least one new formation.

Equipment

- Music: "Tinikling," Kimbo (KEA 8095, 9015)
- Eight sets of Tinikling poles

Warm-Up Activities (5 minutes)

Tinikling Steps

To the Tinikling music, and without the poles, the students practice any of the steps they have learned. Have them experiment with turns. See Grades 6-8: Rhythmic Activities, Lessons 11 to 15, pages 196, 199, 201, 202, and 203.

Skill-Development Activities (20 minutes)

Line Formation

Arrange the children in groups of four, each group with two sets of poles.

1. Describe Line Formation.
   - Two sets of poles are arranged about six feet apart for each group.
   - The object is to dance down the set of poles and return to the original spot.
   - The student performs the Basic Tinikling Step through the first set of poles, takes three small running steps to get in position for the traditional step at the second set of poles, takes three running steps to turn around and get into position to step in the opposite direction (turns around so that right side is to the poles), and then begins the Basic Tinikling Step again, going back to the starting point.
2. Have the students practice Line Formation with poles stationary.
3. Have them practice Line Formation to the music with poles striking.
4. Rotate strikers.

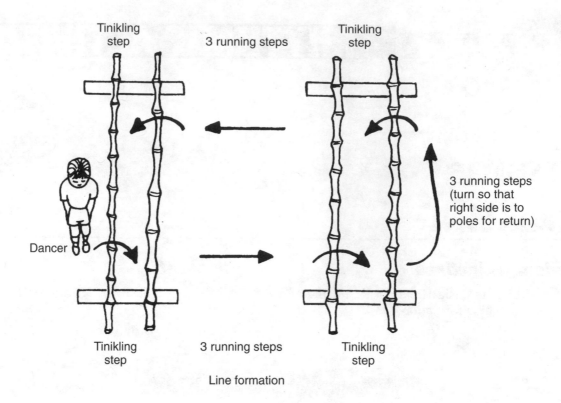

Line formation

Square Formation

Arrange the children in two groups, each group with four sets of poles arranged in a square.

1. Describe the Square Formation.

    - The dancer starts with a Tinikling Step at one set of poles.

    - Taking three running steps, the dancer circles to get into position for the return step.

    - After the return step, the dancer takes three running steps to get into position at the next set of poles, and so on.

    - Four dancers can dance at a time, each starting at a different set of poles. The student performs the Turning Step at each set of poles and then takes three running steps to get in position for the step at the next set of poles.

2. Have the students practice the Square Formation with poles stationary.

3. Have the students practice the Square Formation while striking poles to music.

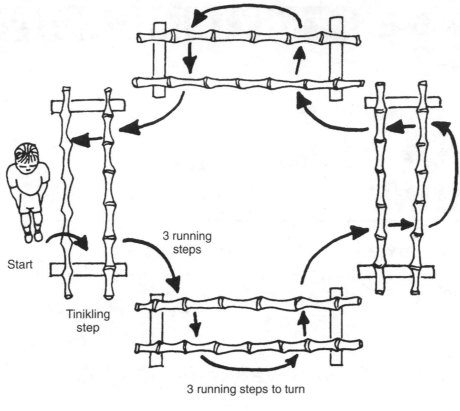

Start

Tinikling
step

3 running
steps

3 running steps to turn

Square formation

Tinikling: Square or Line

Divide the children into two or more groups, with groups of four within each group. The groups perform individually either the Square Formation or the Line Formation.

LESSON 17
TINIKLING

Student Objectives

- Perform the Two-Foot Step and the Cross-over Step.

Equipment

- Music: "Tinikling," Kimbo (KEA 8095, 9015)
- One set of Tinikling poles for each group of four students

Warm-Up Activities (5 minutes)

Follow the Leader

The leader selects a Tinikling step and performs the step in place or moving about the area. The group imitates the movement of the leader. See Grades 6-8: Rhythmic Activities, Warm-Ups, page 172.

Skill-Development Activities (20 minutes)

Two-Foot Step

Arrange the children in groups of four. Each group has a set of poles. The students begin with their right sides to the poles.

1. Describe and demonstrate the Two-Foot Step.

   Count 1: Jump in place with feet together.

   Counts 2 and 3: Jump twice with two feet between the poles.

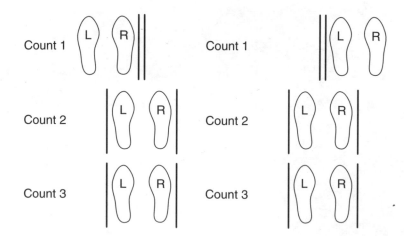

2. Have the children practice the Two-Foot Step with poles stationary.

3. Have the children practice the Two-Foot Step while striking the poles to music.

Crossover Step

The students begin with their right sides to the poles.

1. Describe and demonstrate the Crossover Step.

Count 1: Step in place with the left foot.

Count 2: Step between the poles with the right foot.

Count 3: Hop* on the right foot between the poles.

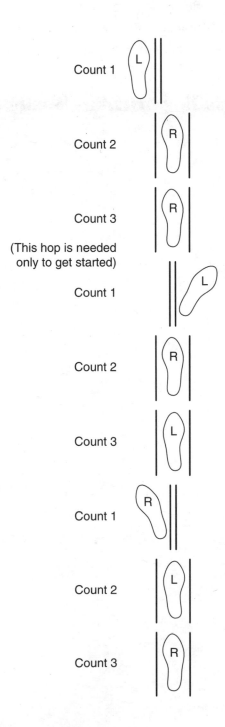

Count 1

Count 2

Count 3

(This hop is needed
only to get started)

Count 1

Count 2

Count 3

Count 1

Count 2

Count 3

Count 1: Cross over the right foot with the left foot, and step to the right side of the poles. (This is a crossover step. The left foot crosses over the right foot and weight is on the left foot outside the pole. The right foot is lifted, but it stays behind the left foot.)

Count 2: Step between the poles with the right foot.

Count 3: Step between the poles with the left foot.

Count 1: Cross over the left foot with the right foot, and step to the outside of the poles on the left side.

Count 2: Step between the poles with the left foot.

Count 3: Step between the poles with the right foot.

*This hop is needed only to get started.

2. Have the students practice the Crossover Step with poles stationary.

3. Have the children practice the Crossover Step while striking poles to music.

Concluding Activities (5 minutes)

Tinikling Steps

The students perform the following steps:

> Basic Tinikling Step
> Two Steps In
> Crossover Step
> Turning Step
> Two-Foot Step
> Straddle Step

LESSON 18
TINIKLING

Student Objectives

- Adjust the Basic Tinikling Step to 4/4 time.

Equipment

- Music: "Seven Jumps," Victor 45-6172
- Music: "Walk Right In" from *Contemporary Tinikling Activities*, Kimbo (KEA 8095)
- One set of Tinikling poles for every four students

Warm-Up Activities (5 minutes)

Seven Jumps

Arrange the children in a circle.

1. Have the children Step-Hop around the circle to music.
2. When the music stops, sound a tone. The children touch their right knees to the floor on the tone; they then stand and prepare to Step-Hop when the music resumes.
3. Each time the music stops include an additional tone, indicating that the children should touch an additional body part to the floor, in the following order: right knee, left elbow, right elbow, head, head covered with arms, stomach.

Skill-Development Activities (20 minutes)

Pole Striking for Tinikling Step in 4/4 Time

Arrange the children in groups of four, each group with a set of poles.

1. Describe and demonstrate 4/4 Pole Striking: The strikers hit the poles together on Counts 1 and 2 and on the crossbars on Counts 3 and 4.
2. Have the children listen to 4/4 music and clap along. Say to the children: *Clap, clap, snap, snap to music.*
3. Have the students practice 4/4 Pole Striking.

4/4 Tinikling Steps

The students begin with their right sides to the poles.

1. Describe and demonstrate Counts 1 to 4.

     Count 1: Step in place with the left foot.

     Count 2: Hop in place on the left foot.

     Count 3: Step between the poles with the right foot.

     Count 4: Step between the poles with the left foot.

2. Have the students practice Counts 1 to 4 with poles stationary. Say to the students: *Step left, hop left, right in, left in.*

3. Describe and demonstrate Counts 5 to 8.

     Counts 5 and 6: Step out to the right with the right foot and hop.

     Counts 7 and 8: Step between the poles with the left foot and then with the right foot (lift left).

4. Have the students practice Counts 5 to 8 with poles stationary. Say to the students: *Out right, hop, between left, between right.*

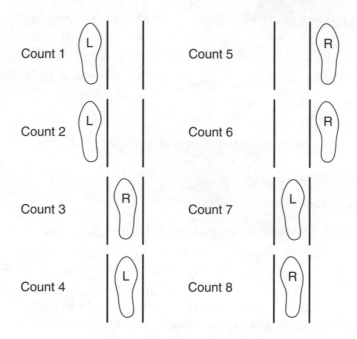

Concluding Activities (5 minutes)

4/4 Tinikling Steps

The students perform the Tinikling Step in 4/4 time to the music while striking the poles.

LESSON 19
TINIKLING

Student Objectives

- Refine Tinikling Steps.
- Advance at least one station during practice.

Equipment

- Record: "Tinikling," Kimbo (KEA 8095, 9015)
- Tinikling poles for six stations
- Tape to mark floor lines

Warm-Up Activities (5 minutes)

Seven Jumps

See Grades 6-8: Rhythmic Activities, Warm-Ups, page 173.

Skill-Development Activities (20 minutes)

Tinikling Stations

Allow each child to select a station, but limit the number at each station to six.

1. Have the children practice and refine Tinikling skills, progressing at their own rates.
2. After a child masters the skills at one station, he or she selects another station.

Diagram of stations

1
Basic step → 2
Simple variations → 3
Formations

6
Routines ← 5
Tinikling step
in 4/4 time ← 4
Complex
variations

Station 1: Basic Tinikling Step
The student will

- perform the Basic Tinikling Step 10 times without a miss, using the lines on the floor;
- strike the Tinikling poles for a dancer to dance through the entire dance;

- perform the Basic Tinikling Step 10 times without a miss; and
- perform the Basic Tinikling Step with a partner.

Station 2: Simple Variations
The student will

- perform Two Steps In 10 times without a miss;
- perform the Straddle Step 10 times without a miss;
- combine one of the above (Two Steps In or Straddle Step) with the Basic Tinikling Step; and
- create a routine using eight Basic Tinikling Steps, eight Two Steps In, and eight Straddle Steps.

When doing the Straddle Step, the student will perform the turning variation five times without a miss.

Station 3: Formations
The student will

- perform the Basic Tinikling Step through two sets of stationary poles in Line Formation without a miss,
- perform the Basic Tinikling Step through two sets of moving poles without a miss, and
- perform the Basic Tinikling Step through four sets of poles in Square Formation without a miss.

Station 4: Complex Variations
The student will

- perform the Two-Foot Step 10 times without a miss,
- perform the Crossover Step 10 times without a miss, and
- combine the Basic Tinikling Step and one complex variation into a routine.

Station 5: Tinikling Step in 4/4 Time
The student will

- strike the poles in 4/4 time for a dancer;
- using the lines on the floor, perform the Tinikling Step in 4/4 time 10 times without a miss; and
- using the Tinikling poles, perform the Tinikling Step in 4/4 time 10 times without a miss.

Station 6: Routines
The student creates a routine using any of the steps already learned.

Concluding Activities

None.

GRADES 6-8 RHYTHMIC ACTIVITIES

LESSON 20
ROPE JUMPING

Student Objectives

- Make progress toward performing variations in double-time footwork using a short rope.

Equipment

- One short jump rope for each child
- Music: Select any good music with a definite beat.

Warm-Up Activities (5 minutes)

Rhythmic Rope Jumping

Arrange the children in scatter formation, each with a jump rope. Play music with a good beat, and allow the children time to practice rhythmic jumping skills using any combination of steps.

Skill-Development Activities (20 minutes)

Arrange the children in scatter formation, each with a short jump rope.

Basic Two-Foot Double Jump

1. Describe and demonstrate the Basic Two-Foot Double Jump: The student jumps on both feet twice for each turn of the rope.

2. Have the students practice the Basic Two-Foot Double Jump.

Basic One-Foot Double Jump

1. Describe and demonstrate the Basic One-Foot Double Jump: The student jumps on one foot twice for each turn of the rope.

2. Have the students practice the Basic One-Foot Double Jump.

Hustle

1. Describe and demonstrate the Hustle.

   - The student runs forward alternating right, left, right, and then kicks with the left foot. This should take two turns of the rope.

   - The student moves backward in the same fashion, beginning on the left foot.

2. Have the students practice the Hustle.

Grapevine

1. Describe and demonstrate the Grapevine: To double-time rhythm, the student steps to the right on the right foot, crosses in back with the left foot, steps to the right on the right foot, and touches the left foot next to the right. The student then repeats the movements, beginning with the left foot.

2. Have the students practice jumping rope using the Grapevine.

Concluding Activities (5 minutes)

Cooperative Rope Routines

Arrange the children in groups of four to six.

1. Ask each group to create a routine, using the Basic Two-Foot Double Jump, the Hustle, and the Grapevine.

2. Each routine created is shared with the class.

GRADES 6-8 RHYTHMIC ACTIVITIES

LESSON 21
ROPE JUMPING

Student Objectives

- Make progress toward performing variations in single-time footwork using a short rope.

Equipment

- One short jump rope for each child
- Music for rope jumping

Warm-Up Activities (5 minutes)

Rhythmic Rope Jumping

See Grades 6-8: Rhythmic Activities, Warm-Ups, page 172.

Skill-Development Activities (20 minutes)

Arrange the children in scatter formation, each with a short jump rope.

Hustle and Grapevine

See Grades 6-8: Rhythmic Activities, Lesson 20, pages 215 and 216.

Two-Foot Singles

1. Describe and demonstrate Two-Foot Singles: The student jumps one time on both feet for each turn of the rope.
2. Have the students practice Two-Foot Singles.

One-Foot Singles

1. Describe and demonstrate One-Foot Singles: The student jumps one time on one foot for each turn of the rope.
2. Have the students practice One-Foot Singles.

Single-Time Straddle

1. Describe and demonstrate the Single-Time Straddle: The feet move apart to the sides and then together. There must be one turn of the rope for feet apart and one turn for feet together.
2. Have the students practice the Single-Time Straddle. Say to the students: *Apart, together, apart, together.*

Scissors

1. Describe and demonstrate the Scissors: The feet move alternately forward and back, one foot forward and the other foot back; and the landing is with weight evenly distributed on the balls of the feet.

2. Have the students practice the Scissors. Say to the students: *Front, back, front, back.*

Schottische

Describe and demonstrate Schottische: This step consists of three steps and a hop. There must be one turn of the rope for each step and hop. Say to the students: *Step, step, step, hop.*

Concluding Activities (5 minutes)

Cooperative Rope Routines

Arrange the children in groups of four to six. Ask each group to combine the basic single jump with any of the variations for a short routine.

RHYTHMIC ACTIVITIES

LESSON 22
ROPE JUMPING

Student Objectives

- Make progress toward being able to perform Side Hits and the Swing Turn.

Equipment

- One short jump rope for each child
- Music for rope jumping

Warm-Up Activities (5 minutes)

Rhythmic Rope Jumping

Arrange the children in scatter formation. The students practice any of the skills learned previously. See Grades 6-8: Rhythmic Activities, Warm-Ups, page 172.

Skill-Development Activities (20 minutes)

Arrange the children in scatter formation, each with a short jump rope.

Scissors and Schottische

See Grades 6-8: Rhythmic Activities, Lesson 21, page 218.

Side Hits

1. Describe and demonstrate Side Hits: The rope strikes the floor directly to the side, alternating sides with each strike.
2. Have the students practice Side Hits.

Swing Turn

1. Describe and demonstrate the Swing Turn.
   - The student jumps two times (Counts 1 and 2), swings the rope to the left side on Count 3 while turning a half turn to the left, and jumps rope backward on Count 4.
   - The student then starts again with two jumps backward (Counts 1 and 2), a swing of the rope to the left on Count 3 while turning a half turn to the left, and a jump forward on Count 4.
2. Have the students practice the Swing Turn.

Cooperative Rope Routines

Arrange the children in groups of four to six. Ask each group to combine Side Hits and Swing Turns with two other steps in a routine.

G R A D E S 6-8 RHYTHMIC ACTIVITIES

LESSON 23
ROPE JUMPING

Student Objectives

- Make progress toward being able to perform the Double Under and the 360 Turn.

Equipment

- One short jump rope for each child
- Music for rope jumping

Warm-Up Activities (5 minutes)

Rhythmic Rope Jumping

See Grades 6-8: Rhythmic Activities, Warm-Ups, page 172.

Skill-Development Activities (20 minutes)

Arrange the children in scatter formation, each with a short jump rope.

Side Hits and Swing Turns

See Grades 6-8: Rhythmic Activities, Lesson 22, page 219.

Double Under

1. Describe and demonstrate the Double Under: The rope is turned twice under the feet during one jump.
2. Have the students practice the Double Under.

360 Turn

1. Describe and demonstrate the 360 Turn: The student jumps forward, hits the rope to the floor on the right side, makes a half turn to the left, jumps backward, makes a half turn to the left, and jumps forward.
2. Have the children practice the 360 Turn.

Concluding Activities (5 minutes)

Double Under and 360 Turn

Arrange the children in scatter formation, each with a short jump rope.

1. The students perform the Double Under and the 360 Turn to music.
2. Have the children each make a routine using Singles, with the Double Under inserted occasionally; and then vary the routine to include the 360 Turn.

LESSON 24
ROPE JUMPING

Student Objectives

- Work toward refining rope jumping skills.

Equipment

- One short jump rope for each student
- Music for rope jumping

Warm-Up Activities (5 minutes)

Rhythmic Rope Jumping

See Grades 6-8: Rhythmic Activities, Warm-Ups, page 172.

Skill-Development Activities (20 minutes)

Rope Skill Stations

Allow each student to select one of the following stations. After mastering the skills at one station, the student can move to another station. For descriptions of the Rock Step, Ski Twist, and Arm Crosses, see *Physical Education for Children: Daily Lesson Plans for Elementary School*, Second Edition—Grades 4-5: Rhythmic Activities, Lessons 10, 13, and 14, respectively.

Station 1: Basic Jumps—Double Rhythm
Using a double-jump rhythm, the student will

- jump forward 10 times,
- jump backward 10 times,
- jump forward with the Rock Step 10 times,
- jump using the Ski Twist 10 times, and
- jump using the Straddle Step 10 times.

Station 2: Basic Jumps—Single Rhythm
Using a single-jump rhythm, the student will

- perform 10 Reverse Toe Taps,
- perform 10 Heel-Toe Steps,
- perform 10 Side Hits, and
- perform 10 Double Side Hits.

Station 3: Intermediate Jumps—Double Rhythm

Using a double-jump rhythm, the student will

- perform 20 Hustle steps;
- perform 20 Grapevine steps; and
- combine 10 Rock steps, 10 Ski Twists, 10 Hustle steps, and 10 Grapevine steps.

Station 4: Intermediate Jumps—Single Rhythm

Using a single-jump rhythm, the student will

- perform 20 Scissors;
- perform 20 Schottische steps; and
- combine 10 Two-Foot Singles, 10 Arm Crosses, 10 Scissors, and 10 Schottische.

Station 5: Advanced Jumps—Single Rhythm

Using a single-jump rhythm, the student will

- perform 10 Swing Turns,
- perform three Double Unders, and
- perform five 360 Turns.

Station 6: Routines

The student creates a routine using any of the steps already learned.

Concluding Activities (5 minutes)

Rope Jumping Routines

Choose one of the following routines, and have the students perform the movements to music.

Basic Routine (Single-Jump Rhythm)

Two-Foot Basic Step (8 counts)

Alternate Foot Step (8 counts)

Toe Taps (8 counts)

Side Hits (8 counts)

Repeat from the beginning.

Intermediate Routine (Single-Jump Rhythm)

Two-Foot Basic Jump (8 counts)

Double Side Hits (8 counts)

Scissors (8 counts)

Swing Turn (8 counts)

Repeat from the beginning.

Advanced Routine (Single-Jump Rhythm)

Two-Foot Basic Step (8 counts)

Side Hits (8 counts)

Swing Turn (8 counts)

Two-Foot Basic Step (8 counts)

Schottische (16 counts)
360 Turn (8 counts)
Two-Foot Basic Step (8 counts)

GRADES 6-8

GYMNASTICS

The goal of the gymnastics program is to develop the skills of traditional and creative activities by exploring movement alone, with a partner, and in relationship to apparatus and small equipment. At this level tumbling and balance stunts are refined and combined into creative routines. Basic jumps, rolls, and partner support activities are presented from simple to complex, with the more difficult movements building upon the lower level activities. Through gymnastics, students can gain confidence in their bodies by developing strength, flexibility, balance, and coordination.

UNIT ORGANIZATION

The 24 lessons in this section are sequenced from simple to complex and allow students to participate in a wide variety of challenging movement tasks. Early in the unit, time is provided for review and practice on balances, splits, and jumps. The more advanced stunts, such as the Handstand and Handstand variations, require a considerable amount of balance and strength; they may need spotting. For these more difficult exercises, a description of the spotting technique is included. The students practice floor exercise routines and are asked to develop their own routines as well. A series of partner support stunts are included; in two lessons students create a routine of partner and group stunts. Finally, activities with small and large apparatus offer a variety of challenging activities for this age group.

LESSON DESCRIPTIONS

The gymnastics warm-up section describes a routine that can be used over the entire unit. It includes 11 different exercises designed to develop strength, muscular endurance, flexibility, agility, and coordination. Lesson 1 is devoted to the review of the Forward Roll, the Backward Roll, and several variations of each. Cooperative learning groups are used for practice. Lesson 2 continues with the review and practice of balances, splits, and jumps that have been learned at lower grade levels. Students are asked to combine three different movements into a sequence. The Handstand, Handstand variations, and the Cartwheel are presented in Lesson 3. This lesson also describes the technique for Handstand spotting.

In Lesson 4, time is spent refining and improving technique for the basic rolls, balances, jumps, and splits. Lessons 5 through 8 focus on basic tumbling skills in a Floor Exercise Routine. The concepts of passes and fillers are introduced in these lessons. In Lessons 9 through 12, students are asked to invent a routine that contains tumbling, balances, strength skills, and a variety of locomotor skills. The routine is expected to cover the entire floor area and reflect changes in tempo. Lesson 13 is devoted to partner stunts; each student is matched to a partner of equal size and practices stunts such as the Flying Angel, Double Roll, and Partner Flip. More advanced partner stunts are offered in Lesson 14. In Lessons 15 and 16, the students create a routine that includes partner or small-group stunts.

Lessons 17 through 20 focus on creative movements with hoops, balls, and streamers. In Lessons 19 and 20 students create a routine using one or more pieces of small equipment. Lessons 21 through 24 describe activities for ladders, beams, vaults, and ropes. Lesson 21 offers opportunities for practice on the large equipment in a station formation, and Lessons 22 through 24 introduce routines for each piece of equipment.

TEACHING TIPS AND LESSON MODIFICATIONS

In gymnastics, students must have sufficient time to refine traditional tumbling skills and balance stunts before they can become competent at more advanced levels. It is important for the teacher to make certain that students are practicing at a level that is within the limits of their abilities. For some students remedial work on the more basic skills will be needed. Never allow students to perform gymnastics activities beyond their capabilities. Variations in rolls, for example, should not be attempted until the basic Forward Roll is mastered. It is important to stress to the students that the gymnastics program is not meant to be competitive. The goal is for students to progress at their own rates and move to more difficult skills only when a level of proficiency is gained at the basic level.

Throughout the entire unit, emphasize refining the quality of movement. Many times students are not motivated to persist at an activity long enough to develop the expected level of competency. One way to encourage students to concentrate on quality and control is to offer opportunities for variations and adaptations. Ask students to generate new ideas, and always allow enough time for experimentation and exploration. Offer many opportunities for students to create novel movement sequences, and encourage students to demonstrate their routines.

After the initial demonstration of a stunt or skill, reinforce the critical elements of the movement during practice. Emphasize the importance of starting and finishing positions, as well as smooth transitions between the separate skills in a sequence or routine. During cooperative learning sessions, encourage students to analyze the movement quality of their peers and offer feedback to improve performance.

SAFETY ISSUES

Students should be made aware of safety requirements related to gymnastics activities. Remind students to work at their own rates and never attempt stunts they do not feel comfortable with. In many stunts a spotter is needed, and these stunts should never be practiced alone. Always ensure that there is a student to act as a spotter; this person should be of similar physical size. Teachers must instruct the students how to spot; they must make sure students understand how to assist and support others before attempting skills that could result in injury.

There must be clearly established rules for the students to follow during practice. For example, practice should occur only on the mats, and for most activities only one student at a time should be allowed on the mat. Students must understand about taking turns and using the equipment only as it is intended. Arrange the mats or apparatus to allow sufficient space for individual or group practice, and ensure that students stay in the designated practice areas.

Check all apparatus and small equipment often, making sure it is in good condition and safe. Ensure that the floor is free of glass, splinters, and other hazards.

Table G4.1: Unit Plan for Grades 6-8: Gymnastics

Week 9: tumbling	Week 10: tumbling	Week 20: partner stunts
Monday: warm-up, rolls, variations Tuesday: warm-up, splits, balances, jumps Wednesday: warm-up, handstand, variations, cartwheel Thursday: warm-up, practice Friday: warm-up, practice	Monday: warm-up, floor exercise routine Tuesday: warm-up, floor exercise routine Wednesday: warm-up, floor exercise routine Thursday: warm-up, free routines Friday: warm-up, routine practice	Monday: warm-up, partner stunts Tuesday: warm-up, partner stunts Wednesday: warm-up, partner stunts Thursday: warm-up, partner stunts Friday: warm-up, partner stunts
Week 21: partner stunts	**Week 27: small equipment**	**Week 28: large equipment**
Monday: warm-up, partner stunts Tuesday: warm-up, partner stunts Wednesday: warm-up, partner stunts Thursday: warm-up, stunt routines Friday: warm-up, stunt routines	Monday: warm-up, hoops, balls, and streamers Tuesday: warm-up, hoops, balls, and streamers Wednesday: warm-up, hoops, balls, and streamers Thursday: warm-up, routines Friday: warm-up, routines	Monday: warm-up, ladder, beam, vault, and ropes Tuesday: warm-up, ladder, beam, vault, and ropes Wednesday: warm-up, ladder, beam, vault, and ropes Thursday: warm-up, routines Friday: warm-up, routines

Note: This table provides an example of a way to organize the gymnastics unit. Feel free to use this plan or devise one of your own.

WARM-UPS

Arrange the children in a long line at the edge of the mats, which should be laid out end to end.

Back Arch

Lying on the stomach with arms and legs extended, the student moves the head back as far as possible until the chest lifts off the floor, being sure to keep legs together; the student then return to starting position. Repeat five times.

Back Push-Ups

Lying on the back with hands under the shoulders and feet close to the seat, the student pushes with the arms until the back is as high off the floor as possible. If necessary, hands and feet should be walked in toward each other.

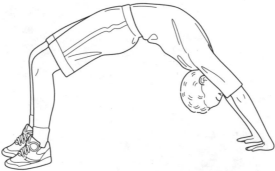

Dorsal Back-Curl

Lying on the stomach with arms and legs extended, the student lifts the arms, head, and chest off the ground while lifting the legs off the ground. The exercise should be repeated 30 times, with a rest after each 10, if necessary.

Pike Stretch

Sitting with the legs straight ahead and together with toes pointed, the student grasps the ankles (or calves) and pulls the body gently down and forward keeping the back straight, sits up, flexes the ankles (points toes toward face), and then reaches for the toes with the arms (keeping the back straight). The entire exercise should be repeated 10 times.

Push-Ups

The student begins with as many Push-Ups as possible in one minute, trying for 25 at first and then increasing.

Run and Skip

The student runs and skips for two minutes, alternating and changing directions on command. The student should lift the body as high as possible off the ground. The arms should have an exaggerated swing on the skipping; this helps to lift the body.

Single-Leg Stretch

Sitting cross-legged, the student grasps the inside of the right foot with the right hand and straightens the right leg upward, using the left hand to help balance if necessary, and then repeats the exercise with the left foot. The entire exercise should be done five times.

Sit-Ups

The student does regular Bent Knee Sit-Ups with arms crossed on the chest.

Straddle Stretch

Sitting on the floor with legs spread and the insides of the legs pointed toward the sky (or ceiling), the student reaches both arms forward to the toes of one foot, sits up straight, and then reaches for the other foot. The student should repeat this 10 times, trying to get the chest to the knee.

Torso Stretch

Standing with feet shoulder width apart and arms extended overhead, the student reaches as far left as possible, returns to straight, then leans right, center, front (keeping the back straight), center, and back. The entire exercise should be repeated 10 times.

V Sit-Ups

Lying on the back on the floor with arms and legs extended, the student lifts legs, arms, and upper body off the mat to meet in the air and then returns to starting position. The exercise should be repeated 10 times.

Stretching Warm-Up Routine

Straddle Stretch (repeat 10 times)

Pike Stretch (repeat 10 times)

Single-Leg Stretch (repeat 5 right and 5 left)

Back Arch (repeat 5 times)

Back Push-Ups (repeat 10 times)

Torso Stretch (repeat 10 times)

Endurance Conditioning Warm-Up Routine

Dorsal Back-Curl (repeat 30 times, resting after each 10, if necessary)

V Sit-Ups (repeat 10 times)

Push-Ups (repeat as many times as possible in one minute; 25 = good)

Sit-Ups (repeat 30 times)

Run and Skip (repeat one minute each)

LESSON 1
TUMBLING REVIEW

Student Objectives

- Review and practice Forward and Backward Rolls and variations of rolls.
- Work in a cooperative learning group to improve their own technique and that of others in the group.

Equipment

- Six or more mats (four by eight feet)

Warm-Up Activities (7 to 10 minutes)

Arrange the children in a long line at the edge of the mats, which should be laid out end to end.

1. Do the stretching components of the Warm-Ups.
2. Do the endurance components of the Warm-Ups.

Skill-Development Activities (15 to 18 minutes)

Rules

Arrange the children in information formation.

1. Read the rules to the children.
   - Rule 1: *Only one person is allowed on the mat or equipment at a time.*
   - Rule 2: *Use a spotter for new or difficult skills.*
   - Rule 3: *Practice only on the mats.*
   - Rule 4: *Always warm up before working out.*
   - Rule 5: *Do not talk when the teacher talks.*
   - Rule 6: *Wait quietly for your turn.*
2. Ask if the children have questions.

Forward Roll

Arrange the children in small groups of five or six, with one group at each mat.

1. Describe and demonstrate the Forward Roll.
   - Bending forward and placing hands on the mat shoulder distance apart, the student looks at the stomach and bends arms to accept increasing amounts of body weight while the legs decrease support.

- As the center of gravity moves forward, the body overbalances and rolls forward with the impact on the shoulder blades. The body continues to roll in a curved position.
- The legs bend at the knees and accept weight as the shoulders leave the mat.
- The student returns to standing position with arms extended overhead.

2. Review guidelines for cooperative learning.

   Each student is responsible for his or her own work and the work of other students in the group. The group is not successful unless all students accomplish the goal.

   Students must observe and help each other.

   Each student must try hard.

3. In cooperative learning groups, have the students practice the Forward Roll until they each get at least two tries.

Backward Roll

1. Describe and demonstrate the Backward Roll.
   - Standing with arms extended overhead and the back toward the length of the mat, the student bends the legs to a squat position while moving the hands to the shoulders (palms up) and the chin to the chest and overbalances backward to begin the roll, remaining in a tuck position.
   - As the hands contact the mat, they should push to lift the body (hips, legs, and torso) over the head. The head and neck should not support weight and should touch the mat as little as possible.
   - As the feet contact the mat, the arms straighten until the weight is supported by the feet.
   - The student ends by standing with arms extended overhead.

2. In cooperative learning groups, have the children practice the Backward Roll until they each get at least two tries.

Forward Roll Straddle

1. Describe and demonstrate the Forward Roll Straddle. This is actually two consecutive rolls.

   - Beginning in closed standing position with arms extended above the head, legs straight, and feet together, the student bends forward and places hands on the mat shoulder distance apart, looks at the stomach, and bends arms to accept increasing amounts of body weight while the legs decrease support.

   - As the center of gravity moves forward, the body overbalances and rolls forward with the impact on the shoulder blades. The body continues to roll in a curved position. The legs are straight and spread apart in straddle position.

   - For the first roll, the landing is on the legs with the feet spread, body bent slightly forward, and arms extended forward.

   - The second roll begins immediately from this straddle position (there is no hesitation), with the head tucking under.

- The body continues forward with a shoulder-blade landing. The recovery is with feet closed, as in the regular Forward Roll. The student ends in the original standing position.

2. In cooperative learning groups, have the students practice the Forward Roll Straddle until they each get at least two tries.

Forward Roll Pike

1. Describe and demonstrate the Forward Roll Pike: Standing with legs straight and feet together (closed position), the student rolls, finishing in the sitting position with legs extended forward and never bending the legs.

2. In cooperative learning groups, have the students practice the Forward Roll Pike until each gets at least two tries.

Donkey Kick

1. Describe and demonstrate the Donkey Kick: With hands on the mat shoulder distance apart, the student kicks both feet up and back, momentarily supporting weight on the hands, and lands on the feet.

2. In cooperative learning groups, have the children practice the Donkey Kick until each gets at least two tries.

Diving Forward Roll

1. Describe and demonstrate the Diving Forward Roll.

   - This is a variation of the Forward Roll. The roll begins with a jump (or a run and jump), going immediately into the Forward Roll (catching the weight on the arms).

   - At first the student puts his or her hands on the mat and jumps to a Donkey Kick to begin the roll (rather than moving to the squat that usually starts the roll).

   - With practice, the jump can occur before the hands make contact.

2. In cooperative learning groups, have the students practice the Diving Forward Roll until each gets at least two tries.

Backward Roll Straddle

1. Describe and demonstrate the Backward Roll Straddle.

   - The roll begins in a straddle balance position. The hands move between the legs as the torso moves forward to lower the body.

   - The hips move back and down until the seat touches the mat.

   - The body immediately rolls backward while the legs remain in the straddle position. The recovery is to the straddle balance position.

2. In cooperative learning groups, have the students practice the Backward Roll Straddle until each gets at least two tries.

Backward Roll Pike

1. Describe and demonstrate the Backward Roll Pike.

    - Beginning in a sitting position with the legs straight and feet together, the student reaches forward to the toes and, using momentum, rolls backward, keeping the legs straight. This requires strength and flexibility.

    - The finish is done by pushing up to standing position (never bending the knees).

2. In cooperative learning groups, have the students practice the Backward Roll Pike until each gets at least two tries.

Shoulder Roll

1. Describe and demonstrate the Shoulder Roll.

    - Sitting with the back to the length of the mat and legs extended to the front, the student reaches forward to the toes and, using momentum, rolls backward immediately, turning the head to the side.

    - The leg opposite the direction of the head turn bends at the knee. The knee is placed on the mat near the back of the head and as close as possible to the shoulder. Weight is supported by the hands and one knee, with the other leg extended.

2. In cooperative learning groups, have the students practice the Shoulder Roll until each gets at least two tries.

Concluding Activities (5 minutes)

Activity Practice

Tell the children: *Practice the activity that was most difficult for you.*

GYMNASTICS

LESSON 2
TUMBLING REVIEW

Student Objectives

- Review and practice balances, splits, and jumps.
- Work in a cooperative learning group to improve their own technique and that of others in the group.

Equipment

- Six or more mats (four by eight feet)

Warm-Up Activities (5 to 7 minutes)

Warm-Up Routine

See Grades 6-8: Gymnastics, Warm-Ups, page 231.

Skill-Development Activities (18 to 20 minutes)

Arrange the children in small groups and assign each group to one of the mats.

Straddle Splits

1. Describe and demonstrate Straddle Splits.
   - In a standing position, with legs straight and shoulder distance apart, the student slowly lowers the body as the feet move farther from the midline.
   - The object is to get the legs as close to parallel to the ground as possible.
2. In cooperative learning groups, have the students practice Straddle Splits until each student gets at least two tries.

Front Splits

1. Describe and demonstrate Front Splits.

   - Beginning with one leg pointing forward (toes straight ahead) and the other turned out and to the rear (inside arch is pointing forward), the student slowly lowers the body as the legs move apart.

   - The object is to get the legs parallel to the ground.

2. In cooperative learning groups, have the students practice Front Splits until each student gets at least two tries.

Arabesque

1. Describe and demonstrate the Arabesque.

   - Standing on one foot, the student lowers the torso forward and down, keeping the back straight, while the nonsupporting leg rises to a position parallel to the ground.

   - The torso stops approximately parallel to the ground.

   - The arms are extended to the side so the thumbs are even with the face. (Variation: The arm on the side of the nonsupporting leg is held back near the hip, and the arm on the side of the supporting leg is held forward in front of the face.)

   - Balance should be maintained for 2 to 10 seconds.

2. In cooperative learning groups, have the students practice the Arabesque until each student gets at least two tries.

Needle Scale

1. Describe and demonstrate the Needle Scale.

   - The object is to stand on one foot and, grasping the supporting ankle, get as close as possible to a split position.

   - Beginning in a scale (Arabesque), the student balances on one leg with the other leg extended to the rear, keeps the arms close to the sides, bends the torso, grasps the ankle as the nonsupporting leg is lifted as high as possible into the air, balances, and then recovers by reversing the process.

2. In cooperative learning groups, have the children practice the Needle Scale until each student gets at least two tries.

Knee Scale

1. Describe and demonstrate the Knee Scale: The child begins on all fours, with knees together and hands about four inches apart. He or she extends one leg to the rear with the toes pointed, lifting the leg as high as possible and looking forward. The student uses the hands and one knee to support the torso parallel to the floor.

2. In cooperative learning groups, have the children practice the Knee Scale until each student gets at least two tries.

Heel Slap

1. Describe and demonstrate the Heel Slap.

   - The student jumps up from both feet, reaches back with the arms, and lifts the feet toward the seat.

   - The object is to touch the heels with the hands just under the seat and then land on both feet.

2. In cooperative learning groups, have the students practice the Heel Slap until each student gets at least two tries.

C-Jump

1. Describe and demonstrate the C-Jump: The student jumps high, curving the back, bending the legs, and extending the head and arms back, trying to touch the feet to the head.

2. In cooperative learning groups, have the students practice the C-Jump until each student gets at least two tries.

Toe Touch

1. Describe and demonstrate the Toe Touch: Beginning standing, the student jumps up, lifting the legs parallel with the ground in straddle position (with the feet as far apart as possible), and reaches for the toes with the hands, keeping the head high and looking straight ahead.

2. In cooperative learning groups, have the children practice the Toe Touch until each student gets at least two tries.

Run and Leap

1. Describe and demonstrate the Run and Leap: The student takes several small steps (running) and then a long exaggerated one, which is the leap, and continues with several steps, another Leap, and so on.

2. In cooperative learning groups, have the children practice the Run and Leap.

Run and Jump

1. Describe and demonstrate the Run and Jump.

   - The student begins running and then takes off (jumps) from one foot, landing on two feet. The jump can be for height or distance.

   - If the purpose is height, the angle of takeoff is steep, and the arms move straight overhead.

   - If the purpose is distance, the takeoff is low, and the arms reach toward the landing target.

2. Have the students practice the Run and Jump in cooperative learning groups.

Concluding Activities (5 minutes)

Skill Combinations

Ask each student to perform the following combinations:

- One jump, one scale, and one roll
- One arm balance, one roll, and one scale

GYMNASTICS

LESSON 3
TUMBLING

Student Objectives

- Review and practice the Handstand, Handstand variations, and the Cartwheel.
- Work in a cooperative learning group to improve their own technique and that of others in the group.

Equipment

- Six or more mats (four by eight feet)

Warm-Up Activities (5 to 7 minutes)

Warm-Up Routine

See Grades 6-8: Gymnastics, Warm-Ups, page 231.

Skill-Development Activities (18 to 20 minutes)

Handstand

Arrange the children in small groups and assign each group to a mat.

1. Describe and demonstrate the Handstand.
   - The arms support weight with hands shoulder distance apart on the mat.
   - Beginning in a standing position with arms overhead and one leg extended forward (this will be the support leg), the student steps forward on the support leg, reaching for the mat with the arms, and lowers the torso, keeping the body in a straight line (similar to performing the scale) with the nonsupporting leg.
   - When the arms are supporting the weight, the supporting leg kicks upward until the entire body forms a straight line. Important: The back should not have a large arch, and the legs should be lifted as high as possible to eliminate much of the arch.
2. In cooperative learning groups, have the children practice the Handstand until each student gets at least two tries. Use spotting if necessary.

Handstand Spotting

Spotting is done best from the side with one hand toward the child's back, providing support under the shoulder to protect the child's head in case his or her arms "give out," and the other arm on the front of the thigh to facilitate balance.

Handstand Forward Roll

1. Describe and demonstrate the Handstand Forward Roll.

   - This is an extension of the Handstand, with the extension beginning when balance is achieved.
   - The roll begins by tucking the head (looking at the ceiling or sky, with chin on chest) and slightly bending the arms.
   - The arms gradually bend until the shoulder blades touch the mat. From here the movement proceeds just like a Forward Roll to a standing position.

2. In cooperative learning groups, have the children practice the Handstand Forward Roll until each student gets at least two tries. Use spotting if necessary.

Cartwheel

1. Describe and demonstrate the Cartwheel.

   - The cartwheel is a side entry and exit to the Handstand, and it should not be attempted by anyone who cannot do the Handstand without help.
   - Beginning with the side facing the length of the mat, arms extended overhead, weight on the back foot (away from the movement), and the front foot pointed, the student turns the head and looks at a spot on the mat several inches in front of the extended toe and steps on that foot as the other foot leaves the mat.
   - The arms continue to move down until the front hand touches the mat and supports the weight; as the other hand makes contact with the mat, both feet should be in the air, with visual focus on the mat between the hands.
   - The feet continue to move overhead until a Handstand (with legs in a straddle) is achieved. (The legs should be straight.) The legs continue over the body and to the mat. The sequence is hand, hand, foot, foot, with only two body parts on the mat at one time.

2. In cooperative learning groups, have the students practice the Cartwheel until each
   student gets at least two tries. Use spotting if necessary.

Backward Roll Extension

1. Describe and demonstrate the Backward Roll Extension.

    *   The roll begins as a regular Backward Roll.
    *   When the hips are directly over the head, the arms push up to extension, the legs straighten, and the body is in a momentary Handstand.
    *   The feet then drop to the mat, and the body returns to a standing position.

2. Have the children practice the Backward Roll Extension in cooperative learning groups.

Split Handstand

1. Describe and demonstrate the Split Handstand: On entry to the Handstand, the lead leg is allowed to continue movement, but the supporting leg is not raised to vertical. The critical part is to have the legs split evenly front and back.

2. In cooperative learning groups, have the children practice the Split Handstand until each student gets at least two tries.

Arabian Handstand

1. Describe and demonstrate the Arabian Handstand: The student assumes a Split Handstand position and then bends both knees.

2. In cooperative learning groups, have the children practice the Arabian Handstand until each student gets at least two tries.

Yogi Handstand

1. Describe and demonstrate the Yogi Handstand: Once into a regular handstand, the student inverts the hips so that the feet are visible to the front and the hips are overhead.

2. In cooperative learning groups, have the students practice the Yogi Handstand.

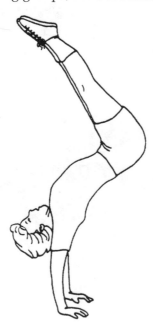

Concluding Activities (5 minutes)

Follow the Leader

The students at each mat select a leader.

1. The leader can select any skill already introduced and practiced.
2. The other students in the group perform the skill selected.

LESSON 4
TUMBLING

Student Objectives

- Work in a cooperative learning group to improve their own technique and that of others in the group.
- Practice a variety of tumbling skills.

Equipment

- Six or more mats (four by eight feet)

Warm-Up Activities (5 to 7 minutes)

Warm-Up Routine

See Grades 6-8: Gymnastics, Warm-Ups, page 231.

Skill-Development Activities (18 to 20 minutes)

Skills Practice Stations

Arrange the children in cooperative learning groups at the individual mats. Challenge the children to practice skills from each of the following four categories:

Balance skills: Handstand, Scales

Tumbling skills: Rolls, Cartwheel

Jumps and leaps

Splits

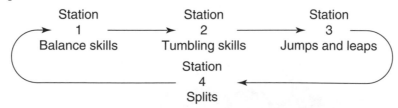

Concluding Activities (7 to 10 minutes)

Skills Demonstrations

Select one skill from each category and ask the children to demonstrate it.

LESSON 5
TUMBLING ROUTINE

Student Objectives

- Demonstrate basic tumbling skills.

Equipment

- Six or more mats (four by eight feet)

Warm-Up Activities (5 to 7 minutes)

Warm-Up Routine

See Grades 6-8: Gymnastics, Warm-Ups, page 231.

Skill-Development Activities (18 to 20 minutes)

Floor Exercise

Arrange the children around two mats that are placed end to end.

1. Explain the pass to the children: *A pass is several tumbling skills grouped together. A floor exercise routine has several passes, with other activities between the passes.*

2. Explain the filler to the children: *Fillers are strength, flexibility, and dance moves that go between tumbling passes.*

Floor Exercise Routine

Pass 1
Run, to takeoff, to a Round-Off, to jump and turn, to a Diving Forward Roll. Have the children practice Pass 1.

Filler 1
Scale facing forward, to turn and split, to roll with legs together into a Pike Position, to Backward Roll Pike, to standing position. Have the children practice Filler 1.

Pass 2
Cartwheel, to half turn Backward Roll Extension, to Backward Roll Straddle, to standing position. Have the children practice Pass 2.

Filler 2
C-Jump, to Forward Roll Pike, to Shoulder Roll, to Knee Scale, to a stand. Have the children practice Filler 2.

Pass Three

Skip and takeoff, to a Round-Off, to Backward Roll, to half turn, to Handstand, to Forward Roll, to a stand. Have the children practice Pass Three.

Concluding Activities (5 minutes)

Floor Exercise Description

Arrange the children in information formation. Ask the children if they can define the following terms and then provide them with the definitions.

Floor Exercises: This is an Olympic and AAU Gymnastics event for both men and women; it combines tumbling, balance, and strength movements (and, for women, dance) into routines set to music.

Compulsory Routines: These are required routines made up by a panel of experts and learned by the gymnasts. These routines allow all the gymnasts to be compared to each other on the same skills.

Free Routines: These are original routines, composed for the individual performer, so gymnasts can show off their creativity and individual strengths.

Judging for Scores: Routines are rated for difficulty (how hard the stunts are) and execution (how well the individual performed the stunts). The top score is 10.

LESSONS 6 TO 8
TUMBLING ROUTINE

Student Objectives

- Practice a Floor Exercise Routine.

Equipment

- Six or more mats (four by eight feet)

Warm-Up Activities (5 to 7 minutes)

Warm-Up Routine

See Grades 6-8: Gymnastics, Warm-Ups, page 231.

Skill-Development Activities (18 to 20 minutes)

Grades 6-8 Floor Exercise Routine

Arrange the mats in formation for the floor exercise routine. Arrange the children in five groups, and assign each group to one of the three passes or two fillers.

Pass 1

This pass begins in corner A and goes to corner C: Run, to takeoff, to Round-Off, to jump and turn, to Diving Forward Roll.

Filler 1

Scale facing corner C, to turn to face B and split, to roll with legs together into a Pike Position, to Backward Roll Pike, to a stand.

Pass 2

This pass goes to corner B: Cartwheel, to half turn Backward Roll Extension, to Backward Roll Straddle, to a stand facing C.

Filler 2

C-Jump, to Forward Roll Pike, to Shoulder Roll, to Knee Scale (still facing C), to a stand.

Pass 3

This pass goes to D: Skip to takeoff, to Round-Off, to Backward Roll, to half turn to Handstand, to Forward Roll, to a stand.

1. Remind the children of the parts of the routine by having one person in each group demonstrate each section (filler or pass) after you describe it.
2. Allow all children in each group to practice their parts; then rotate groups to the next section of the routine, so that each child gets to practice the entire routine each day.

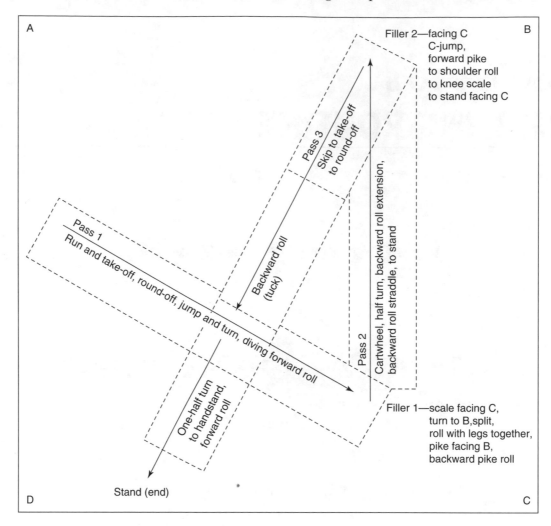

Concluding Activities (5 minutes)

Floor Exercise Routine

Move the mats into floor exercise formation and allow one-third of the children to try the entire routine each day. The other children can watch or practice the following skills:

> Run and Leap
>
> Run and Jump
>
> Skipping forward
>
> Skipping backward
>
> Skip backward, knee turn, skip forward

LESSONS 9 TO 12
CREATIVE GYMNASTICS ROUTINE

Student Objectives

- Develop a Floor Exercise Routine with the following characteristics:

   Covers the entire floor area

   Contains tumbling, balances, strength skills, and a variety of locomotor skills (run, walk, skip, hop, leap)

   Exhibits changes in tempo (contains both fast and slow movements, and pauses)

Equipment

- Six or more mats (four by eight feet)

Warm-Up Activities (5 to 7 minutes)

Warm-Up Routine

See Grades 6-8: Gymnastics, Warm-Ups, page 231.

Skill-Development Activities (18 to 20 minutes)

Free Routines

Arrange the mats in pairs end to end.

1. Describe the three characteristics the routines must have:

   Cover the floor area (all four corners and the middle).

   Include changes of tempo (slow and fast movements, and pauses).

   Include tumbling (Roll, Cartwheel, Round-Off), balances (Handstand, Scale, Split), strength (Handstand, Backward Roll Extension), and a variety of locomotor skills.

2. Allow 15 minutes for students to work on creative routines.

Concluding Activities (5 minutes)

Routine Practice

1. Encourage the children to seek help from other students or from you as they design their routines. Establish a pattern for the mats and ask some of the students to practice their whole routine. Students must make their routines fit the established pattern.

2. Ask for volunteers to perform their routines.

LESSON 13
PARTNER STUNTS

Student Objectives

- Perform partner stunts.
- Work cooperatively with a partner.

Equipment

- Six or more mats (four by eight feet)
- Playground balls (one for each pair of students)

Warm-Up Activities (5 to 7 minutes)

Warm-Up Routine

See Grades 6-8: Gymnastics, Warm-Ups, page 231.

Skill-Development Activities (18 to 20 minutes)

Double Roll

1. Describe and demonstrate the Double Roll.
   - Match each child to a partner of equal size, and assign two or three pairs to each mat.
   - One child in each pair lies flat with knees bent. The other child stands near the shoulders of the child lying down, bends, and grasps his or her ankles.
   - The standing partner then begins to do a Forward Roll; this action lifts the partner who was lying down up off the mat. This continues.
2. Have the children practice the Double Roll.

Shoulder Balance

1. Describe and demonstrate the Shoulder Balance.
   - One student (the base) is lying down on back with knees bent.
   - The other student (the top) mounts by standing between the base's knees and leaning, shoulders forward, to the extended arms of the base.
   - The base braces the top's shoulders, and the top holds the base's knees and kicks legs up to a Handstand position.
2. Have the children practice the Shoulder Balance.

Spotting for Shoulder Balance

1. Spotters stand on either side of the base near the base's waist.
2. They guide and balance the top by holding the thighs, being careful not to interfere with the base's grasp.

Side Stand

1. Describe and demonstrate the Side Stand.
   - One partner (the base) assumes the all-fours position, and the other partner (the top) stands at the base's side.
   - The top places both hands under the near side of the base's torso and then lays both arms over the base's back, kicking into an arm support (similar to a Handstand) and balancing.
2. Have the children practice the Side Stand. Use spotting if necessary.

Spotting for Side Stand

1. One spotter stands at the head of the base, the other at the base's feet.
2. The spotters grasp the top's shoulder, giving support, and the top's ankles or thighs, aiding balance.

Back Support

1. Describe and demonstrate the Back Support.

    *   One partner (the base) is lying down with legs straight and extended at a 45-degree angle.
    *   The other partner (the top) stands with his or her back to the base, at the base's feet.
    *   The base puts both feet in the lower back of the top.
    *   The partners grasp hands, and the base lifts the top off the ground. Balance is maintained with the top directly over the base.

2. Have the students practice the Back Support with spotting.

Spotting for the Back Support

The spotters stand on each side of the base, each gently holding a shoulder and thigh of the top.

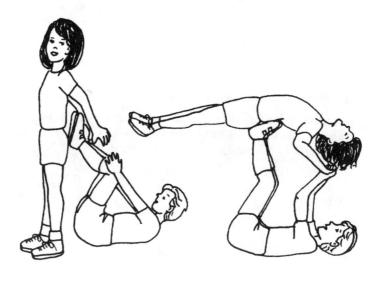

Ball Lift

1. Describe and demonstrate the Ball Lift.

    • Partners lie on the ground facing each other, with a playground ball between and touching their heads.

    • The partners try to stand and do not allow the ball to fall. No hands can be used!

2. Have the children practice the Ball Lift.

Flying Angel

1. Describe and demonstrate Flying Angel.

    • One partner (the base) stands with feet wider than shoulder width apart. Knees should be bent.

    • The other partner (the top) mounts by stepping on the right thigh with the right leg and on the left thigh with the left leg.

    • The base grasps the knees of the top. The top should be standing tall with a slightly arched back while the base is in a semi-squat position.

2. Have the students practice Flying Angel.

Back-To-Back Get-Up

1. Describe and demonstrate the Back-to-Back Get-Up.

   • Standing back-to-back, the partners lock elbows and sit with knees bent and heels close to their seats.

   • The partners push against each other and try to stand, returning to the starting position.

2. Have the students practice Back-to-Back Get-Up, with spotters if necessary.

Partner Flip

1. Describe and demonstrate the Partner Flip.

   • Standing back-to-back with elbows locked, one partner leans forward lifting the other partner off the ground.

   • The lifted person bends legs to the chest and rolls over partner's back to a standing position (partners will now be facing).

2. Have the children practice the Partner Flip with spotting.

Jump Through

Arrange the children in groups of three.

1. Describe and demonstrate the Jump Through.
   - The three children hold hands forming a circle.
   - One child tries to jump over the joined arms of the other two children. All three children lift the jumper's weight. Each person should have a turn.
2. Have the children practice the Jump Through.

Triple Roll

1. Describe and demonstrate the Triple Roll.
   - The three children in each group are in hands-and-knees position, three feet apart from each other. All should be facing the same side of the mat.
   - The middle child begins to roll to the right, and the child to the right hops over the middle child and rolls toward the left child, who jumps to the middle over the rolling child. This continues.
2. Have the students practice the Triple Roll.

Concluding Activities (5 minutes)

Wheelbarrow Relay Race

Assign each child a partner. Push two mats together for a double length. Divide the pairs among the mats for three equal-size teams. Each pair on each team does the Wheelbarrow to the end of the mat, turns, and comes back as quickly as possible in relay sequence.

LESSON 14
PARTNER STUNTS

Student Objectives

- Attempt a new mount for the Back Support.
- Practice small-group stunts.

Equipment

- Six or more mats (four by eight feet)

Safety Tip

- Always use spotters for the Mount to Back Support.

Warm-Up Activities (5 to 7 minutes)

Warm-Up Routine

See Grades 6-8: Gymnastics, Warm-Ups, page 231.

Skill-Development Activities (18 to 20 minutes)

Mount to Back Support

Match children with partners and arrange two or three pairs at each mat.

1. Describe and demonstrate the Mount to Back Support.

   - One partner (the top) does a Handstand near the legs of the other partner (the base).

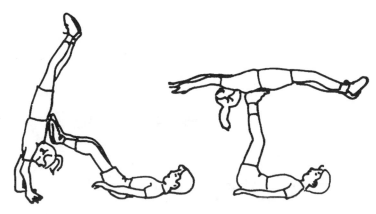

- The base places feet on the back of the top, while the top arches into the Back Support position.
- One spotter stands on each side of the base, reaching for the feet and shoulders of the top.

2. Have the children practice the Mount to Back Support with spotters.

Mount to Front Support

1. Describe and demonstrate the Mount to Front Support.

   - One partner (the base), who is lying flat with legs vertical, places both feet on the hips of the other partner (the top), who is standing near the legs of the base. The partners hold hands.
   - The two partners balance with the top directly over the base. When balance is achieved, they let go of hands.

2. Have the students practice the Mount to Front Support with spotters.

Mount to Front Support Spotting

The spotters stand on each side of the base, guiding the top and holding his or her shoulders and thighs.

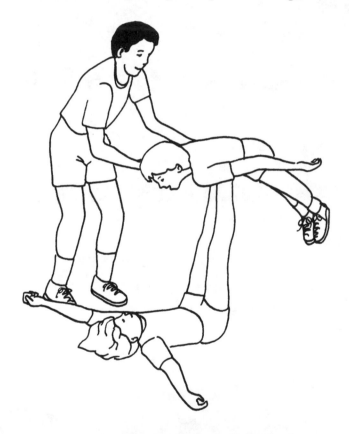

Concluding Activities (5 minutes)

Leapfrog Relay

Divide the children into equal-sized groups; children in each group should be approximately the same size. Arrange each group in a line with about three or four feet between children.

1. All the children in a group squat, using hands for support and balance.

2. On a signal, the last child in each line begins leaping over the other children in the line, one at a time. The leaping is done by putting the hands on the shoulders of the child being leapt over, jumping with legs in a straddle, and landing in front of the base child.

3. After leaping over all children in the line, the leaper squats at the front of the line and prepares to be leapt over.

4. The winner can be determined in two different ways:

   The first group to cover a specified distance (this is easier for the teacher to determine).

   The first group to leap and return to the original order, so the last child is again last in line.

The second method is better if the children in the groups are of greatly different size, where larger children may cover more distance on a leap.

LESSONS 15 AND 16
PARTNER STUNTS

Student Objectives

- Participate in creating a routine of partner and group stunts.

Equipment

- Six or more mats (four by eight feet)

Warm-Up Activities (5 to 7 minutes)

Warm-Up Routine

See Grades 6-8: Gymnastics, Warm-Ups, page 231.

Skill-Development Activities (18 to 20 minutes)

Stunt Routines

Arrange the children in small groups at the mats.

1. Each group creates a routine that includes several partner or small-group stunts.
2. Remind students of the stunts: Flying Angel, Back Support, Side Stand, Triple Roll, Double Roll, Shoulder Balance, Partner Flip, Back-to-Back Get-Up, Jump Through, Front Support, and Ball Lift.
3. The next day, after about 10 minutes of practice, ask if any groups want to demonstrate their routines for the class.
4. Spend the last part of the second day working on the Wave and the Caterpillar.

Wave

The children form a line by the side of the mat, facing the end of the mat.

1. Describe the Wave: The first child does a front fall, the next child follows immediately, and so on, until all the children are lying on the mat.
2. Have the children practice the Wave.

Caterpillar

The children form a long line, holding hands with the persons in front and in back of them. To hold hands they reach between their legs, holding one hand in front and one in back.

1. Describe and demonstrate the Caterpillar.
   - The first person in line does a Forward Roll to the Forward Roll Pike sitting position.
   - While continuing to hold hands, the rest of the children in the line walk over that child and roll as they reach the front of the line.
2. Have the children practice the Caterpillar.

Concluding Activities (5 minutes)

Wave and Caterpillar

Place all the mats in a row, and have all the children perform the Wave and the Caterpillar together.

LESSON 17
HOOPS, BALLS, AND STREAMERS

Student Objectives

- Practice with small equipment.

Equipment

- Six or more mats (four by eight feet)
- One hoop, one playground ball (8 1/2-inch), and one streamer per child

Warm-Up Activities (5 to 7 minutes)

Warm-Up Routine

See Grades 6-8: Gymnastics, Warm-Ups, page 231.

Skill-Development Activities (22 to 24 minutes)

Boomerang

Arrange the children in scatter formation, each with a hoop.

1. Describe and demonstrate the Boomerang: The object is to roll the hoop forward and make it roll back again with backspin. Backspin is achieved by a quick downward thrust by the wrist just before release. The arm is making a rolling motion while the wrist and hand are putting on backspin.

2. Have the students practice the Boomerang.

Run Through

1. Describe and demonstrate the Run Through: With the hoop rolling, the student runs at the same speed as the hoop, parallel to the hoop; and then quickly turns, bends, and runs through the rolling hoop.

2. Have the children practice the Run Through.

Toss and Catch

1. Describe and demonstrate the Toss and Catch: The student tosses the hoop into the air and catches it.

2. Have the students practice the Toss and Catch.

Hula on Body Parts

1. Describe and demonstrate Hula Hooping: The student moves the hoop in a circular motion on various body parts (hips, wrist, ankle, neck, and so on).

2. Have the students practice Hula Hooping.

Figure Eight

Gather the hoops and give each child a streamer.

1. Describe and demonstrate the Figure Eight: The student moves either arm (with the streamer) in a circle on one side of the body, crosses the arm over in front of the body, makes a circle on the other side of the body, and continues this pattern.

2. Have the children practice the Figure Eight.

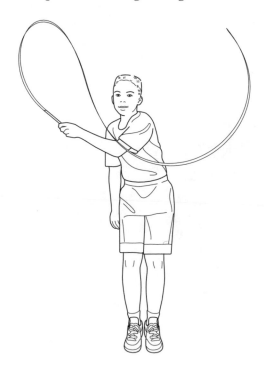

Circles

1. Describe and demonstrate Circles: using the entire arm, the student makes large circles with the streamer overhead, in front, and beside the body.

2. Have the children practice Circles.

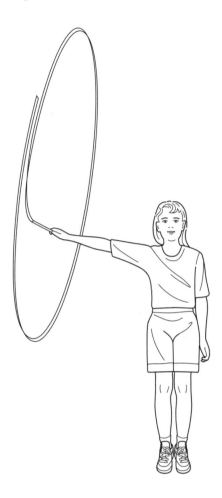

Draggin'

The student turns in a circle with the streamer following and dragging on the ground.

Toss and Catch With Streamer

1. Describe and demonstrate the Toss and Catch: The student throws the streamer into the air and catches the handle as it drifts back down. A more difficult variation of the same skill is to toss, run, and catch the streamer.

2. Have the children practice the Toss and Catch.

Toss and Catch With Ball

Collect the streamers, and give each child a ball.

    1. Describe and demonstrate the Toss and Catch.

        • With arms straight, the student tosses the ball above the head.

- Beginning with legs bent, the student lifts the body to tiptoe as the ball is tossed.
- As the ball falls, the arms give with the ball as it is caught.

2. Have the children practice the Toss and Catch.

Walk and Bounce

1. Describe and demonstrate the Walk and Bounce
   - The student bounces the ball with every step, catching the ball and bouncing it with straight arms extended in front of the body.
   - The ball should bounce directly in front of the body, at arm's distance.

2. Have the children practice the Walk and Bounce.

Forward Roll With Ball

Holding a ball in one hand with arm extended to the side, the student performs a slow roll forward with no hands. The shoulder rotates so that the ball stays in the palm of the hand. Have the children practice Forward Roll With Ball.

Toss in Front, Catch in Back

With straight arms, the student tosses the ball high and slightly backward and then moves a step forward and reaches back to catch the ball with straight arms.

Miniroutine

Line up all the children on line **X** with streamers. Lay out hoops, balls, and mats as in the figure.

1. Describe and demonstrate the Miniroutine: The student does three Figure Eights, runs two steps and turns, runs two steps into a hoop, picks up the hoop to overhead position parallel to the ground, tosses and catches the hoop, hulas on the right arm, rolls a Boomerang, tosses and catches, runs and rolls the hoop forward, drops the hoop over the body to the floor near the ball, picks up the ball, tosses it from right to left and from left to right hands, tosses front to back, walks forward bouncing and catching, puts the ball in the right hand, and does a Forward Roll on the mat with ball in hand. The end!

2. Have the children practice the Miniroutine with verbal cues.

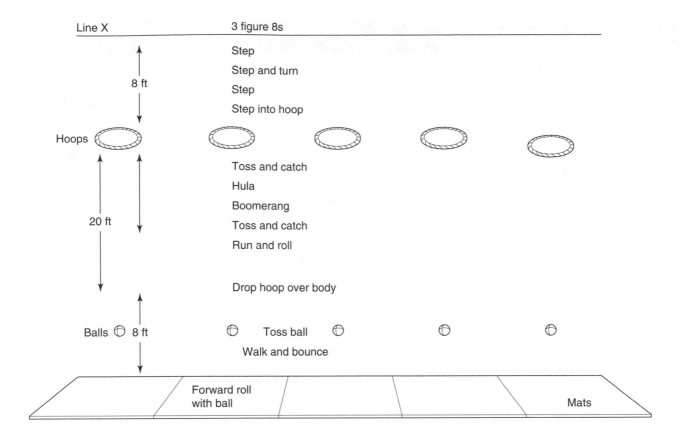

Line X   3 figure 8s

8 ft

Step
Step and turn
Step
Step into hoop

Hoops

Toss and catch
Hula
Boomerang
Toss and catch
Run and roll

20 ft

Drop hoop over body

Balls 8 ft   Toss ball
Walk and bounce

Forward roll with ball

Mats

Concluding Activities (1 minute)

Miniroutine

Have the children practice the Miniroutine as a group.

GYMNASTICS

LESSON 18
HOOPS, BALLS, AND STREAMERS

Student Objectives

- Practice with balls and hoops.

Equipment

- Six or more mats (four by eight feet)
- One hoop and one playground ball per child

Warm-Up Activities (5 to 7 minutes)

Warm-Up Routine

See Grades 6-8: Gymnastics, Warm-Ups, page 231.

Skill-Development Activities (15 minutes)

Down the Chute

Arrange the children in scatter formation. Each child has a ball.

1. Describe and demonstrate Down the Chute: The student holds the ball in one hand, with that arm raised slightly and the other arm slightly down, the two arms making

a straight line; and rolls the ball down the arm, across the shoulders, and into the opposite hand.

2. Have the children practice Down the Chute.

Back-to-Front Toss

1. Describe and demonstrate the Back-to-Front Toss.

   - Holding the ball in front of the body, the student rolls and swings the ball down and back so that momentum keeps the ball in contact with the hand until the hand reaches a position parallel to the ground in back of the body.

   - The ball should fly upward and back over the head where it can be caught in front of the body.

2. Have the children practice the Back-to-Front Toss.

Circle Dribble

1. Describe and demonstrate the Circle Dribble: The student dribbles the ball in a circle around the body without moving the feet.

2. Have the students practice the Circle Dribble.

Circle and Toss

1. Describe and demonstrate Circle and Toss: Beginning with the ball in front of the body in the right hand, the student moves the ball to the right in a circle to the back of the body, releasing the ball at the left side and catching the ball high and to the front.

2. Have the children practice Circle and Toss.

Bounce and Catch

1. Describe and demonstrate Bounce and Catch: Holding the top side of the hoop and facing the open side, the student bounces the hoop hard against the ground and, as it rebounds, catches it.

2. Have the children practice Bounce and Catch.

Hula Catch

1. Describe and demonstrate the Hula Catch: The student hulas the hoop on the arm or leg. As the hoop rolls up, the student pulls the arm (or leg) out and allows the hoop to fly into the air, catching it on a body part and continuing the hula motion.

2. Have the children practice the Hula Catch.

Concluding Activities (5 minutes)

Partner Hoop Activities

Assign each child a partner. Partners attempt to toss and catch two hoops or two balls simultaneously. Have them try rolling and catching two balls or two hoops.

GRADES 6-8

GYMNASTICS

LESSONS 19 AND 20
HOOPS, BALLS, AND STREAMERS

Student Objectives

- Compose a brief routine using one or more pieces of small equipment.

Equipment

- Six or more mats (four by eight feet)
- One hoop, one ball, and one streamer for each child

Warm-Up Activities (5 to 7 minutes)

Warm-Up Routine

See Grades 6-8: Gymnastics, Warm-Ups, page 231.

Skill-Development Activities (18 to 20 minutes)

Equipment Routines

Arrange the children in pairs or small groups.

1. Allow the groups to select two or three types of equipment. The groups are to create a routine using the equipment. The routine should have the following characteristics:

   - It uses two or three different types of equipment.
   - It includes five movements with each type of equipment.
   - It has a definite beginning and end.

2. Have all the children in the group perform all parts of the routine.

3. Allow the children practice time.

4. During the second day, observe each routine and then, at the end of the second day, ask for volunteers to present their routines to the class.

Concluding Activities

None.

LESSON 21
LADDER, BEAM, VAULT, AND ROPES

Student Objectives

- Practice on the large equipment.

Equipment

- Six or more mats (four by eight feet)
- Two ropes or one set of rings
- Three long balance beams (18 inches high)
- One or more vaulting cubes (24 to 36 inches high, 12 to 36 inches wide, and 12 inches deep)
- One horizontal ladder

Warm-Up Activities (5 to 7 minutes)

Warm-Up Routine

See Grades 6-8: Gymnastics, Warm-Ups, page 231.

Skill-Development Activities (18 to 20 minutes)

Hand-Over-Hand Walk

Arrange the children in small groups at each of the four equipment stations.

1. Describe and demonstrate Hand-Over-Hand Walking: Beginning by holding weight with both hands on the first rung of the horizontal ladder, the student reaches for the second rung with one hand, the third rung with the other hand, and so on.
2. Have the children practice Hand-Over-Hand Walking.

Skin the Cat

1. Describe and demonstrate Skin the Cat: Grasping one rope (or ring) in each hand and lifting the legs up, the student bends the legs until the knees are near the chest, rolls the head and torso backward until the body is parallel to the ground, extends the legs, and continues the circle; the student stops when the feet point at the ground and then reverses the movement back to starting position.

2. Have the children practice Skin the Cat.

Climbing the Rope

1. Describe and demonstrate Climbing the Rope: Using hands to pull the body upward, the student grips the rope with the feet to stop slipping downward when the hands must regrip.

2. Have the children practice Climbing the Rope.

Straddle Dismount

1. Describe and demonstrate the Straddle Dismount: From a standing position, the student jumps off the beam. While in the air, the student splits the legs, trying to touch toes in a straddle position, and then lands on both feet.

2. Have the children practice the Straddle Dismount.

Straddle Vault

1. Describe and demonstrate the Straddle Vault: From a running start, the student puts hands on the box between the legs, lifting the body off the floor with the legs in a straddle position; moves over the cube; and lands on the opposite side with feet together.

2. Have the children practice the Straddle Vault.

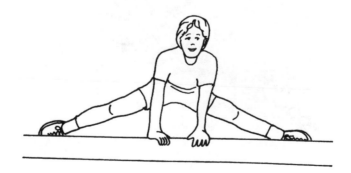

Apparatus Stations

After three or four minutes at a station, each group rotates to the next station.

Station 1: Ladder
Hand-Over-Hand Walk

Station 2: Balance Beam
Walking
Leaping
Running
Turning

Station 3: Ropes
Skin the Cat
Climbing

Station 4: Vaulting Cube
Straddle Vault

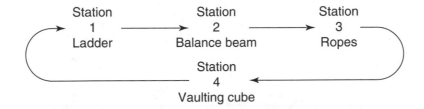

Concluding Activities (5 minutes)

Follow the Leader

A leader selects the movement sequence to perform at each piece of equipment. The students in the group must follow the leader.

LESSONS 22 TO 24
LADDER, BEAM, VAULT, AND ROPES

Student Objectives

- Combine skills on each of three pieces of equipment.
- Attempt new vaults.

Equipment

- Six or more mats (four by eight feet)
- Two climbing ropes or rings
- One horizontal ladder
- Three long balance beams (18 inches high)
- Vaulting cubes

Warm-Up Activities (5 to 7 minutes)

Warm-Up Routine

See Grades 6-8: Gymnastics, Warm-Ups, page 231.

Skill-Development Activities (18 to 20 minutes)

Beam Routine

1. Describe the Beam Routine.
2. Ask a child to perform the Beam Routine as you give verbal instructions.
3. Tell the student: *Mount the beam at the end; walk with high kicks for three or four steps; lean into a scale; stand up; run to the end of the beam; jump and turn around; walk three or four steps; do a Forward Roll; walk backward; turn to face the opposite direction; run to the end of the beam; and end with a Straddle Dismount.*

Rings/Rope Routine

1. Describe the Rings/Rope Routine.
2. Ask a child to perform the Rings/Rope Routine as you give verbal instructions.
3. Tell the student: *Jump to a hang; perform Skin the Cat; roll back, supporting weight so that hands are at your sides and are not extended above your head as in a mount; press the arms as far out as possible and hold (cross position); dismount by performing a fast Skin the Cat and dropping from a leg-over position to the feet.*

Horizontal Ladder Routine

1. Describe the Horizontal Ladder Routine.

2. Ask a child to perform the Horizontal Ladder Routine as you give verbal instructions.

3. Tell the student: *Walk hand over hand to the middle of the ladder; do a double jump (with both hands on one rung, jump both hands to the next rung); swing forward and lift your legs so that they touch the rung in front of you; and hang by your knees, releasing your hands. Regrip your hands in their original position; drop your legs down; turn to the opposite direction; make a large swinging arch; and drop to both feet.*

Flank Vault

1. Describe the Flank Vault.

2. Ask for a volunteer to demonstrate the Flank Vault: From a running approach, the student places both hands on the box, swinging both legs to one side and over the box, lifting one hand off the box, and lands with one side facing the box. The hand of the leg-swinging side should be on the box, and the other arm should be extended upward.

Flank Vault With Quarter Turn

Arrange the children in small groups at the four stations.

1. Describe the Flank Vault With Quarter Turn variation.

2. Ask for a volunteer to demonstrate the Flank Vault With Quarter Turn.

   • From a running approach, the student places both hands on the beam, swinging both legs to one side and keeping the legs straight and together.

   • As the legs clear the beam, the student makes a quarter turn so that the landing is with the back to the beam.

3. Have the groups practice at each station about five minutes and then rotate to the next station.

4. Informally observe the children at the stations.

Extension Activities

Ask the students to compose routines.

Concluding Activities

None.

Health instruction during the middle school years can help shape positive health-related attitudes and behaviors. Healthy lifestyles begin with the formation of positive values and habits; teachers can assist students in satisfying their wants and needs in constructive and responsible ways. The ability to make important health-related decisions requires education and practice.

UNIT ORGANIZATION

This section offers 10 lessons that focus on decision making for a healthy lifestyle. These health lessons, which can be taught either in the classroom or on the playground, are designed to help students deal with peer pressure and to say "no" to activities that could be harmful, unsafe, or illegal. These lessons do not create a complete health program; they are intended to be a starting point for those teachers who would like some activities to assist students in developing a healthy lifestyle. If health education is an important part of your program, you might want to develop additional lessons.

The 10 lessons presented here can be grouped together as a unit, or they can be used on Fridays or rainy days.

LESSON DESCRIPTIONS

Health Lesson 1 addresses developing positive feeling about oneself and leads students through a discussion of personal traits and characteristics that can make them feel good about themselves. Lesson 2 discusses both healthy and unhealthy ways to express feelings as a form of communication. Lesson 3 addresses decision making and how decisions can affect health. The focus of Lesson 4 is dealing with disappointment in healthy ways.

Lesson 5 presents ways to resist peer pressure in situations that could be harmful or unhealthy. Lessons 6 and 7 present strategies for saying "no" to alcohol and drugs. Lesson 8 discusses the characteristics of responsible people. Goal setting is the topic of discussion in Lesson 9. Lesson 10 summarizes the preceding lessons by discussing high-level wellness, as well as the physical, social, and emotional components of health.

HEALTH CONCEPTS

A positive self-concept helps students communicate with friends, deal with stress, set realistic goals, and make healthy decisions. A good way to develop positive feelings about oneself is to remember that all individuals have some unique and positive traits. Another way is to maintain satisfying relationships with others.

Emotional health is part of high-level wellness. Conflict occurs in most everyone's life and can cause anger, frustration, and disappointment. There are healthy, acceptable ways to deal with conflict, but there are also unacceptable ways to approach stressful situations. Healthy ways to deal with conflict include physical exercise and sharing feelings without blaming others. Unhealthy ways to deal with anger or disappointment include fighting or swearing.

Peer pressure is part of growing up and can significantly affect health-related decisions if not dealt with responsibly. Individuals should resist pressure from friends to engage in behaviors that are harmful to their health and well-being. Responsible behavior is fundamental to a healthy lifestyle.

CONCLUSION

Total health and well-being include physical, social, and emotional components. These elements enable individuals to accomplish their goals, perform at adequate levels, and make healthful decisions about their lives.

Table F4.1: Unit Plan for Grades 6-8: Health

Week 29: health concepts	Week 30: health concepts
Monday: self-concept	Monday: saying no
Tuesday: expressing feelings	Tuesday: saying no
Wednesday: making decisions	Wednesday: responsible behavior
Thursday: feelings	Thursday: setting goals
Friday: peer pressure	Friday: high-level wellness

Note: This is one way to organize these lessons. More likely you will want to use lessons throughout the year rather than planning all fitness instruction in one unit. In any curriculum plan, the fitness assessment is repeated at the end of the year.

HEALTH

LESSON 1
DEVELOPING POSITIVE FEELINGS ABOUT ONESELF

Student Objectives

- Distinguish between liking yourself and being selfish.
- Identify positive traits they possess.

Concept-Development Activities (20 minutes)

Define Key Terms

> **Self-Concept:** The feelings a person has about himself or herself.
>
> **Positive Self-Concept:** Good or positive feelings a person has about himself or herself.
>
> **Positive Behavior:** Behavior that is responsible and usually shows that a person has positive feelings about himself or herself.
>
> **Selfish Behavior:** Behavior that fulfills personal desires with little concern for the feelings or needs of others.

1. Introduce this concept: *Everyone needs to develop traits that will make them feel good about themselves.*

2. Discuss the importance of developing positive feelings about yourself. *All of us are individuals with some positive traits. We are all unique—there is absolutely no one else exactly like you. What are some things that make other people interesting and different? (Size, where they live, how they dress, or what they like to eat.)*

3. Tell the children: *There are personal traits and characteristics that can make us feel good about ourselves. We all need to use these positive traits to develop good relationships with our friends. What are some positive traits that you can develop that will help you to have better relationships with others?*

   (Be a good listener.

   Always be honest and direct.

   Be pleasant and try to brighten the day for others.

   Be real rather than artificial.

   Try to show others that you care about them.)

4. Tell the children: *Some students think only about their own wants and needs and have little consideration for the desires or feelings of their friends. This is selfish or self-centered behavior. Selfish behavior can keep you from having positive relationships with your friends.*

Identifying Strengths

Each student writes his or her name on the top of a sheet of paper. The paper is pinned or taped to the student's back.

1. The students walk around the room; on a signal they stop and choose a partner.
2. Each person writes something positive about his or her partner on the sheet.
3. The activity is repeated and another partner is selected. Continue until each student has had time to collect statements from 10 to 12 people.
4. The statements written on the backs of their partners should pertain to either a physical or a personality characteristic. Examples might be *You have pretty blue eyes,* or *You are always smiling.*
5. Collect the statements and read them to the class in random order. Have the children try to identify the student by the characteristics.

Concluding Activities (10 minutes)

Identifying My Own Strengths

Arrange children in groups or five or six.

1. Students are asked to write down a list of five positive traits they think they have. The traits should be those that will help them to develop good relationships with their friends.
2. After they have identified five traits, ask them to select the one they believe is the most desirable, and have them share their selection with the group.

LESSON 2
EXPRESSING FEELINGS

Student Objectives

- Explain why communication with your friends and family is important.
- Distinguish between healthy and unhealthy ways to express feelings.

Concept-Development Activities (20 minutes)

Define Key Terms

Communication: A way of letting another person know what your thoughts and feelings are.

Healthy Ways to Communicate: Expressing feelings that you have about an event or situation without blaming another person.

Unhealthy Ways to Communicate: Showing anger by blaming another person rather than expressing feelings.

Anger: An emotion out of control.

1. Discuss healthy and unhealthy ways of expressing feelings: *It is important for us to communicate our feelings, thoughts, likes, and dislikes to our friends and family members. We need to develop ways of communicating that are healthy rather than unhealthy. Healthy ways of communicating feelings focus on the events or behaviors and the results but do not blame the person responsible. You want to share how you feel, but you do not want to shame the person. It is unhealthy for you to try to hurt the person responsible rather than expressing how you feel.*

2. Provide some examples of healthy and unhealthy ways to communicate.

   Situation: *Your friend borrowed your favorite vest and left it outside overnight. It rained and the vest got wet. You wanted to wear it this evening.*

   Healthy Response: *That was one of my favorite vests and it got wet. I was planning to wear it this evening, but I have another one that I like almost as well.*

   Unhealthy Response: *You are irresponsible; you don't take care of anything.*

Healthy Communication

Arrange children in groups of five or six.

1. Present the following situations. Students are to create healthy and unhealthy ways to communicate their feelings. For each situation, allow some time for group discussion, and then ask the students in each group to share their responses.

Situation 1: *Your friend said he would come by your house at 4:30. You waited even though your older brother asked you to go to the movies. Your friend didn't show up and didn't call. When you see him the next day he says he decided to go visit another friend instead.*

Situation 2: *You share a secret with your friend and ask her not to tell anyone. A week later you learn that at least 10 other students have the information.*

2. Introduce the following concept: *It is okay to be angry, but anger must be expressed in appropriate ways.*

3. Discuss appropriate ways to express anger: *We all have feelings of anger, and it is normal to have these feelings. However, we must develop appropriate and healthy ways to express angry feelings and thoughts. You should not express your anger in ways that will cause harm to other people. This means that you can never use a physical response, such as striking or kicking. You should not use language that will harm another person's self-image. Telling a person he or she is dumb or stupid is not appropriate.*

Ways to Express Anger

Arrange children in groups of five or six.

1. Present the following situation. Ask children to create healthy and unhealthy ways to express their feelings about the situation. After time for discussion, ask each group to share their responses.

   Situation: *Your friend borrowed your new softball glove for the weekend. After the game, your friend forgot the glove at the ball park, and it was stolen. You worked hard to earn enough money to buy the glove, and you are angry about losing it.*

2. Introduce the following concept: *Two people together are never without some form of communication.*

3. Discuss how communication can be verbal or nonverbal: *There are ways to communicate your feelings without speaking a word. This is nonverbal communication, which can take the form of body language, such as gestures, postures, or facial expressions. These all include doing something with your body to convey your feelings. Another way to express displeasure or disapproval is failing to respond verbally or to show any positive body language.*

4. Provide an example of nonverbal communication: *You ask your friend if you can walk home with her from school.* (Responses might be

   a nod of the head and a motion with the hand,

   no response at all, or

   a shake of the head and a frown.)

   The nod and the hand motion tell you that your friend wants you to join her.

   No response, or the shake of the head and a frown make you feel unwelcome.

Concluding Activities (10 minutes)

Communicating Feelings With Movement and Gesture

Arrange children in groups of five or six. The children are asked to show various feelings using non-verbal communication. Examples might be fear, worry, anger, excitement, or jealousy.

GRADES 6-8

HEALTH

LESSON 3
MAKING DECISIONS

Student Objectives

- Explain the steps one needs to take when making decisions.
- Explain what it means to act in responsible ways.

Concept-Development Activities (20 minutes)

Health Concept

1. Introduce the following concept: *Individuals make daily decisions that affect their health and the health of others.*

2. Discuss decision making and the steps a person should take to assure that his or her decisions are responsible: *We are faced with decisions daily, and sometimes the decisions to be made are difficult ones. We make decisions that can affect our health, our safety, and our happiness. Sometimes our decisions can result in illegal behavior or can hurt another person. There are some things we can do and think about any time we are faced with making a decision.*

3. Discuss the steps to take in making responsible decisions:

   Clearly define the situation. *Think through what the question is. You might even write the problem down or state the situation out loud to yourself. If you are required to make a quick decision, there might not be time to write the problem down; however, you must take time to at least think about the situation. Do not ever act without thinking.*

   Consider all of the possible actions you can take. *If there is enough time, you might make a list of possible actions, or discuss the possibilities with a friend or a responsible adult.*

   Never act without considering several courses of action. *Before deciding which action you will take, you should ask yourself a series of questions:*

   Will the action be harmful to me or to others?, Will the action put my safety or the safety of others in jeopardy?, Is the action illegal?, Will the action make me feel good about myself?, and Will the action be consistent with the rules set by my parents and my teachers? Based on the answers to the questions you asked yourself, make a decision.

   Evaluate the results. *Act according to your decision, but be reflective. Think about the action you took, and determine if the decision and the behavior were responsible.*

4. Present the following situation to explain the decision-making process.

   Situation: *Jim, Grant, Sue, and Melinda are at the park. Jim takes out two hand-rolled cigarettes and hands one to Sue. He suggests that Sue share hers with Grant and that Melinda can smoke with him. Melinda recognizes the cigarette as marijuana and is very uncomfortable.*

   What should Melinda do?

5. Ask the children the following questions:

   What is the problem? (Melinda is uncomfortable because of the marijuana and doesn't know what action to take.)

   What are her choices? (She can give in and join her friends in smoking. She can leave. She can tell her friends that she does not approve of smoking marijuana, and she does not want to be involved.)

   What are the possible consequences of each action? (If Melinda leaves or tells her friends that she does not approve of smoking marijuana, she may lose her friends. If she agrees to smoke, her parents may find out, and the action is against their guidelines. If she agrees to smoke, she will be breaking the law and could be arrested.)

   What is the decision? (Melinda decides to leave.)

   How would Melinda evaluate her decision? (She might lose three friends, but she did not put herself in a position to engage in an illegal act and one that is against her parents' rules. She feels good about herself and is certain that she can find other friends to socialize with.)

Concluding Activities (10 minutes)

Making Decisions

Arrange children in groups of four to six. Present the following situation and ask each group to use the decision-making process to select a course of action.

   Situation: *Julie, Sam, Mark, and Jeanie are at a softball game. Julie mentions that she has a friend in the parking lot who has some beer, and he is willing to share it with the four of them.*

   Mark does not want to participate but does not know how to handle the situation. What should Mark do?

LESSON 4
DEALING WITH DISAPPOINTMENT

Student Objectives

- Identify healthy ways of acting and feeling when needs cannot be satisfied.
- Explain why it is important to share hurt feelings.

Concept Development Activities (20 minutes)

Health Concept

1. Introduce the following concept: *Every person has some needs that cannot be met right away.*

2. Discuss the importance of dealing with disappointments in healthy ways: *We all have times in our lives when we can't do exactly what we want and when things don't go exactly as we would like.*

3. Get students to give some examples of times when things didn't go the way they wanted them to. (Examples might be

     you are tired and want to go to bed, but your parents are visiting friends;

     you are hungry, but you are on the bus and still an hour away from home;

     you are lonely, but all your friends are out of town;

     you are scheduled to play tennis, and it rains; or

     you had planned to go to a movie, and your parents decide that you should not go.)

4. Ask students to think about things they might do if what they really wanted or needed was not available. (Examples might be

     you can keep everything to yourself and say nothing;

     you can talk to a friend and tell him or her how disappointed you are; or

     you can try to do something fun that might get your thoughts away from your disappointment.)

5. Discuss the importance of expressing feeling rather than keeping them inside: *There are times when you are hurt and disappointed by your friends and sometimes by your family. There are people who will make fun of the way you look, and they might call you names. Sometimes your parents or your friends might tell you that you are worthless or a bad person. Some students have a tendency to criticize others and say hateful things.*

6. Explain how important it is to recognize and share hurt feelings: *If your friend calls you stupid, you have several ways that you can react. You can pretend that it does not hurt*

and simply smile and blow it off. This reaction is an example of keeping your feelings on the inside, and that is not healthy. If you do not share your true feelings and you try to appear happy when you are actually sad, the hurt will get worse. Holding hurt feelings inside can actually make you physically ill. You may start having headaches or other physical symptoms, and you may be unable to sleep at night.

7. Tell the students: *The healthy way to deal with hurt feelings is to share them. First try to identify why you had your feelings hurt. Then think of ways to express your feelings in healthy ways. A good way is to share your feelings with a friend or a mature adult.*

Concluding Activities (10 minutes)

Dealing With Hurt Feelings

Arrange children in groups of four to six. Present the following situation; then ask each group of children to identify the feeling and offer ways to express it. Students should explain why it is important to share hurt feelings.

> **Situation:** *Sue and Mindy have planned to room together at summer camp. One week before leaving Sue announces to Mindy that she would rather room with Kathy. How should Mindy deal with her feelings?*

LESSON 5
DEALING WITH PEER PRESSURE

Student Objectives

- Identify situations where they need to say "No."
- Demonstrate ways to resist pressure from peers.

Concept-Development Activities (20 minutes)

Health Concept

1. Introduce the following concept: *It is important to learn to say "NO" in certain situations.*

2. Discuss situations where an adolescent might need to deal with pressure from peers: *There will be times when your friends will try to talk you into engaging in behaviors that are unhealthy and perhaps dangerous, and we all need to think ahead and be ready to act. You need to identify situations where you want to say "No," and say it in such a way that your friends believe you and accept your decision. It takes planning and practice to be able to resist pressure.*

3. Have students suggest some situations where they felt uncomfortable and wanted to say "No" to suggestions from their friends.

   (To take drugs

   To smoke cigarettes

   To steal from the local athletic store

   To make nasty comments about a friend

   To slip out of the house at night after everyone is asleep

   To cheat on a test

   To take a knife to school)

4. Ask students to give reasons why these are situations where they need to resist pressure from their friends. Ask them the types of behaviors they need to resist.

   (Behavior that is illegal

   Behavior that is harmful to their health

   Behavior that is unsafe

   Behavior that will hurt others

   Behavior that is against the rules of their parents or the school

   Behavior that is not responsible)

5. Discuss ways to say "No": *In situations where you decide that you should resist pressure from your friends to engage in behavior that you disapprove of, there are several things you can do to be more effective. First, you need to look directly at your friends and speak clearly and firmly. Be assertive and say "No, I will not smoke cigarettes." Do not apologize for your decision, and do not say "No thank you, I'm not interested."*

6. Discuss follow-up actions that they should take: *When your friends try to pressure you into engaging in behavior that you disapprove of, in addition to saying "No," you should try to help them understand why you make the decisions you do. Explain to your friends that it is unwise to choose actions that are unsafe, unhealthy, disrespectful to others, or illegal. Do what you can to influence your friends. You might suggest an alternative or simply try to talk them out of engaging in the risky behavior.*

7. Tell the students: *If you cannot influence your friends, then you should avoid them. Do not put yourself into situations where you are pressured to engage in behaviors that you disapprove of.*

Concluding Activities (10 minutes)

Saying "No" to Friends

Arrange students in groups of four to six. Present the following situations and ask each group to role-play each situation.

Situation 1: *Frank, Judy, and Anna are visiting Joseph; his parents have gone to the grocery store. Frank suggests that Joseph take the keys to the second car so the four of them can go for a ride. Joseph knows this is risky, unsafe behavior that is against his parents' rules as well as being illegal, since they are not old enough to drive. Joseph does not want to go along but Frank, Judy, and Anna try to convince him that it would be a thrill and that no one would ever find out.*

Situation 2: *Tim and Carla are walking home from school when Carla suggests that they stop by the drugstore. As they are walking up and down the aisles, Carla says that she can put a pack of cigarettes in Tim's backpack without being seen. They can then smoke on the way home. Tim is not interested and does not want to be involved in such behavior.*

GRADES 6-8

LESSON 6
SAYING "NO" TO ALCOHOL

Student Objectives

- Explain how drinking affects your ability to make responsible decisions.
- Create ways to say "No" when pressured to drink.

Concept-Development Activities (20 minutes)

Health Concept

1. Introduce the following concept: *Alcohol is the number one drug problem in the nation today. Alcohol is a depressant that dulls your senses and interferes with your ability to make wise decisions.*

2. Discuss how alcohol can interfere with wise decision making: *Alcohol acts as a depressant on the nervous system. Depressants slow down the activity of the brain and nervous system. In small amounts, alcohol acts like a tranquilizing drug, making the user feel relaxed, less tense, and less inhibited.*

3. Have students suggest some behaviors they might engage in if they were less inhibited.

   (Might disobey your parents, thinking you can get by with it

   Might take risks when riding your bicycle in traffic, and not really care about the danger

   Might be more inclined to break the law, and go along with friends who want to experiment with drugs)

4. Tell the students: *When you drink alcohol, you are less concerned with your safety and the safety of others. You are less concerned with following the rules set by your parents. You are more likely to break the law. Students who drink small amounts of alcohol cannot make responsible decisions and are more likely to engage in behaviors that might be unhealthy and irresponsible.*

5. Explain more about the risks of drinking alcohol: *Not everyone who uses alcohol is a problem drinker. Many people drink alcohol in moderation and are sensible. These are responsible users. However, excessive use of alcohol is abuse. Abuse of alcohol can lead to alcoholism. Alcoholism is a disease caused by drinking large amounts of alcohol over a relatively long period of time. You can never become an alcoholic if you never start drinking.*

6. Discuss the serious problems associated with alcohol abuse: *People who abuse alcohol seldom get the most out of life. They tend to argue and fight with other people, get angry, and do embarrassing things; they act silly and immature, act irresponsibly, and tend not to meet*

their obligations; they tend to lose good friends and family members who try to help them. Alcohol abuse takes the quality out of living.

7. Tell the students: *You should say "No" when pressured to drink alcohol. When you get older, you might decide you want to drink in moderation, but at this time it is best to say "No."*

Concluding Activities (10 minutes)

Saying "No" To Drinking

Arrange students in groups of five or six.

1. Present the following situations and ask each group to role-play each situation.

   Situation 1: *Tony, Sam, and Maggie go to Rita's house to listen to music. When they get into the house Rita announces that her parents are not home, and she has alcoholic drinks for everyone to enjoy. Tony, Sam, and Maggie go along with the plan and have a few drinks. Tony suggests that they try smoking. Sam, Maggie, and Rita cannot think clearly because of the alcohol and agree to smoke. Maggie then convinces the group that they should go to the house next door and spray paint the outside walls. Tony, Sam, and Rita cannot think clearly because of the alcohol and agree to spray paint the house just for kicks.*

2. Allow the students to use their imaginations to come up with other ideas that would result in poor decision making and risky or unhealthy behaviors.

   Situation 2: *Tony, Sam, and Maggie go to Rita's house to listen to music. When they get into the house Rita announces that her parents are not home and she has alcoholic drinks for everyone to enjoy. Tony immediately says, "My parents have a rule against me going into your house if your parents are not home. And No, I do not want any alcohol." Tony tries to influence Sam and Maggie to make responsible decisions and say "No" to the alcohol. After some discussion, Tony, Sam, and Maggie agree that they should go to Sam's house down the street to listen to music. They invite Rita to join them and off they go.*

3. Hold a discussion about the two situations and the influence of alcohol on decision making.

4. Have students offer other possible situations that might happen.

LESSON 7
SAYING "NO" TO DRUGS

Student Objectives

- Explain why adolescents should say no to drugs.
- Create ways to say "No" when pressured to use drugs.
- Identify strategies that peers might use to influence their friends.

Concept-Development Activities (20 minutes)

Health Concept

1. Introduce the following concept: *It is unwise to consider using any drug that is illegal.*

2. Discuss the characteristics of marijuana and explain why students should say "No" when peers pressure them to smoke marijuana: *Marijuana is a mild hallucinogen that causes behavioral changes in some individuals. Happy people can become sad. Calm people become nervous and anxious. Clear-thinking people become confused. People experience a distortion of time, space, and distance. We do not know everything about marijuana, but we do know that it is an illegal drug and should therefore be avoided.*

3. Discuss some things that peers might say to persuade you to smoke marijuana: *Pretend you are at a party, and everyone there is smoking marijuana except you. You are not interested, but you must stay at the party until your ride is ready to leave. You say "No" in a firm, clear way but your peers continue to try to get you to participate. What are some comments they might make to get you to join in?* (Some examples might be

   don't be a party pooper,

   let your hair down and have some fun,

   you will never have any fun in life if you don't try some new things,

   try it just this once; nobody will ever know, or

   you can't be our friend if you are going to be a prude.)

4. Ask the students: *What are some arguments you could make to your friends to let them know why you will not smoke marijuana?*

   (I don't want to smoke.

   It is illegal and I will not break the law.

   Smoking is bad for your health.

   It can change your behavior, and you will not make responsible decisions.

   We don't know enough about what marijuana can do to our health.)

5. Discuss the validity of the arguments used.

Concluding Activity (10 minutes)

Saying "No" to Marijuana

Arrange students in groups of six. Role-play the following situation.

> **Situation:** *Six students are at a party together. Five are smoking marijuana, and one is resisting. The five smokers try to convince the nonsmoker to join them.*

Giving Advice

Keep the same groups. Students are asked to respond to the following situation.

> **Situation:** *You have a friend who shares with you a problem that she has. Her new boyfriend smokes marijuana and wants to get some crack to try. He tells your friend that if they are to continue seeing each other she must try smoking marijuana. What is your advice for your friend?*

Students discuss the issue and arrive at a solution that they all agree is right. Responses are shared with the other groups.

LESSON 8
CHARACTERISTICS OF RESPONSIBLE PEOPLE

Student Objectives

- Identify characteristics that lead to responsible behavior.
- Explain that sometimes undesirable characteristics are not noticeable when you first meet a person.

Concept-Development Activities (20 minutes)

Health Concept

1. Review the following concept: *One is not capable of loving and respecting another person unless one loves and respects oneself first.*

2. Discuss the behaviors one should expect from others: *We want our friends to treat us with respect. Respect means that someone likes you because he or she admires you for the person you are and treats you in ways that let you know you are admired. Before people can respect others, they must first like who they are. They must believe they are important and have a contribution to make to society. People who like themselves will not put themselves down or make excuses for mistakes. Everyone makes mistakes and a self-loving person will expect to do so. There is no reason to blame oneself or others. A self-respecting person would not choose to engage in unsafe, risky, or unhealthy behavior.*

3. Discuss other characteristics you should look for in others: *Responsible individuals will be up front and honest with their friends. If you share your secrets with them, you can be pretty sure they will not tell others. They are trustworthy and dependable. If they tell you they will meet you at four o'clock, they will make every effort to do so. If they agree to help you with a task, you can relax and depend on the help.*

4. Tell the students: *Responsible people are consistent. If you know them, you don't have to worry about surprises such as emotional outbursts or fits of anger. They share their feelings in healthy ways. They follow the rules set by their parents, the school, and community officials.*

   Responsible people set goals and work toward meeting those goals. They make plans for their lives and realize that in order to be happy and successful there might be some struggle. They realize that they can't have everything they want immediately, but that they have to plan and work toward success.

   Responsible people work to have good relationships with others. They respect and like themselves so they are able to respect others.

5. Introduce the following concept: *There are some characteristics that are noticeable when you first meet a person but others that you are not aware of until you have been around him or her for some time.*

6. Have students identify characteristics that are noticed immediately. (Examples might be size, hair color, eye color, and other physical attributes.)

7. Have students identify characteristics that you can know about a person by just being in the same school. (Examples might be the person is athletic and a good musician. He or she wears expensive clothes and drives a recent model car.)

8. Have students identify characteristics that you can't know about a person until you are around them for a while. (Examples might be they are insecure, they take drugs, and they criticize and make fun of others.)

Concluding Activities (10 minutes)

Describing a Person I Would Like To Know

Arrange students in groups of five or six. Ask each group of students to make a list of desirable characteristics that are not noticeable about a person immediately but are ones that you would like your friends to have.

GRADES 6-8

LESSON 9
SETTING GOALS

Student Objectives

- Identify what they want to accomplish in life.
- Identify the obstacles they might encounter that will keep them from reaching their goals.

Concept Development Activity (20 minutes)

Health Concept

1. Introduce the following concept: *Reaching your goals in life takes responsible planning.*

2. Discuss the importance of planning ahead: *We all need to think ahead and plan what we want to do with our lives. We can all come up with a list of "Hoped for Items."*

3. Have the students make a list of positions or places in life that they hope to achieve. Have them make a dream list. (Examples might be

   I hope to have a lot of money;

   I hope to have a happy marriage;

   I hope to be successful in a career;

   I hope to have good health;

   I hope to have healthy children;

   I hope to live in a big, beautiful house;

   I hope to be a movie star;

   I hope to be a professional athlete; or

   I hope to be an artist.)

4. Tell the children: *We need to realize that some of the things we put on our "Hoped for Items" list might not be realistic. For example, it is not likely that many of us will become movie stars or professional athletes. However, there are many positions in life that are possible. In order to accomplish goals, we must plan and work hard, but many things are possible.*

5. Have the students make a list of goals that are possible for them. (Examples might be

   to be a physician,

   to get a college degree,

   to have a happy family,

   to travel and see the world,

   to gain the respect of my peers,

to make enough money to do the things I want to do,

to have good health, and

to be happy.)

6. Tell the children: *Many things are possible with hard work, but we need to start planning now. It might be helpful to reflect on some of the situations we want to avoid.*

7. Have the students make a list of situations they want to avoid in life. (Examples might be

to be poor,

to be unemployed, or

to be alone, without friends.)

8. Discuss how irresponsible decision making today might keep you from achieving your goals tomorrow. Give examples of some health-related decisions such as taking drugs and becoming an addict, being arrested and put in jail for shoplifting, or becoming parents at a young age.

Concluding Activities (10 minutes)

Planning for the Future

Arrange students in groups of five or six. Each student should share his or her goals with others in the group. The group should discuss what the student can do to make it easier to reach those goals and what decisions might make it harder or perhaps impossible to reach the goals.

LESSON 10
DEVELOPING HIGH-LEVEL WELLNESS

Student Objectives

- Explain that high-level wellness includes physical, mental, social, and emotional aspects of health.
- Identify activities that will contribute toward a high level of wellness.

Concept-Development Activities (20 minutes)

Health Concept

1. Introduce the following concept: *Total health and well-being includes physical, social, and emotional components.*

2. Discuss the importance of being a well-rounded individual with a variety of interests: *To attain a high level of wellness, we must consider our physical, mental, social, and emotional needs; and plan activities that will contribute to our overall health. If we expect to attain a balance among the four components, we must plan our time. We need to arrange time in our lives to participate in activities that will make contributions in each of the four areas: physical, mental, social, and emotional.*

3. Have children think of activities that can contribute to one's physical health. (Examples might include joining a tennis group, planning an after school fitness program, taking a long walk on the weekend, starting to lift weights, or organizing a neighborhood soccer game.)

4. Tell the children: *We also need to engage in activities that will stimulate our thinking. We need to plan some activities on our own that are done outside of school.*

5. Have children think of activities that can contribute to one's mental health. (Examples might include reading for pleasure, learning to play chess or bridge, figuring out a difficult puzzle, assisting a friend with his or her math homework, or putting together a difficult model.)

6. Tell the children: *To attain a balance in our lives we must plan time for social interactions with our friends or family.*

7. Have children think of social activities that are pleasurable and will contribute to overall health. (Examples might include spending time visiting with a grandparent, taking a younger brother or sister for a bike ride, discussing future plans with a friend, inviting a friend to join you to make hamburgers, or joining a club such as Boy Scouts or Girl Scouts.)

8. Tell the children: *Finally, it is important to select activities that make us feel good. These will contribute to our emotional health.*

9. Have students think of activities that might contribute to the emotional aspects of health. (Examples might be giving clothes you no longer wear to Goodwill, assisting an older neighbor with his or her yard work, volunteering to make Christmas gifts for the needy, or visiting a nursing home.)

Concluding Activities (10 minutes)

Planning Activities for a Healthy Lifestyle

Students make a list of activities they hope will achieve balance in their lives and contribute to overall health and wellness. The plan should include specific times and dates for the activities to be accomplished.

The lessons in this section can be used when physical education classes are held in the classroom, whether by choice or by chance. Sometimes weather may prohibit you from going outdoors, and there may be no indoor facility available. At times, assembly programs or other events might require a change in the regular schedule, making it necessary for the physical education classes to meet in a classroom. Classroom activities can help us reach our physical education goals, but it takes careful planning.

UNIT ORGANIZATION

The 10 lessons in this section present activities and skills that are meant to be exciting, challenging, and fun. Shuffleboard, Twister, Bowling, and Balloon Volleyball are included. Some new games are included as well; for example, Lesson 8 presents Lummi Sticks, a partner hand-eye coordination activity, which is perfect for small areas. Also included in this section are three fitness lessons for small areas. Although the unit offers some opportunities for competition, more attention should be given to learning the skills and cooperating with others in a small space.

LESSON MODIFICATIONS

These lessons can be modified to match the space available. The size of the play area can be made larger or smaller, and the number of different activities selected for one class period can be increased or decreased. The 10 lessons presented here are intended to get you started; there are also numerous lessons in the regular program that can be successfully taught in a classroom.

The Fitness Hustles, as well as many of the other Fitness lessons, are appropriate for most small areas. The fitness concepts that are included in each fitness lesson can be pulled out and presented at any time. The Health lessons would be an excellent choice for classroom presentation. Many of the rhythmic lessons and some of the gymnastics activities can also be adapted to classroom activity, especially if the furniture can be rearranged. Careful selection and teaching of these activities can make classroom presentations a meaningful part of the overall program.

LESSON 1
RECREATIONAL GAMES

Student Objectives

- Cooperate by taking turns.
- Demonstrate aiming by hitting a target with a disk.
- Demonstrate the use of varying forces by stopping a disk at specified places and bumping a disk out of play.
- Demonstrate a correct Four-Step Approach.
- Roll a softball so the ball remains in contact with the ground after release.

Equipment

- Two shuffleboard sets, or four brooms with the straw cut off and nine margarine containers filled with sand
- Masking tape or cloth tape
- Two softballs or two rubber bowling balls
- Two Twister games, or two sheets with 10-inch dots of various colors painted on them and two spinners

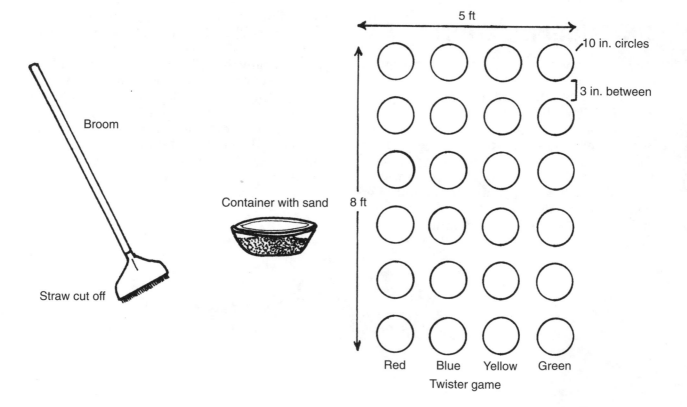

Broom

Straw cut off

Container with sand

5 ft

10 in. circles

3 in. between

8 ft

Red   Blue   Yellow   Green

Twister game

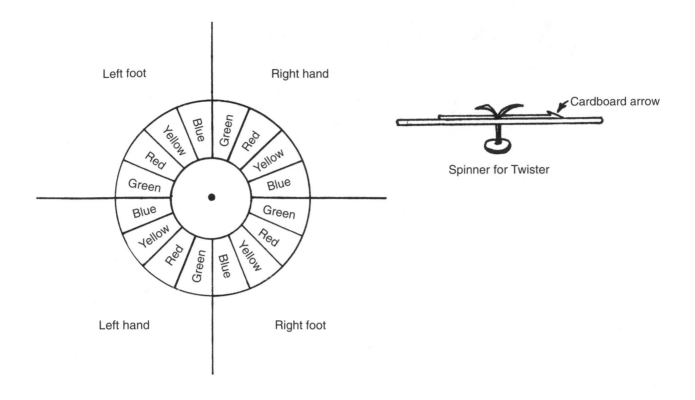

Left foot   Right hand

Left hand   Right foot

Cardboard arrow

Spinner for Twister

Skill-Development Activities (30 minutes)

Shuffleboard Skills (5 minutes)

Arrange students along ends of the shuffleboard court.

1. Have the students practice pushing a disk with a cue so that the disk stops in the triangle at the opposite end of the court.
2. Have the students use various amounts of force to bump disks in the triangle out of the triangle while keeping the bumping disk in the triangle.

Four-Step Approach (5 minutes)

1. The student begins by standing with feet together and hands together holding the ball, palms up, at waist height in front of body. The torso leans slightly forward.
2. Both hands move forward, with the hand holding the ball moving a little beyond the free hand.
3. At the same time, the foot on the side of the body holding the ball moves forward a step. As the foot makes contact with the ground, the downswing should be in progress.
4. The ball goes back, passing the line of the body as the next step occurs, and begins to move upward behind the body.
5. As the ball reaches the top of the backswing, the third step begins, which is a quick step with the ball hesitating before the forward motion.
6. The forward swing is a downward and forward motion with the last step, which turns into a slide to the release and follow through.

Four-Step Delivery (9 minutes)

1. The Four-Step Approach is used with a ball in the Four-Step Delivery. The object is to have the ball touch the ground as the foot slides after the last step and rolls forward.

2. The ball should remain in contact with the ground at all times.

3. The ball should move toward the target and eventually roll over the target.

Twister (2 minutes)

Four players play in two teams with teammates beginning at the same end of the board.

1. Explain the rules for Twister.

2. Begin with two to four players standing on the dots at the long ends of the playing board.

3. Have one of the players (if you have two or four children in the group) or the referee (if you have three or five children in the group) spin the spinner.

4. All players must move the body part indicated by the spinner to a dot of the color indicated by the spinner.

5. No two players can use the same dot, nor can one player have two body parts on the same dot. The game continues until a player cannot make the appropriate move, falls, or touches an elbow or knee to the board.

Skill Practice (9 minutes)

Arrange the children in six groups. Rotate groups to a new activity every four or five minutes so that each group tries each activity.

1. Two groups practice Four-Step Delivery bowl for five minutes, trying to roll the ball over an X taped on the floor 30 to 60 feet from the starting line.

2. Two groups play Twister for five minutes.

3. Two groups practice Shuffleboard Skills for five minutes.

LESSON 2
RECREATIONAL GAMES

Student Objectives

- Cooperate with others by taking turns.
- Demonstrate an understanding of the basic rules for Shuffleboard and Bowling.
- Demonstrate correct form for the Four-Step Delivery when aiming at bowling pins.

Equipment

- 2 shuffleboard sets, or 4 broomsticks and 16 margarine containers filled with sand (8 each of 2 different colors)
- Masking tape or cloth tape
- 20 plastic bottles (2-liter)
- 2 softballs or 2 rubber bowling balls
- 2 Twister games, or 2 sheets with 10-inch dots of various colors painted on them and 2 spinners

Skill-Development Activities (30 minutes)

Doubles Shuffleboard

Partners stand behind opposite triangles on the shuffleboard court.

1. Explain the rules for Doubles Shuffleboard.

   - Red disks are played from the right of the head court and from the left of the foot, or opposite, court; black disks are played from the other side.

   - To determine which color disks a pair gets, the opponents in the head court push one disk each to the far end line. The player with the disk landing closest to the end line gets a choice of team color.

   - To begin, the four red disks are lined up in the right half of the 10-off area of the head court, and the black disks are placed in the left half of the 10-off area of the head court.

   - Reds play first in the first game of a match (a three-game series). A red disk is pushed from the head court to the foot court.

   - This play is followed by an opponent pushing a black disk. This routine continues until all disks are played.

   - When all eight disks have been played, the second round begins from the foot court. The second game is started by black, and the third game begins with red. Additional rules surrounding play are as follows:

A player may not step over the baseline.

A player may not step onto the other half of the court to make a play.

A player must remain seated when play is toward his or her end of the court.

A player may not interfere with the opponent's play and may not talk during the opponent's shot.

The disk must be wholly in one side of the 10-off area to start play.

A player may not hit a disk twice or hesitate in hitting a disk.

A player may not leave the court during play.

A player may not coach a teammate.

A player may not step on the court or shoot before the opponent's disk stops.

2. Demonstrate the play for Doubles Shuffleboard.

Bowling

1. Describe the rules for Bowling.

   - Each game is made up of 10 frames. During each frame, each player has a chance to knock all the pins down.

   - In a frame, the first player rolls the ball at the pins. If all the pins fall on the first roll, it is called a strike, and that player's turn is over. If some pins are missed, the player gets a second roll to knock down the remaining pins. If all the pins are knocked down in two tries, it is called a spare.

   - Each player completes the first frame (rolling one or two balls as described above) before any player goes to the second frame. If a player steps beyond the fault line, the roll does not count.

2. Demonstrate play for Bowling.

Skill Practice

Divide the children into six groups. Two groups play Shuffleboard, two groups Bowl, and two groups play Twister.

LESSON 3
RECREATIONAL GAMES

Student Objectives

- Practice scoring for Bowling and Shuffleboard.
- Participate in an elimination tournament.

Equipment

- 2 shuffleboard sets, or 4 broomsticks and 16 margarine containers filled with sand (8 each of 2 different colors)
- Masking tape or cloth tape
- 20 plastic bottles (2-liter)
- 2 softballs or 2 rubber bowling balls
- 2 Twister games, or 2 sheets with 10-inch dots of various colors painted on them and 2 spinners

Skill-Development Activities (30 minutes)

Shuffleboard Scoring

Describe and demonstrate these steps to Shuffleboard Scoring:

1. When all eight disks in a half-round have been played, the score of the first half-round is tallied.

2. Only disks that stop wholly within a scoring area receive the points from that area.

3. Disks that touch a line do not score. For every disk in or touching the line of the 10-off area, 10 points are deducted. A game is 75 points.

4. The first half-round is followed by another half-round, which begins again with red. The second game is started by black, and the third game begins with red.

5. Five points are deducted every time a player steps over the baseline, steps onto the other half of the court to make a play, or interferes with an opponent's play. Ten points are deducted when a disk is played that is not fully in either the right or the left 10-off area; or when a player hesitates or hits a disk twice, leaves the court, talks during an opponent's shot, coaches a teammate, or shoots before the opponent's disk stops.

Bowling Scoring

Describe these steps for Bowling Scoring:

1. Each pin knocked down in a frame is worth one point unless all the pins are knocked down within a frame (one or two rolls).

2. When less than 10 pins are knocked down with the two balls, the number of pins knocked down with each ball is written in the small boxes (the first ball goes in the left box, and the second ball goes into the right box).

3. When a strike is made (all 10 pins on the first ball in a frame), an X is placed in the small left box; when a spare is made (all 10 pins in two balls in a frame), a slash (/) is placed in the right box.

4. The running total score is placed in the large box.

5. The reward for a strike is to add extra points to the 10 points in the strike frame; these points are determined by the pins knocked down with the next two balls. Therefore, the next two balls count twice. They are added to 10 for the strike, and they also count for the current frame.

6. The reward for a spare is the addition of points from the next one ball after the spare. This ball also counts twice, once for the spare and once for the current frame.

7. In the figure below, Bonnie knocked down 7 pins with her first ball and 2 pins with the second ball, scoring neither a strike nor a spare. Her total for Frame 1 is 7 + 2 = 9. In Frame 2, she knocked down 9 pins on the first ball and missed the last pin on her second ball. She scored 9 more points for a cumulative total of 18 (9 + 9) in Frame 2. In Frame 3, she rolled a strike—all 10 pins knocked down with the first ball. Scoring for Frame 3 now depends on her next two balls, where she rolls a 7 and a 2. Her score for Frame 3 is 10 + 7 + 2 = 19, giving her a running total of 37 in Frame 3.

8. Scoring continues through the 10 frames. In the 10th frame, players getting a spare or strike are allowed an extra ball or two for three balls in the final frame to obtain their reward.

9. If a player knocked down all of the pins with the first ball in every frame—12 strikes in a row—the total score would be 300 points (see Gordon's score).

Demonstrate Bowling Scoring using the example given in the figure and also based on game play.

NAME	1	2	3	4	5	6	7	8	9	10	TOTAL
GORDON	X 30	X 60	X 90	X 120	X 150	X 180	X 210	X 240	X 270	X X X 300	300
ANN	X 20	7/ 40	X 60	18/ 80	X 100	9/ 120	X 140	9/ 160	X 180	9/ X 200	200
JOHN	7/ 17	9/ 32	5/ 51	9/ 69	18/ 88	9/ 106	18/ 123	7/ 139	6/ 156	7/ 9 175	175
BONNIE	7 2 9	9 - 18	X 37	7 2 46	7/ 66	X 86	6/ 105	9/ 124	9/ 144	X 9/ 164	164

Two-Person Twister Tournament

Arrange the children in six groups and assign each group to either a Shuffleboard, Bowling, or Twister tournament. Rotate the children among the three activities.

1. Describe a Two-Person Twister Elimination Tournament: This game is played like the four-person Twister game, but the winner of each game plays against the children in a group that has not yet played.

2. Once all the children have played, those who lost play the current champion until all but one child has lost two times.

3. Have the children walk through a sample tournament.

4. Select a group of four or five children, place two on the Twister board, declare one the winner, replace the loser with another child, declare a winner, replace the loser with the first child to have lost, declare a winner, replace the loser with the second child to have lost, and so on.

LESSON 4
RECREATIONAL GAMES

Student Objectives

- Practice scoring for Bowling and Shuffle-board.
- Participate in an elimination tournament.
- Learn an offensive and defensive strategy for Shuffleboard.

Equipment

- 2 shuffleboard sets, or 4 broomsticks and 16 margarine containers filled with sand (8 each of 2 different colors)
- Masking tape or cloth tape
- 20 plastic bottles (2-liter)
- 2 softballs or 2 rubber bowling balls
- 2 Twister games, or 2 sheets with 10-inch dots of various colors painted on them and 2 spinners

Skill-Development Activities (30 minutes)

Bowling Scoring

See Grades 6-8: Classroom Activities, Lesson 3, page 318.

Shuffleboard Scoring

See Grades 6-8: Classroom Activities, Lesson 3, page 318.

Variations

Place a pilot on the shuffleboard court. A pilot is a disk that is not meant to score or bump. It is placed on the court to block the entrance to the scoring area by the opponent or to protect a later shot. One placement for pilots is at the tip of the triangle on the outside.

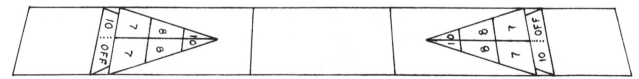

Team Elimination Twister

Arrange the children in six groups and assign two groups to each activity. Rotate children after eight minutes at an activity.

This game is played as regular Four-Person Twister (see Grades 6-8: Classroom Activities, Lesson 1, page 314). Two children play against two other children, with winners from the two games playing each other and losers playing each other.

Sample for Eight Children (four pairs or teams):

Game 1: A plays B

Game 2: C plays D

Game 3: Winners of Games 1 and 2 (Winner of this game is overall winner).

Game 4: Losers of Games 1 and 2

Game 5: Loser of 3 plays winner of 4 (Winner of this game is consolation winner).

Sample for 10 Children (five pairs or teams)

Game 1: A plays B

Game 2: C plays D

Game 3: Winner of Game 2 plays E

Game 4: Winner of Game 1 plays winner of Game 3 (Winner of this game is overall champ.)

Game 5: Loser of Game 1 plays loser of Game 2.

Game 6: Winner of Game 5 plays loser of Game 3

Game 7: Winner of Game 6 plays loser of Game 4 (Winner of this game is consolation champ.)

LESSON 5
FITNESS

Student Objectives

- Perform flexibility, muscle endurance, and cardiovascular endurance exercises.

Skill-Development Activities (30 minutes)

Fitness Stations

Arrange the children in six groups and assign each group to a fitness station. The children will rotate through the six stations three times (taking approximately 22 minutes).

Fitness stations

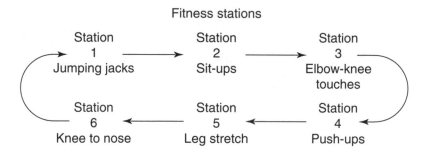

| Station 1 Jumping jacks | Station 2 Sit-ups | Station 3 Elbow-knee touches |
| Station 6 Knee to nose | Station 5 Leg stretch | Station 4 Push-ups |

1. Describe and demonstrate each station (three to five minutes).
2. Ask the children to perform as many repetitions as possible for one minute and then rotate to the next station (allow them 15 seconds to rotate).

Station 1: Jumping Jacks

The student begins standing with feet together and arms low at sides, jumps, lands with feet to the sides in a straddle as the arms clap overhead, and then jumps back to starting position.

Station 2: Sit-Ups

Sit-Ups are performed with knees bent and arms crossed on chest.

Station 3: Elbow-Knee Touches

The student stands with feet shoulder distance apart. The first movement is touching the left knee with the right elbow while lifting to a tiptoe position. Then the student returns to the starting position and reverses the movement, so that the left elbow touches the right knee.

Station 4: Push-Ups

The student performs Push-Ups with the body straight, lowering the body until the chest touches the floor and then returning to starting position.

Station 5: Leg Stretch

Sitting, the student stretches in Straddle position to the left, right, and center; in Pike position, the student stretches forward with toes flexed and extended.

Station 6: Knee to Nose

Beginning in all-fours position on hands and knees, the student moves chin to chest while bringing one knee forward. After the knee and nose touch or come as close together as possible, the leg is extended backward and the head is lifted up and back. The student repeats the exercise and then changes to the opposite leg.

Cool Down

Everyone walks slowly around the room, taking deep breaths and exhaling slowly, for one minute.

LESSON 6
PROGRESSIVE FITNESS GAME

Student Objectives

- Perform flexibility, muscle endurance, and cardiovascular endurance exercises.

Skill-Development Activities (30 minutes)

Fitness Stations

Arrange the children in fitness teams. Children within a team should be of similar ability. Assign one member of each team to each of the six stations. (See Grades 6-8: Classroom Activities, Lesson 5, page 322.)

1. On a start signal, begin a timer and have each child perform the required repetitions of the exercise at his or her station.

2. When finished, each child moves to the next station and gently taps a teammate who moves on to the next station, finished or not (this means that only one member of a team will be at any station). This continues until all the children on a team have done each station three times.

3. Once a team has completed three rounds of the six stations, they should walk quietly to you to get their time; they then can begin the cool-down process. This continues until all teams have finished and cooled down.

4. The first team to finish can be given a small reward or be recognized by class applause.

Station 1: Jumping Jacks
50 repetitions.

Station 2: Sit-Ups
30 repetitions.

Station 3: Elbow-Knee Touches
100 repetitions.

Station 4: Push-Ups
20 repetitions.

Station 5: Leg Stretch
30 repetitions, Straddle; 10 repetitions, Pike.

Station 6: Knee to Nose
30 repetitions each leg.

Cool Down

The children walk slowly around the room until they are cool (have stopped sweating and have heart rates of 100 or less). Allow the children to get a drink of water and return to their seats.

CLASSROOM ACTIVITIES

LESSON 7
FITNESS SELF-EVALUATION

Student Objectives

- Perform flexibility, muscle endurance, and cardiovascular endurance exercises.
- Perform self-test activities and record results.

Equipment

- One sit-and-reach box
- One scale
- One yardstick or measuring stick (for height)
- One skinfold caliper
- Three stopwatches, watches with second hands, or timing clocks
- One bench (18 inches) or a sturdy chair
- Eight pencils
- One self-testing sheet and one pencil for each child

Skill-Development Activities (30 minutes)

Resting Heart Rate

Give each student a self-testing sheet.

1. While they are sitting quietly, ask the children to count their resting heart rates (pulse rates) for 10 seconds. Repeat two more times.

2. If one score is 3 greater or less than the other two scores, use the average of the other two scores.

3. If any child obtains scores with extreme differences in the three scores, help that child take his or her pulse.

4. If the scores are similar, take either the mode (the score that occurs most often) or the mean (average of the three).

5. Multiply the resting heart rate by six and record the total on the self-testing sheet. For additional information on taking heart rate, see chapter 2 of *Physical Education for Children: Concepts Into Practice* by Thomas, Lee, and Thomas.

Fitness Testing Stations

Arrange the children in partners and assign two pairs (four children) to each station. Children rotate to the next station as they finish measuring each other and recording their performances.

Station 1: Standing Height
The children remove their shoes and measure their standing height against a wall.

Station 2: Weight
The children remove their shoes and measure their weight to the nearest pound.

Station 3: Sit-Ups
The children do Bent Knee Sit-Ups with arms crossed on chest and record the number of repetitions in one minute.

Station 4: Push-Ups
With the body straight and hands and feet in contact with the ground, the child lowers the chest to the ground and then returns to full arm extension. Each child records the number of repetitions she or he performed continuously.

Station 5: Sit-and-Reach
Sitting with feet against the box, the student reaches, keeping the knees straight, and holds the position for one second. Each child records the number on the box that corresponds to the reach.

Station 6: Step Test (see Grades 4-5, Classroom Activities, Lesson 5, "Highsteppers")
Each child records the length of time she or he performed continuous stepping.

Station 7: Skinfolds
Children measure each other and record the tricep and subscapula sum.

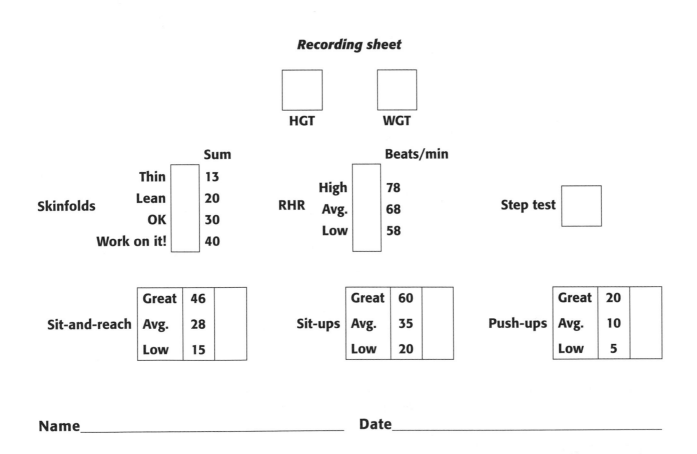

Recording sheet

Name_____   Date_____

LESSON 8
LUMMI STICKS

Student Objectives

- Participate in Lummi Stick activities.

Equipment

- Two rhythm sticks for each child

Skill-Development Activities (30 minutes)

Partner Tapping

Arrange partners in scatter formation, sitting cross-legged facing each other. Each child has two sticks.

1. Describe and demonstrate Partner Tapping: For Partner Tapping use the following pattern—tap sticks down, tap sticks together, touch right stick to partner's right stick, tap own sticks together; repeat, touch left stick with partner's. Say to the children: *Down, together, right, together; down, together, left, together.*

2. Have the children practice Partner Tapping.

Partner Tossing

1. Describe and demonstrate Partner Tossing: Each child tosses his or her right stick to the partner's right side and catches the partner's right stick. Repeat with left sticks.

2. Perform the following sequence:

   Tap down, tap together, toss right, tap together. Say to the children: *Down, together, right, together.*

   Tap down, tap together, toss left, tap together. Say to the children: *Down, together, left, together.*

3. Have the children practice the sequence.

Partner Flipping

1. Describe and demonstrate Partner Flipping: The sticks are tilted forward so that the ends can be tapped to the floor. Flip the stick by tossing it up and catching it in the air, giving it a half turn.

2. Perform the following sequence:

   Tap front and flip.

   Tap down, tap together, toss right, toss left. Say to the children: *Front-tap, flip, down, together, right, left.*

3. Have the children practice the sequence.

Creative Tosses

Each pair of children creates a unique sequence of tosses and flips. Ask for volunteers to show their routines.

LESSON 9
NEW GAMES

Student Objectives

- Participate in three games requiring cooperation.

Equipment

- One carpet square per child
- Music

Skill-Development Activities (30 minutes)

Cookie Factory

1. Select two to four students (leaving an even number of remaining students) to be cookies. The remaining students form a double line (the oven), facing each other with arms joined by grasping the forearm with the hand.

2. Explain that the oven has to bake the cookies.

3. Help the first cookie to climb onto the arms of the pair at the end of the line, lying on his or her stomach.

4. The oven moves the cookie by lifting, leaning, and wiggling their arms while supporting the cookie.

5. The cookie is passed through the pairs to the end of the oven, where you help the cookie out of the oven.

6. Continue with the remaining cookies.

Cooperative Musical Squares

Form a row of carpet squares; the number of squares should be equal to the number of students.

1. Describe Cooperative Musical Squares.

   - Start the music. The children walk around the squares. Remove two or three squares.

   - When the music stops, the children stand on squares. Some children will have to share squares.

   - Continue until it is impossible for the children to balance on the squares. The purpose is to help each other by holding on, balancing, standing on tiptoe, and so on.

2. Have the children play Cooperative Musical Squares.

Human Chair

Arrange the children in a line (the line can be a curve, a spiral, or any other shape).

1. Specify the front of the line so that each child stands facing the back of the next person.

2. The last person in the line pretends to be sitting in a chair by squatting down with bent knees.

3. The person in front of the squatting person sits on that child's thighs. The chair person will help to balance the sitting person.

4. This continues until all children are seated in a chainlike chair.

5. Variation: The human chair walks! On verbal cues, the first person (the one with no person on his or her lap) begins by taking a small step. Everyone else takes a small step with the same foot. Continue for 10 steps or until the group loses balance.

LESSON 10
RECREATIONAL GAMES

Student Objectives
- Play a game that requires striking.

Equipment
- Several balloons
- One piece of string (20 to 30 feet long)

Skill-Development Activities (30 minutes)

Balloon Volleyball

Move the desks and chairs to clear a space for the game. Run a string through the middle of the play area. If the desks and chairs are not movable, run the string between two rows so that approximately half the children are on each side. Two teams are arranged on either side of the string, which is tied five to six feet off the ground. The playing area can be marked with tape, or you can simply designate boundaries and then decide when a balloon has left the playing area.

The children should be spread three to four feet apart. Taped Xs on the floor are helpful for keeping children in position. This game can be played from chairs (or desks) if the space is limited or if the chairs cannot be moved. The playing area is determined by the amount of space (if the room is small and the playing area will be small), the arrangement of chairs (if you are playing from chairs), or the number of children on a team (the more children, the more space is needed).

Describe the steps for Balloon Volleyball:

1. Each team begins with 15 points.
2. Toss the balloon to the team on one side of the string. The children on that side of the string hit the balloon (staying in their positions as much as possible) until it goes over the string; the other team hits the balloon until they return the balloon over the string.
3. If the balloon touches the ground, goes out-of-bounds (hits a desk or goes out of the playing area), or is caught by a child, play stops. The team that hit the balloon out-of-bounds, caught it, or failed to keep the balloon in the air loses a point.
4. While play is stopped the children change positions, so that the children in the back row move to the front row, the front row moves to the middle, and the middle row moves to the back.
5. Play resumes with you tossing the balloon to the team that did not start play on the last round.
6. The game ends when one team has zero points.
7. Have the students practice Balloon Volleyball (as you explain the rules again).

8. Have the children play Balloon Volleyball. Here are some variations:

Have the students play with more than one balloon.

Place a weight in the balloon (a penny, marble, sand).

Have the students play with one hand behind the back.

APPENDIX EVALUATION FORMS

TYPES OF EVALUATION FORMS

The following evaluation forms are arranged by activity category: Games and Sports, Rhythmic Activities, and Gymnastics. There are three types of evaluation forms: checklists, rating scales, and skill test scoring forms.

CHECKLISTS

There are two types of checklists. The first type of checklist is used to evaluate an entire group of students. Place one student's name in each row or column as indicated on the checklist. Observe each student, checking the appropriate box when a skill is performed correctly. The second type of checklist is for separate evaluation of individuals. Fill in the student's name, his or her class, and the observation date at the top of the form. Then check "yes" if the skill is completed correctly or "no" if the skill is not completed correctly. Both types of checklists can tell you which skills you need to stress in class and can help you give feedback to the children about which skills they need to practice.

RATING SCALES

Rating scales are used to follow the development of skills in an individual child over a period of time. Write the child's name on the scale and the date of the first observation in the space above the first column. In each column, place a 3, 2, or 1 corresponding to the student's ability level when performing each skill. You can add other items to the list of skills as needed. The next time you observe the child, place the date of this second observation over the second column and follow the same procedure. You may want to space your observations; for example, record the ratings in September, December, and May. This records the development of a child's skills across time.

For children without mature or developmentally appropriate motor patterns, you should provide extra instruction by including additional instruction on those patterns. Then fill in the numbers that are appropriate for the demonstrated characteristic, taking into account the developmental levels of the children.

SKILL TESTS

The third type of evaluation form is the skill tests scoring form. To use skill tests scoring forms, fill in the student's name, his or her class, and the observation date. Then have the child complete the test. Record his or her score(s) using the standards listed. These standards can be used to motivate the children to attain higher scores.

GRADES 6-8: CHECKLIST FOR SOCCER

Name_____ Class_____

Observation date_____

Dribbling

	Yes	No
Advances ball with short kicks.		
Taps ball with insides of alternating feet.		
Keeps ball close and in control.		

GRADES 6-8: SKILL TESTS FOR SOCCER

Name_____ **Class** _____

Observation date _____ **Dribbling score** _____

Dribbling

Description: Arrange five cones at 10-foot intervals with the first cone five feet from a starting line. The student starts behind the line and on the "go" signal, dribbles around the cones in zigzag, both going down and returning to the starting line. The score is the number of seconds it takes to dribble the course.

Standards

15 seconds or less = excellent
16 to 22 seconds = average
23 seconds or more = poor

GRADES 6-8: CHECKLIST FOR BASKETBALL

Name_____ **Class**_____

Observation date_____

Lay-Up Shot

        Yes No

Approaches board at 45-degree angle.

Lifts body up by jumping from foot opposite shooting arm.

Releases ball at top of jump.

GRADES 6-8: SKILL TEST FOR BASKETBALL

Name _____ **Class** _____

Observation date _____ **Shooting Score** _____

Shooting

Description: Student stands under the basket with a basketball. On the "go" signal the student shoots the ball, recovers it, and shoots again. The objective is to make as many baskets as possible in 30 seconds. Any shot can be used. The score is the number of baskets made.

Standards

10 or more = excellent
    5 to 9 = average
 4 or fewer = poor

GRADES 6-8: CHECKLIST FOR SOFTBALL

Name_____ Class_____

Observation date_____

Batting

	Yes	No
Faces plate with feet comfortably apart.		
Keeps eyes on pitcher.		
Holds bat shoulder high and slightly behind back foot.		
Swings bat parallel to ground.		
Shifts weight at moment of impact.		

GRADES 6-8: SKILL TEST FOR SOFTBALL

Name_____ **Class** _____

Observation date _____ **Fielding score** _____

Fielding Ground Balls

Description: Mark an area 20 feet by 20 feet. The student stands in the marked area. A thrower rolls 20 balls to the student from a line 30 feet away. The score is the number of balls the student is able to field cleanly.

Standards

15 to 20 = excellent
7 to 14 = average
6 or fewer = poor

GRADES 6-8: SKILL TESTS FOR VOLLEYBALL

Name_____   Class _____

Observation date _____   Serving score _____

Volleying score _____

Serving

Description: Mark the court into three zones. The server gets 10 trials to serve the ball from the service line over the net. The score for each serve is determined by the zone the ball lands in. The final score is the total number of points after 10 serves (total points possible = 30).

Standards

21 to 30 = excellent
11 to 20 = average
10 or fewer = poor

Volleying

Description: Mark a line on a wall 10 feet high and parallel to the floor. Mark a restraining line on the floor six feet from the wall. The student stands behind the restraining line and on a "go" signal tosses the ball against the wall, so that it hits above the 10-foot line, and then volleys in succession against the wall. The score is the number of successful volleys in one minute. The tossed balls do not count. If the ball goes out of control, another ball is handed to the student.

Standards

12 and above = excellent
6 to 11 = average
5 or fewer = poor

GRADES 6-8: CHECKLIST FOR TRACK AND FIELD

Name_____ Class_____

Observation date_____

Triple Jump

	Yes	No
Approaches board with run.		
Takes off on one foot.		
Uses hop, step, and jump pattern.		
Lands on two feet.		

High Jump

	Yes	No
Approaches bar at slight angle.		
Lifts inside foot over bar, with rear leg following.		
Keeps legs straight during jump.		
Lands on lead foot with knees bent.		

GRADES 6-8: SKILL TESTS FOR FOOTBALL

Name_____ Class _____

Observation date _____ Forward pass score _____

Punting score _____

Forward Pass

Description: On a marked football field, the student passes a football for distance. Allow three passes, measuring each. The longest pass is recorded.

Standards

70 feet or over = excellent
50 to 69 feet = average
49 feet or under = poor

Punting

Description: On a marked football field, the student punts a football for distance. Allow three punts, measuring each. The longest punt is recorded.

Standards

70 feet or over = excellent
50 to 69 feet = average
49 feet or under = poor

GRADES 6-8: RATING SCALE FOR FOLK AND COUNTRY DANCE

Name_____   Class_____

Skill	Date_____ First 3 2 1*	Date_____ Second 3 2 1	Date_____ Third 3 2 1
Performs dance steps using correct step sequence:			
Basic Polka			
Two-Step			
Heel-Toe Polka			
Alley Cat			
Performs dance movements and steps to music:			
Basic Polka			
Two-Step			
Alley Cat			
Remembers step sequence for folk and country dances:			
Weggis Dance			
Pattycake Polka			
Freeze			
Cotton-Eyed Joe			
Hoya			

*Note: 3 = nearly always, 2 = sometimes, 1 = seldom

GRADES 6-8: RATING SCALE FOR RHYTHMIC ROUTINES

Name_____ Class_____

Skill	Date_____ First 3 2 1*	Date_____ Second 3 2 1	Date_____ Third 3 2 1
Jumps rhythmically using the following skills:			
Straddle			
Scissors			
Schottische			
Creates Rhythmic Rope-Jumping routine.			
Tinikling			
Performs Basic Tinikling Step to 3/4 rhythm.			
Performs variations of Basic Tinikling Step:			
Two steps In			
Straddle			
Crossover			
Performs Basic Tinikling Step to a 4/4 rhythm.			
Creates Tinikling Step routine.			

Note: 3 = nearly always, 2 = sometimes, 1 = seldom

GRADES 6-8: CHECKLIST FOR EVALUATION OF THE FLOOR EXERCISE ROUTINE

Each pass and filler is worth two points if well done. Those who have trouble get one point on that portion, and those who can't or won't do the pass or filler get zero.

Name	Pass 1	Filler 1	Pass 2	Filler 2	Pass 3	Total

GRADES 6-8: CHECKLIST FOR EVALUATION OF FREE FLOOR EXERCISE ROUTINES

This form needs to be used in connection with the lesson on floor exercises in "Grades 6-8: Gymnastics." Children's names go across the top; use "+" to indicate the presence of characteristic and "−" to indicate its absence.

Name

Skills

Cover complete mat area

    A

    B

    C

    D

    Middle

Change in tempo

Tumbling

    Roll

    Cartwheel

Balance

Strength

    Handstand

    Backward Roll Extension

Variety in locomotor patterns

Amelia Lee, PhD, is a professor and chair of the department of kinesiology at Louisiana State University. In addition to her 25 years of experience as a teacher educator, Dr. Lee taught physical education at elementary schools in Louisiana and Texas for 10 years. She has published many articles on children's learning and motivation in physical education and has served as a physical education consultant to more than 20 school districts. Dr. Lee is a member of the American Educational Research Association (AERA), and she has received the Scholar Lecture Award from the AERA's Special Interest Group on Learning and Instruction in Physical Education. She is a member of the American Alliance for Health, Physical Education, Recreation and Dance (AAHPERD) and has received an Honor Award from AAHPERD's Curriculum and Instruction Academy. Dr. Lee earned her doctorate in physical education from Texas Woman's University in 1972.

Katherine T. Thomas, PhD, is an associate professor of health and human performance at Iowa State University, where she teaches a variety of teacher education and motor development courses. Dr. Thomas also has taught at Arizona State University, Southeastern Louisiana University, and Southern University, Baton Rouge. Her research and numerous publications focus on skill acquisition in sport and exercise and the relation of physical activity to health. She has external grant funding in excess of $800,000 to study physical activity and is the physical activity consultant for the USDA's Team Nutrition. However, Dr. Thomas calls her early professional experiences as a graduate assistant and as an instructor in elementary schools and a college teaching laboratory the most relevant to the writing of this book. These experiences enabled her to find out firsthand what does and doesn't work in a physical education class.

Dr. Thomas is a member of AAHPERD and the North American Society for the Psychology of Sport and Physical Activity (NASPSPA). She received her doctorate in physical education from Louisiana State University in 1981.

Jerry R. Thomas, EdD, has taught elementary physical education methods and children's motor development for more than 30 years. Currently, he is a professor and chair of the department of health and human performance at Iowa State University. Dr. Thomas also has taught as a professor at Florida State, Louisiana State, and Arizona State Universities. He has written more than 125 published papers, including many on children's motor skills. Dr. Thomas is former president of the American Academy of Kinesiology and Physical Education and NASPSPA. In addition, his scholarly work in physical activity has earned him the titles of C.H. McCloy Lecturer for children's control, learning, and performance of motor skills; Alliance Scholar for AAHPERD; and Southern District AHPERD Scholar.

THE COMPANION BOOK FROM HUMAN KINETICS

Physical Education for Children
Daily Lesson Plans for Elementary School

Katherine T. Thomas, PhD; Amelia M. Lee, PhD; Jerry R. Thomas, EdD
2000 • Paper • 1,192 pp
ISBN 0-87322-681-X • $29.00 ($43.50 Canadian)

This book has been a big hit with physical educators since it came out in 1989. Now it's available in a new edition that keeps all the best features of the original, adds new material, and improves the presentation, all while making the information more affordable!

Physical Education for Children: Daily Lesson Plans for Elementary School includes 437 lessons for grades K-5. The activities become more challenging as you progress through the grade levels, and new activities are added at the higher levels. For each level, you'll find units of lesson plans on the following topics: organization, fitness, games and sports, rhythmic activities, gymnastics, health, and classroom activities.

COME CHECK OUT THE NEW HUMAN KINETICS WEBSITE!

The Human Kinetics Website (**www.humankinetics.com**) provides a key medium through which HK works to improve the quality of people's lives through physical activity. There is something for everyone—news about the latest sport psychology study, new country line dances, running software, basketball practice plans, strength training exercises for people over 50, physical activity games for children, fitness assessment software for personal trainers—the list goes on and on. If it is human-powered, you'll find it at humankinetics.com.

ALSO BE SURE TO VISIT THE AFA WEBSITE!

The AFA's mission is to improve young people's fitness and health by promoting physical activity and other healthy behaviors. Our objective is to provide a national resource center for fitness and activity-related products and services and to create new programs, often in cooperation with others, to promote physical activity and fitness throughout life.

On this website (**www.americanfitness.net**) you'll find top-quality educational, assessment, and training resources that you can use to enhance youth fitness whether you're a physical educator, fitness professional, or youth program administrator.

To request more information or to order, U.S. customers call 1-800-747-4457, e-mail us at **humank@hkusa.com**, or visit our website at www.humankinetics.com. Persons outside the U.S. can contact us via our website or use the appropriate telephone number, postal address, or e-mail address shown in the front of this book.

Human Kinetics
The Information Leader in Physical Activity

2335